T0209216

INCORPORATING ENGAGED RESEARCH IN SOCIAL DEVELOPMENT

Exemplars and Guidelines for Social Work and Human Services

Wassie Kebede *and* **Alice K. Butterfield, Editors**

INCORPORATING ENGAGED RESEARCH IN SOCIAL DEVELOPMENT EXEMPLARS AND GUIDELINES FOR SOCIAL WORK AND HUMAN SERVICES

iUniverse books may be ordered through booksellers or by contacting:

iUniverse
1663 Liberty Drive
Bloomington, IN 47403
www.iuniverse.com
844-349-9409

ISBN: 978-1-6632-2014-1 (sc)
ISBN: 978-1-6632-2015-8 (hc)
ISBN: 978-1-6632-2016-5 (e)

Library of Congress Control Number: 2021906703

Print information available on the last page.

iUniverse rev. date: 04/26/2021

CONTENTS

TABLE OF FIGURES AND TABLES

PREFACE

This book emerges from our years of joint teaching experience as international and local faculty at Addis Ababa University, School of Social Work. In Ethiopia, social work education began as a diploma-level of training program in 1959 at the then Haile Selassie I University (now Addis Ababa University), but closed shortly after the Ethiopian socialist regime came to power in 1974. After an absence of 30 years, there was a revitalization of social work education, the consequence of a serendipitous encounter between Dr. Alice Butterfield, Professor at the Jane Addams College of Social Work, University of Illinois Chicago who came to Ethiopia in 2001 as a member of a People-to-People delegation focused on understanding the emergence of HIV/AIDS in the country and the late Professor Seyoum Gebreselassie. Dr. Seyoum held a dual doctorate in social work and sociology from the University of Michigan, and served in a variety of faculty and administrative positions at Addis Ababa University for more than 30 years. Discussions with Department of Sociology faculty, such as Professors Seyoum Gebreselassie and Andargachew Tesfaye who had social work backgrounds, focused on reopening social work education as part of the University's five-year plan. Their conversations led to a two–year period of investigation and preparation that culminated in the reopening of the School of Social Work at Addis Ababa University. The School launched its MSW program in 2004, and in 2006 a PhD in Social Work and Social Development was initiated through admitting eight students from the first MSW graduating class. Just two years later in 2008, a Bachelors in Social Work program began (Kebede, 2014). Between 2006 and 2020,

1492 social workers graduated from the School of Social Work, Addis Ababa University. This includes 589 that graduated with a Bachelors in Social Work, 863 with a Masters in Social Work, and 40 students earned a doctorate in Social Work and Social Development. Of note, 507 (34%) of those who obtained a social work degree were female.

When AAU's School of Social Work reopened in 2004 there were few Ethiopian faculty members with expertise in the profession. International faculty played important roles in the School's early efforts. Unforgettable contributions in the establishment and flourishing of the new social work programs at AAU were Professors A.K Butterfield, Abye Tasse, Melese Getu, Nathan Linsk, James Rollin, Margaret Adamek, Errol S. Bolden, Larry, W. Kreuger, Robert L. Miller, Sandy Wexler, Deborah Zinn, James Scherrer, Valerie Chang, Richard S. Kordesh, Sandhya Jossi, Rosemary Sarri and many others. Students in the newly established PhD program who were employed as faculty members, were assigned as co-instructors with the international faculty in the MSW program. This was done with the understanding that the doctoral students would be mentored to take over full responsibility for the curriculum and teaching. Doctoral students also were involved in the day-to-day academic and administrative affairs of the School. The opportunity to play these leadership roles contributed to a sense of ownership of AAU's social work education programs that the majority of those who were in leadership continue to feel today. The student leadership role ended in 2011 when Dr. Wassie Kebede, the first to receive a doctorate in the new program, assumed the position of Dean (Johnson Butterfield, Tasse & Linsk, 2009).

Over time, other universities in Ethiopia began to send Lecturers, as either PhD or MSW students from their respective departments, to AAU's School of Social Work. Many of these graduates have since returned to their home universities and launched social work schools/ departments. In about 15 years since social work education was re-established in Ethiopia, a total of 13 universities (11 public and two private) have started social work education programs. Among them, AAU and the University of Gondar now run full programs of BSW, MSW and PhD studies (Kebede, 2019). In line with international social work education and training standards (International Federation of Social Workers, 2019; Sewpaul, 2010), social work research in Ethiopia is well appreciated and incorporated into the social work curriculum at all educational levels. Students are taught its importance for practice and have the opportunity to demonstrate their understanding and skills during the production of their theses and dissertations.

Engaged social work research has been an integral part of social work training. Engagement has been interpreted in a number of ways including university-community partnerships, students' action research, and in thesis and dissertation projects required for graduation. Social work curriculum requires community-engaged teaching whereby students are exposed to direct practice in community settings while taking courses at various levels (BSW, MSW and PhD). This engagement promoted the establishment of a university-community partnership through Asset Based Community Development in the Gedam Sefer neighborhood (Yeneabat & Butterfield, 2012). Engaged/ action research started by graduate student served as a catalyst to initiate the ABCD model (Butterfield, Kebede & Gessesse, 2009). Field practicum at BSW and MSW levels are other components for students' engagement in community-based learning. Through their practicum, students produced action-oriented reports through direct participation in community projects. Some courses that required students to conduct participatory/engaged research at the MSW level are Integrated Social Work Methods, Models of Community Development and Practice, and Social Development and Models of Change. In some cases, the action research reports produced by students served as inputs to design community development projects. At the PhD level, the course Action Research and Models of Social Change extensively involved students in engaged research in partnership with community groups.

Social work engaged research continues to be encouraged by AAU's School of Social Work, which has prioritized this model of research. To best prepare students for their future professional careers, the School works diligently to foster MSW and PhD students' knowledge of and skills in community-engaged projects. Community-engaged research, as a model of social work research, has also been incorporated in the curricula of other Ethiopian social work education programs. Graduates of AAU's School of Social Work have taken the model to their home universities and have integrated action research as a component of engaged research into their curricula and university-community partnerships.

This book has grown out of our experiences of teaching courses that engaged students and ourselves in different action research projects. We have been teaching courses which are action research oriented and accumulated critical experience in how to engage ourselves and our students with local communities, how to document action research results and link such results to local development initiatives, and influence social development policy at the local levels.

The book is organized in 12 Chapters under three main categories. The first chapter introduces readers to engaged research and models of social change. Chapter two looks at development issues in Ethiopia in view of engaged research. We offer this context of engaged research in Ethiopia as a protype for extrapolating development policies that can be looked at, compared and contrasted, to those in other countries of the world. Chapters 3-11 are presenting the results of the engaged research of former PhD students, now faculty at various universities in Ethiopia. These chapters are dedicated to promoting the scholarship of young researchers, our former students. Without such opportunity, their work would remain unpublished and unable to find "a route to their colleagues elsewhere" (Butterfield & Abye, 2012, p. 211). In Chapter 12, we present our experience and the importance of involving faculty and students in engaged research. We emphasize the implementation of engaged research through coursework. We believe the book has paramount importance for educators, researchers and practitioners in social work and other human service disciplines who appreciate the contribution of engaged research to social development.

Wassie Kebede, MSW, PhD
Alice K. Butterfield, MSW, PhD

References

Butterfield, A., Kebede, W., & Gessesse, A. (2009). Research as a catalyst for asset-based community development: Assessing the skills of poor women in Ethiopia. *Social Development Issues, 31(2)*, 1-14.

Butterfield, A.K., & Abye T. (2012). Learning from Africa: Publication and research. *Journal of Community Practice, 20*(1-2), 211-217.

International Federation of Social Workers. (2019). Global Standards for Social Work Education and Training. Available at: https://www.ifsw.org/global-standards-for-social-work-education-and-training/#preamble

Johnson Butterfield, A.K., Tasse, A., & Linsk, N. (2009). The Social Work Education in Ethiopia Partnership. In C.E. Stout (Ed.), *The New Humanitarians: Inspiration, Innovations, and Blueprints for Visionaries*, Volume 2 (pp. 57-83). Westport, CT: Praeger.

Kebede, W. (2014). Social work education in Ethiopia: Celebrating the re-birth of the profession. In H.Spitzer, J. Twikirize, & G. Wairire (Eds.). *Professional Social Work in East Africa: Towards Social Development, Poverty Reduction and Gender Equality* (pp. 161-172). Kampala: Foundation Publishers.

Kebede, W. (2019). Social work education in Ethiopia: Past present and future. *International Journal of Social Work, 6(1)*, 1-17.

Sewpaul, V. (2010). Professionalism, postmodern ethics and the Global Standards for Social Work Education and Training. *Social Work/Maatskaplike Werk, 46*(3).253-262. Available at: https://socialwork.journals.ac.za/pub/article/view/156/143

Yeneabat, M., & Butterfield, A.K. (2012). "We can't Eat a Road:" Asset-based community development and the Gedam Sefer community Partnership in Ethiopia. *Journal of Community Practice, 20*(1-2), 134-153.

CHAPTER 1

OVERVIEW OF ENGAGED RESEARCH AND MODELS OF SOCIAL CHANGE

Alice K. Butterfield, Wassie Kebede

Defining Engaged Research

Engaged research is defined in many ways in the literature. The Irish Universities Association (2017, p.4) define engaged research as:

> A wide range of rigorous research approaches and methodologies that share a common interest in collaborative engagement with the community and aim to improve, understand or investigate an issue of public interest or concern, including societal challenges. Engaged research is advanced with community partners rather than for them.

According to James (n.d., p.1) engaged research "is committed to making a positive difference in the world. It is engaged ethically and reciprocally with others. …It is a commitment witnessed by others to fulfil the terms of an agreed relationship."

Engaged research methods and approaches go by a variety of different names, including action learning research, action-oriented research, collaborative inquiry, community action research, community service learning, community-university partnership, community empowerment research, emancipatory research, and engaged scholarship. Despite different names, all of these methods and approaches emphasize the active engagement of community members, organizations, and stakeholders in scanning problems, soliciting data/information, analyzing data, proposing action frameworks and participating in the change process, and evaluating outcomes. All anticipate the engagement of stakeholders as active research participants and decision makers, not just as recipients of the findings and outcome of the research.

Community engagement is defined as "the process of working collaboratively with and through groups of people affiliated by geographic proximity, special interest, or similar situations to address issues affecting the well-being of those people" (National Institute of Health, 2011, p. 3). Thus, community-engaged research focuses on engaging a community as an active partner in all phases of the research process, from problem identification to research design and implementation to data analysis and interpretation to the dissemination of findings (Holliman, 2017). Such research is carried out in order to address community problems and improve community well-being. Figure 1.1 lists just some of the various terminologies that represent varieties of engaged research.

Figure 1A: The Range of Terminologies

Action Learning Research	Action-Oriented Research	Collaborative Inquiry	Community-Action Research
Community-Based Research (CBR)	Community-University Partnership	Emancipatory Research	Feminist Action Research
Indigenous Research Methodology	Knowledge Translation	Organizational Action Research	Participatory Action Research (PAR)
Participatory Evaluation	Participatory Research	Participatory Rural Appraisal	Scholarship of Engagement

Source: Adapted from: Irish Universities Association. (2017, January), page 56.

Community-engaged research benefits the community and the academics who co-create the research with community members. According to Pasika, Oliva, Goldstein and Nguyen (2010, p. 6) regarding the benefits of engaged research to the community, it recognizes community as a unit of identity; builds on strengths and resources within the community; facilitates collaborative partnerships in all phases of the research; integrates knowledge and actions for mutual benefit of all partners; and promotes a co-learning and empowering process that attends to social inequality.

For academics, benefits include facilitating a better understanding of a community's views of prevailing social problems, learning from a community's experiences, and strengthening university-community partnerships. Academics and practitioners have identified many types of engaged research. Brief descriptions of some of the more common methods and approaches of engaged research are noted in Table 1A.

Brief History of Engaged Research

Engaged research, also known as engaged scholarship, has emerged and expanded during the 20th and 21st centuries. Although it has a long history since 1860s, in the United States, engaged scholarship reemerged "at the time of the New Deal and World War II but dramatically expanded during the Civil Rights Era and the Vietnam War" (Willcoxon, 2019, p. 1). Engaged research, as a generic approach was in complete opposition to the positivist and in partial opposition to post-positivist approaches. Epistemologically, engaged research stands in opposition to these traditional approaches. The positivist approach claims that "scientific methodology enables scientists to separate personal values from facts" (Tekin & Kotaman, 2013, p. 82). In positivist research, the researcher is an outsider who is not experiencing the phenomenon he/she is trying to investigate. Since the 1950s, the reductionist approach of positivist research has been criticized. In contradiction to the positivist approach, the post-positivist approach claims that "to study a complex phenomenon, the possibilities, multiple points-of-view and perspectives, and different variables that may affect the proceeding of the whole have to be emphasized" (Tekin & Kotaman, 2013, p. 82). In its early days, during the pre-World War II period, action research, which is an alternative name for engaged research began to function as a bridge between scholarly theories and the application of research in real life.

Table 1A: Types of Engaged Research

Type of Engaged Research	Brief Description
Action Learning Research	"...a strategy utilised by members of a community or an organisation to tackle real life problems by reflecting on their experience as members of that grouping and collaboratively arriving at solutions" (p. 61).
Action-Oriented Research	"...generate knowledge that can be used to address practical concerns of local communities, organizations, and groups and incorporate local understandings of specific practices and issues into projects that usually have some type of change...as an ultimate goal" (p. 61).

Collaborative Inquiry	"...is a participatory, action-based form of research that aims to improve practice and add to knowledge. ...subjects... becoming co-investigators in the inquiry and the [researcher] a full participant" (p. 61).
Community-Action Research	"...collaborative knowledge creation, which is generally initiated with the intent of implementing significant organisational change" (p. 62).
Community-Based Research (CBR)	"CBR projects can adopt multiple approaches and methods but share the common characteristic that the impetus for influence over the research comes from the community and not the external researcher" (p. 62).
Community-University Partnership	"The aim of these programmes is to contribute towards the development of the community in some way. The partnership consists of research programmes, which are conceived, designed and implemented by both the university and the community" (p. 62).
Emancipatory Research	"Emancipatory Research is concerned with the power relations involved in research; and is consciously aware of how these might affect the value placed upon some forms of knowledge over others. The emancipatory research paradigm is based on three key fundamentals: reciprocity, gain and empowerment" (p. 63).
Feminist Action Research	"Feminist Action Research aims to generate knowledge that can address practical concerns of a community. Unlike action research...this approach specifically addresses women's multiple perspectives and attempts to change the conditions of their lives through the pursuit of social justice" (p. 64).
Indigenous Research Methodology	"Indigenous Research Methodology involves analysing the epistemology of a defined indigenous community and then using that analysis to inform a project's research design. [C]ommunity...way of looking at the world actually guides how the research progresses" (p. 64).
Knowledge Translation	"Knowledge Translation is the exchange, synthesis and application of new knowledge between researchers and beneficiaries to implement improved and/or more effective services, products, or processes" (p. 64).
Organizational Action Research	"This is a form of research that places emphasis on understanding how an organisation operates in general... Organisational Action Research can become community-orientated when the work of the organisation impacts upon a community" (p. 64).
Participant Action Research (PAR)	"Participant Action Research is a type of applied social research where, typically, people concerned with the organization under study team up with professional researchers to design projects, gather and analyse data, and utilise the findings in action projects. Participant Action Research requires community members to be active participants in the project design, data collection and analysis, and in the dissemination of findings" (p. 65).
Participatory Evaluation	"...members of a community are centrally involved in designing a project evaluation, gathering and analysing data, drawing conclusions, disseminating results and making recommendations on how to achieve improvements" (p. 65).

Participatory Research	"Participatory Research is a process which combines three activities: research, education and action. It aims to facilitate those who would not normally look upon themselves as researchers to adopt that role and tackle the issues that matter to them in their everyday lives by gathering and assessing data" (p. 65).
Participatory Rural Appraisal (PRA)	"Participatory Rural Appraisal is a collective term for a number of different approaches and methods... emphasises the co-creation of knowledge" (p. 65).
Scholarship of Engagement	"The notion of practicality, reality and serviceability being at the heart of the mission of higher education is central to the principle of Scholarship of Engagement. It challenges the idea that universities should exist separately from the world around them and holds" (p. 65).

Source: Irish Universities Association. (2017, January). Selected from Appendix 1: Glossary of Engaged Methods and Approaches, p. 61-66.

Engaged research can be identified by such names as action research, participatory action research, popular education & participatory research, community based participatory research, and so on. The history and origins of these and other engaged research types are attached to their pioneers. For example, the history of Action Research is attached to Kurt Lewin, a German social psychologist (Masters, 1995). Participatory Action Research is attached to Paulo Freire, a Brazilian philosopher (MacDonald, 2012). "Antonio Gramsci, like participatory democratic theorists, argued that learning occurs through participation itself" (Luckett, Walters & von Kotze, 2017, p. 260). Action research is profoundly a Northern tradition, which emerged mainly from the United States and United Kingdom, whereas participant action research, community based participatory research and others listed above are Southern traditions, originating in Brazil and Italy. Berg (2004) provides an overview of the process of action research, and its use of qualitative research methods. The brief history of each tradition is presented next.

Northern Tradition – Action Research Kurt Lewin

Many scholars agree that the origin of Action Research is tagged to the work of Kurt Lewin, but "there is evidence of the use of action research by a number of social reformists prior to Lewin" (Masters, 1995, p. 1). Kurt Lewin, however, made action research become popular in 1940s when he "constructed a theory of action research, which described action research as "proceeding in a spiral of steps, each of which is composed of planning, action and the evaluation of the result of action" (Kemmis & McTaggert, 1990, p. 8). Action research for Lewin was exemplified by a discussion of problems followed by group decision on how to proceed. Marrow (1969, p. 168) reported that Lewin and his co-workers classified their work into four types of action research, namely

1. Diagnostic action research designed to produce a needed plan of action…2. Participant action research in which it is assumed that the residents of the affected community who were to help effect a cure must be involved in the research process from the beginning…3. Empirical action research was primarily a matter of record keeping and accumulating experiences in doing day-to-day work, ideally with a succession of similar groups…4. Experimental action research, called for controlled study of the relative effectiveness of various techniques in nearly identical social situations (Adelman, 1993, pp. 13-14).

Grundy (1988, p. 353) and McKernan (1991, pp. 16-27) as cited in Masters (1995) lists three general types of action research. Type 1 is the scientific-technical view of problem solving. Type II, is practical-deliberative action research, and Type III is critical-emancipatory action research. Philosophically "action research can be classified as a post-positivist mode of inquiry due to its conditional nature" (Tekin & Kotaman, 2013, p. 86). They further note that "action research views being an insider as an advantage rather than disadvantage because the insider is native to the setting and thus better able to establish the connection needed to conduct a study" (p. 87). The philosophical viewpoints related to legitimizing action research include its appreciation and adherence to praxis, hermeneutics, existentialism, pragmatism, and phenomenology (Susman & Evered, 1978). Appendix A includes

7

Rory O'Brien's (2001) detailed report by which defines action research, explains its evolution, and offers tools for carrying out ethical processes in action research.

Southern Tradition – Participatory Action Research - Paulo Freire

It is hard trace the origin of Participatory Action Research (PAR) to the idea of a single person or a group of persons. PAR is associated to the social movement of the 20th century "… in particular land reform, anti-colonialism, and need for a new research methodology, occurring simultaneously across multiple continents (Glassman & Erdem, 2014, p. 206). Although PAR is considered as a sub-set of action research, the PAR origin is recognized as the work of Paulo Freire with contributions by Budd Hall in his application of Freier's concepts in Tanzania (Hall, n.d.). Freire believed that "critical reflection was crucial for personal and social change. The PAR approach of Freire was concerned with empowering the poor and marginalized members of society" (MacDonald, 2012, p. 37). The uniqueness of PAR to other forms of qualitative research is that "it reflects questioning about the nature of knowledge and the extent to which knowledge can represent the interests of the powerful and serve to reinforce their positions in society" (Baum, MacDougall & Smith, 2006, p. 854). In comparison to conventional research, action research pays special attention to power relationships, and involves participants directly in data gathering and reflective analysis. Rahman 1991 cited in Elliott (2011, p. 5) states that

> the basic ideology of PAR is that a self-conscious people, those who are currently poor and oppressed, will progressively transform their environment by their own praxis. In this process others may play a catalytic and supportive role but will not dominate.

PAR is also distinguished from conventional research by its emancipatory nature to improve the lives of research participants using an action-oriented approach based on research results. As a principle, PAR "democratises knowledge production, secures ownership of the research and improves research quality, leading to a greater likelihood that results will be put into practice" (Amaya & Yeates, n.d., p.3). PAR is not a simple research method, rather it is an approach comprised of a set of principles and practices for originating, designing, conducting, analysing and acting on a piece of research. According to Pain, Whitman and Milledge (n.d., p.3) PAR "goes through a cycle of planning, action, reflection and evaluation."

Miles Horton and Highlander Center – Popular Education and Participatory Research

As reflected in *The Pedagogy of the Oppressed*, Paulo Freire's landmark book is acknowledged as a forerunner of popular education. He argued that education is sexist, racist and favours the powerful (Freire, 1971). In its place, popular education required a high degree of participation expected from everyone to raise levels of consciousness, empower class and group interests to organize, with the overall effort evaluated by PAR outcomes.

In the United States, popular education originated in 1932 with the work of Miles Horton in the founding of the Highlander Folk Center in Tennessee (Horton, Kohl, & Kohl, 1997).

> The school was a place for the oppressed to gather, learn, organize, and make change. Throughout the Great Depression, the school advocated for the working class by providing training for workers and labor organizers. Eventually, the school shifted its focus to Civil Rights. Throughout the 1950's, the school organized literacy and voter registration for Blacks all over the nation [Educators Who Tell the Truth].

After many brief encounters at meetings around the world, Horton invited Freire to Tennessee where they shared and critiqued each other's

9

perspectives and practices on popular education. *We Make the Road By Walking: Conversations on Education and Social Change—Myles Horton and Paulo Freire* is authored from these tape-recorded conversations (Bell, Gaventa, & Peters, 1990).

Popular education is a contested concept and practice and is subject to multiple definitions. Luckett, Walters and von Kotze (2017, p. 257) define popular education as "employing participatory methods for personal development, to acting as part of overtly political anti-capitalist projects. Popular education is rooted in the interests, aspirations and struggles of ordinary people." According to Crowther, Martin and Shaw (1999, p. 4), popular education is "based on a clear analysis of the nature of inequality, exploitation and oppression and is informed by an equally clear political purpose." It also means education that seeks to support organizing or activism for social justice, democracy and environmental goals (Missingham, 2013). Its characteristics include the concrete experiences of the learner in which everyone teaches-everyone learns, a high level of participation, and action for change. The learning process starts with identifying and describing everyone's own personal experience, and knowledge is built upon through various activities done in groups. Methods focus on group rather than individual solutions and stress the creation of new knowledge rather than the passing of existing knowledge through ongoing processes related to time, place, and age. "Popular education is called popular because its priority is to work among the many rural and urban poor who form the vast majority of people" in most developing countries (Arnold & Burke, 1983, p. 7). The authors provide a detailed handbook, include group exercises for adapting the popular education model from Central America to the Canadian context.

Popular education fosters participatory research in that the pedagogy links enabled learners, considered as students, to "engage and enables them to see themselves as agents of social change and not just consumers of pre-packed knowledge" (Missingham, 2013, p. 35). Some basic approaches in popular education and participatory research are to encourage learners to participate in asset-based learning and teaching, dialogue and problem-solving, participatory learning as a collective and deliberative process, and the construction of knowledge, not the passing of knowledge to learners from outside their realm of their experience of reality. In combing popular education with that of participatory research, Streck (2016) identifies five criteria for assessing the quality and validity of participatory methods. These include the issue of social relevance, measures of quality that require descriptive and interpretative thickness, reflexivity, the quality of relations among the stakeholders in the research process, and the practicability of the produced knowledge.

Streck explains three dimensions of collective reflexivity also known as praxis. First, the potential for reflexivity should increase among subjects—a fact inherent in the concept of praxis itself. Quoting Eykeland (2012, p. 40), "Praxis requires sharing and communicating minds in a dynamic community of masters and apprentices. Everyone thereby becomes an experimenter, not an 'experimentee.'" Streck's (2016) second dimension is action reflection exists within history.

> The human being is a being of praxis not only because he can improve his professional practice, but also because he can build a project of his destiny... [noting that] Fals Borda added the concept of *phronesis* to praxis in order to emphasize that it is action reflection targeted at justice (p. 10).

The third dimension relates to the self-knowledge of the researcher, including "knowledge of his/her motivations, interests, limits and emotions...which contain three patterns of relationships: co-humor, relaxed mutual availability and verbal coproduction... creating conditions to make the entire group be in tune." (p. 11).

Community Based Participatory Research

Community Based Participatory Research (CBPR) involves three interconnected goals: research, action and education. CBPR encompasses two perspectives—one from the Northern tradition and the other from the Southern tradition. CBPR draws on two distinct approaches at opposite ends of the continuum: collaborative utilization-focused research with practical goals of system improvement… [and] openly emancipatory research, which challenges the colonizing practices of positivist research and political domination by the elites" (Wallerstein & Duran, 2003, p. 28). The tradition of participatory research arose in the 1970s in Latin America, Asia and Africa, known together as the Southern tradition. CBPR has gained momentum in a number of fields, mainly in education, community development, social work, and public health. CBPR with its appealing model of equal and full partnership with the community at all stages/phases of a research process has become a critical approach for conducting research with vulnerable populations. "CBPR recognizes the importance of involving members of a study population as active and equal participants, in all phases of the research project, if the research process is to be a means of facilitating change" (Holkup, Tripp-Reimer, Salois, & Weinert, 2004, p. 164).

The Kellogg Community Health Scholars Program 2001 defines CBPR in a comprehensive manner. CBPR is

> a collaborative process that equitably involves all partners in the research process and recognizes the unique strengths that each brings. CBPR begins with a research topic of importance to the community with the aim of combining knowledge and action for social change to improve community health and eliminate health disparities (Minkler, Garcia, Rubin, & Wallerstein, 2012, p. 8).

The research dimension of CBPR applies both qualitative and quantitative approaches using various techniques of data gathering, analysis, and compiling results. Administering research in CBPR ranges from conducting quantitative surveys, focus groups, walkability assessments, air monitoring, GIS mapping, and secondary data analysis to the use of randomized control trials to assess community intervention effectiveness (Minkler, Garcia, Rubin, & Wallerstein, 2012). For example, Israel, Coombe, Cheezum et al. (2010) note that CBPR is a critical engagement for capacity building to eliminate policy gaps and health disparities. CBPR stands in two pillars. The first pillar is to be ethical and respond to existing issues of community exploitation and the second pillar is community empowerment (Blumenthal, 2011). Figure 1B illustrates the conceptual model of CBPR.

Figure 1B: Conceptual Model of CBPR

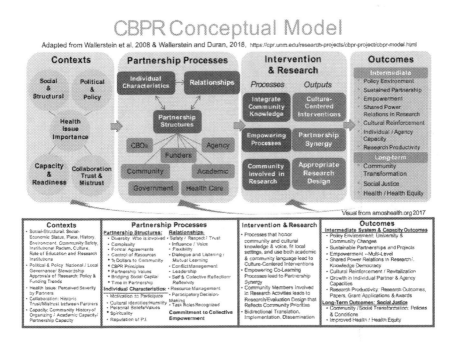

Traditional, Community-Engaged, and Community Based Participatory Research

There are similarities and differences among traditional, community-engaged and community based participatory research approaches.

Community-engaged and community based participatory research (CBPR) have similarity in their objectives as both of them appreciate local issues, though for different purposes. In terms of research design, these two approaches recognize the involvement of community members, yet at various levels of participation. The traditional research approach relies on a scientifically rigorous research design. To recruit and retain research participants, the traditional approach employs probability-based scientific methods whereas the other two approaches use representatives of the community at large. In community-engaged research, participation takes place at the consultation stage, but in CBPR, representatives of the community guide recruitment and are actively involved in the retention of research participants.

Although community-engaged and CBPR emerged historically from two origins, the former originating from Kurt Lewin's Action Research Model (ARM) and the latter from Paulo Freire's Empowerment Education Paradigm (EEP), both have the communality of engaging the community to participate in the research process (Mohatt & Beehler, n.d). However, the lens through which each research tradition—traditional, community-engaged and CBPR—perceive the involvement of community members differs regarding instrument design. Typically, traditional research utilizes research instruments previously tested and verified using psychometric analyses. Community-engaged research adopts instruments from other studies, but tests and adapts them to fit the local context. These two research traditions have communality in that both rely on an already designed instruments. CBPR develops instruments with the help of community members, testing and verifying them with the same population. Table 1B compares and contrasts traditional, community-engaged and community based participatory research.

Table 1B: Comparing Traditional, Community-Engaged Research, and CBPR

	Traditional	Community-Engaged	Community Based Participatory Research
Research Objective	Issues identified based on the epidemiologic data and funding opportunities	Community input in identifying locally relevant issues	Full participation of community in identifying issues of greatest importance
Study Design	Design based entirely on scientific rigor and feasibility	Researchers work with community to ensure study design is culturally acceptable	Community representatives involves with study design
Recruitment & Retention	Approaches based on scientific issues and "best guesses" regarding reaching community members and keeping them involved	Researchers consult with community representatives on recruitment and retention strategies	Community representatives provide guidance on recruitment and retention strategies and aid in recruitment efforts
Instrument Design	Instruments adopted/adapted from other studies, tested chiefly with psychometric analysis method	Instruments adopted from other studies and tested/adapted to fit local populations	Instruments developed with community input and tested in similar populations
Intervention Design	Researchers design interventions based on literature and theory	Community members involved in some aspect of design	Community members help guide intervention development
Analysis & Interpretation	Researchers own the data, conduct analysis and interpret the findings	Researchers share results of analysis with community members for comments and interpretation	Data is shared: community members and researchers work together to interpret results
Dissemination	Results published in peer-reviewed academic journals	Results disseminated in community venues as well as peer-reviewed journals	Community assists researchers to identify appropriate venues to disseminate results; involve in dissemination; results are also published in peer-reviewed journals.

Source: Hartwig, K., Calleson, D., & Wallace, M. (2006). Unit 1: Community-Based Participatory Research: Getting Grounded. In *Developing and Sustaining Community-Based Participatory Research Partnerships: A Skill-Building Curriculum*. [The Complete CBPR Curriculum is available at: www. cbprcurriculum.info]

Action Research Methodology and Process

The methodological essence of action research is based on its research outcomes that satisfactorily address community problems through informed action and reflection (McKay & Marshall, n.d). Methodology is defined as the theoretical framework that supports the methods chosen. It is a perspective taken in research which dictates how the research is approached. Thus, action research methodology is a description of what is involved in this type of research including key characteristics, world views, theoretical positions and the researcher's philosophical stance (Koshy, 2005). Key characteristics of action research include its participatory character, democratic impulse, and simultaneous contribution to knowledge and practice (Carr & Kemmis, 1986). The researcher's philosophical stance or world view is ultimately and primarily to improve practice. Critical theorizing and democratizing research are other elements of the philosophical stance in action research. It is context-bound and involves action (Waterman, Tillen, Dickson, & de Koning, 2001). Theoretically, an element of action research methodology is its "pursuit of meanings and interpretations, which are socially constructed. In theorizing action research, knowledge is the product of a negotiated consensus that contributes to the future harmony of action and elevation of the life course" (Koshy, Koshy & Waterman, 2011, pp. 13-14).

The process of action research is cyclical not linear. There are four distinct stages in doing of action research which include the planning stage, the acting stage the developing stage and the reflecting stage. A reprint of selected portions of Rory O'Brien's (2001) "An Overview of the Methodological Approach of Action Research" in Appendix A provides a detailed look at the definitions, principles and processes of action research, including diagrams that show its reflexive nature between researchers and participants. O'Brien also outlines current types of action research and tools for engaging in action research, include the role of the researcher and research ethics.

Embedding Engaged Research
within Models of Social Change

Social change is simply defined as a shift in the attitudes and behaviors characterizing society (Greenwood & Guner, 2008). Models of social change encompass a number of conceptions that contribute towards change in communities. Some selected models of social change include community development, asset-based community development, social development, community conversation, diffusion of innovation, concept mapping, service learning and social networks. Some are strategies of change, for example, asset-based community development. Others are ways of acquiring evidence, improving skills, and obtaining knowledge, for example, service learning and the diffusion of innovation. Still others are the means and methods to foster togetherness and partnerships, for example, community conversation and social networks. All of these represent different ways, methods, and models for fostering social change. These are described briefly here as part of the broader context in which engaged research can take place.

Community Development is a planned approach to improve the built environment in a local area. Some of the key components of such development include community participation, self-help, collaboration, and integrated solutions to social and economic issues. Typically, community development includes economic development such as improving roads and infrastructure, schools, housing, business development, and so on. In comparison, to top-down social planning models, community development includes the participation and inclusion of people living in the community for access to jobs, infrastructure improvement and services (Johnson Butterfield & Chisanga, 2008). Bottom-up community development necessarily includes community organizing in working with groups, associations, and local government to reach its overarching goal of building community capacity (Capraro,2004). According to Larsen, Sewpaul and Hole (2014, p. 6) "community development addresses community work as a bottom-up approach as sustainable changes are best achieved when people concerned participate in an active way, bringing to the development process their knowledge, skills and experience."

Asset based Community Development (ABCD) is a strategy for sustainable community-driven development. The development of ABCD was spearheaded by the work of Jody Kretzmann and John McKnight (1993) and disseminated through training and consultation via the Asset Based Development Institute (DePaul University, 2021). The Coady Institute in Canada plays a major role in training, networking and implementation of ABCD projects worldwide (Coady Institute, 2021). The focus of ABCD is empowering communities to identify and address their own problems through the local assets available to them. Blickem, Dawson, Kirk et al. 2018 cited in Harrison, Blickem, Lamb et al. (2019) note that:

> A key quality of ABCD practice is the strong emphasis on building and sustaining meaningful relationships within communities and developing networks of reciprocal exchange and acceptable support. This type of approach is in stark contrast to the way disadvantaged communities are often negatively defined as a set of problems, which leaves them feeling demoralized, disempowered, and isolated, in addition to being exposed to increasingly hostile, uncertain, and uninspiring environments (pp. 7-8).

The ABCD approach include citizen-led development, strengths-based community work, community planning and place-making approaches, and working with community capitals. Community capitals include human/intangible capitals such as social capital, political capital, cultural capital, and human capital. Material/tangible capitals include natural capital, financial capital, and built capital (International Association for Community Development, 2009). Applying ABCD for improving the lives of people living in poverty through small and medium enterprise development is also an application of ABCD (Fisher, Geenen, Jurcevic, McClintock, & Davis, 2009). The effectiveness of

ABCD in creating sustainable outcomes and empowering Samoan communities was successful in locally-driven rural development (Fuimaono, 2012). Nurture Development (n.d.) shows the process of implementing asset-based development in practice.

With a focus on child well-being, ABCD has been used successfully in Ethiopia with adults and children living in an impoverished urban slum (Yeneabat & Butterfield, 2010; Butterfield, Yeneabat, & Moxley, 2016). In Ethiopia, ABCD builds on the country's long history of community-based support systems (Cunningham, 2008). These traditional self-help associations are similar to those in other developing countries as reported by Bergdall (2003). Local self-help mechanisms— all of which are asset-based support systems—are synonymous with asset-based development among various ethnic communities in Ethiopia. These include *dabare, eeba ogdi, jige* among the Oromos, *gezma, hera, hera-dana* among the Kambatta, and cooperation, trust and mutual care in the Awramba community. In the Sidama community, the concept is called *affin*i, and *gaze, Iddir and dabo* in the Guraghe community, (Kebede, Getu and Negeri, 2011).

Social Development is another term that has a direct link with community engagement and models of social change. Midgley (1995) provides a detailed description of social development as "an approach to promoting people's welfare that is well suited not only to enhancing the quality of life for all citizens but to responding to the problems of distorted development" (p.7). Economic development is a major emphasis in social development, but one which is enveloped in benefits that comprehensively address poverty and disenfranchisement for local populations. Mohamed, Mohammed and Barom (2020, p.16) list "inclusive social development, society's total development, well-being of the people, social transformation, and improving people's quality of life" as essential features of social development. Nahar's (2014) text analysis of the concept of social development reports that

> Social development does not mean a development of one
> specific issue. Social development means the collective
> development of the whole entity whatever that entity

might be; thus it means growing, advancing, maturing step by step or stage by stage in a unified way and comprehensively covering all aspects and dimensions of such entities as a society (Pawar 2014 cited in Nahar 2014, pp. 5-6).

Simeon, Butterfield, & Moxley (2019) provide a detailed review of social development theory and practice, including locality-based social development that uses a variety of different methods to address local issues.

Community Conversation is a semi-structured way of listening to community members thoughts on various community issues. Community conversations provide a safe place where people can come together to talk about the hopes and goals about their community, their concerns and how they want their community to move forward. The method can be used with one person or many, and can be formal or informal (Harwood Institute for Public Innovation and Community Conversations, 2016). Campbell, Nhamo, Scott et al. (2013, p. 2) identify community conversation as "discussions among local people, guided by a trained facilitator that support critical thinking and problem solving around key community issues."

Diffusion of Innovation is described as "a special type of communication in which the messages are about a new idea" (Rogers, 2003, p. 6). Diffusion is a kind of social change through which alteration occurs in the structure and function of social systems. Diffusion includes the spread of spontaneous or planned new ideas. Alternatively, "diffusion is the process by which an innovation is communicated through certain channels over time among the members of a social system" (p. 37). Dearing and Cox (2018, p. 83) further describe diffusion of innovation as "a social process that occurs among people in response to learning about an innovation such as a new evidence-based approach for extending or improving [for example] health care."

Concept Mapping is a technique used to illustrate and understand relationships between various concepts. "A concept map consists of nodes, arrows as linking lines, and linking phrases that describe the relationship between nodes" (Schwendimann, 2014, p. 1). Concept mapping is used to organize related information in a visual manner. Mapping helps participants to learn quickly and actively. Concept mapping include concepts, usually enclosed in circles or boxes of some type, and relationships between concepts or propositions, indicated by a connecting line between two concepts. Concept mapping can be carried out manually or through software.

Service Learning is widely defined as a form of experiential education that integrates meaningful community service into the curriculum. Service learning contains two main elements, engagement within the community known as service and reflection on that engagement known as learning (Preradovic', 2015). Service learning typically consist of four stages: investigation and preparation, action, reflection and demonstration.

Social Network "refers to an individual's interaction with others, some of whom interact with each other and yet others" (Spetch, 1986, p. 224). Mitchell (1969, p. 2) defines social networks as "linkages among a defined set of persons, with the additional property that the characteristics of these linkages as a whole may be used to interpret the social behavior of the persons involved." Social network research is embedded in many fields including sociology, communication, psychology, social work, and so on. Specifically, researchers apply social network analysis as a method or approach in studying migration, organizations, and community development, as well as health and entrepreneurship. Specific topics of network studies are diverse including "networks of communication, social movements, local power elites, personal networks, informal networks within organizations, virtual networks and many more (Keim, 2011, p. 19).

Overview of the Book

The book consists of 12 chapters. Chapter 2 illustrates development issues in Ethiopia and prospects of engaged research in social work. It highlights the development agenda of Ethiopia, and reviews selected policies that influence the development processes in the country. Both positive and negative accounts of development in Ethiopia are outlined. Some of the positive accounts of Ethiopian development are exemplified in education, health, and social protection. Negative accounts are reflected by corruption, political instability, ethnic violence, migration and unemployment. The context of engaged research is viewed from the policy perspective, and the chapter discusses how policies influence and affect engaged research in Ethiopia.

Engaged research conducted by some former doctoral students who at present are teaching in various universities in Ethiopia and are contained in Chapters 3-11. These reports provide evidence on the way in which engaged research produces critical data for policy formulation and the implementation of action plans. Each chapter demonstrates the way in which action-oriented information can be linked to development-related policies. For example, the study conducted on the Khairat Muslim Women Organization provides evidence of ways to influence women's empowerment and the relationship of Muslim women with family and their education. The chapters entitled Leprosy: Stigma and Discrimination, Reclaiming Health Education, and Exploring Assets of Youth for the Prevention and Control of HIV provide insights about challenges and gaps in the implementation of health policy. Similarly, Supporting People in Poverty through a Local Association, Women and Economic Development, and Building Capacity of Iddirs to Assist Poor Older Adults uncover the importance of community empowerment for local development and social support. Finally, chapters on Student Engagement on Campus-Based Community Policing, and Youth Development in Student Councils illustrate the importance of revisiting policies related to campus and school settings, safety and health prevention, and youth issues.

Chapter 12, the last chapter, presents the involvement of faculty and graduate students in engaged research. It analyzes the exemplars of engaged research as conducted by doctoral students and presents a review of engaged research strategies developed and being implemented by some universities in Ethiopia. The advantages of implementing engaged research to address policy gaps is one focus. Doctoral students give witness to the way in which their engaged and participatory research shaped their areas of scholarship, particularly their dissertation projects. Chapter 12 describes the status of implementing engaged research in social work and related disciplines and concludes by offering practical suggestions for using this book for teaching and implementing engaged research in higher education. Appendix A contains Rory O'Brien's (2001), *An Overview of the Methodological Approach of Action Research*. Appendix B contains sample syllabi from graduate courses in Ethiopia and the United States for teaching engaged and action research. In teaching engaged research, readers are encouraged to include this book as required reading in undergraduate and graduate courses. Readers are encouraged to contact the editors for further assistance in developing or applying this book to teaching engaged research methods. A complete resource manual for carrying out community-engaged research with community-based organizations is provided online by Pasick, Oliva, Goldstein, and Nguyen (2010).

References

Adelman, C. (1993). Kurt Lewin and the origins of action research. Education Action Research, 1(1), 7-24.

Amaya, A.B., & Yeates, N. (n.d.). Participatory action research: New uses, new contexts and new challenges. PRARI Working Paper 15-6. Available at: https://www.open.ac.uk/socialsciences/prari/files/working_paper_6_en.pdf

Arnold, R., & Burke, B. (1983). *A Popular Education Handbook: An Educational Experience Taken from Central America and Adapted to the Canadian Context.* Canada: Ontario Institute for Studies in Education, Adult Education Department. Available at: https://eric.ed.gov/?id=ED289024

Baum, F., MacDougall, C., & Smith, D. (206). Participatory action research. *Journal of Epidemiol Community Health, 60,* 854-857. Available at: https://jech.bmj.com/content/jech/60/10/854.full.pdf

Bell, B., Gaventa, J., & Peters, J. (Eds). (1990). *We Make the Road by Walking: Conversations on Education and Social Change—Myles Horton and Paulo Freire.* Philadelphia, PA: Temple University Press. Available at: https://codkashacabka.files.wordpress.com/2013/07/we-make-the-road-by-walking-myles-and-paolo-freie-book.pdf

Berg, B.L. (2004). Chapter 7. Action Research. In *Qualitative Methods for the Social Sciences* (5th Edition), pp. 195-208. Boston: Pearson. Available at: https://www.academia.edu/1823730/Qualitative_research_methods_for_the_social_sciences?auto=download

Bergdall, T. (2003). Reflection on the catalytic role of an outsider "in Asset Based Community Development" (ABCD). Available at https://community-wealth.org/sites/clone.community-wealth.org/files/downloads/paper-bergdall.pdf

Blickem, C., Dawson, S., Kirk, S., Vassilev, I., Mathieson, A., Harrison, R., Bower, P., & Lamb, J. (2018). What is asset-based community development and how might it improve the health of people with long-term conditions? A Realist Synthesis. *SAGE Open, 8*(3), 1-13.

Blumenthal, D.S. (2011). Is community based participatory research possible? *Am J Prev Med., 40(3),* 386-389.

Butterfield, A.K., Yeneabat, M., & Moxley, D. (2016). 'Now I know my ABCDs': Asset Based Community Development with Ethiopian primary school children. *Children & Schools, 38*(4), 199-207.

Campbell, C., Nhamo, M., Scott, K., Madanhire, C., Nyamukapa, C., Skovdal, M., & Gregson, S. (2013). The role of community conversations in facilitating local HIV competence: Case study from rural Zimbabwe. *BMC Public Health, 13, 354.*

Capraro, J.F. (2004). Community organizing + community development = community transformation. *Journal of Urban Affairs, 26*(2), 151-161.

Carr, W., & Kemmis, S. (1986). *Becoming Critical: Education, Knowledge and Action Research.* London: Deakin University Press.

Coady Institute. (2021). ABCD. https://coady.stfx.ca/themes/abcd/

Crowther, J., Martin, I., & Shaw, M. (1999) (Eds.) *Popular Education and Social Movements in Scotland Today.* Leicester: NIACE.

Cunningham, G. (2008). Stimulating asset based and community driven development: Lessons from five communities in Ethiopia. In A. Mathie & G. Cunningham (Eds.), *From Clients to Citizens: Communities Changing the Course of their own Development* (pp. 263-298). Warwickshire, UK: Practical Action Publishing.

Dearing, J.W., & Cox, J.G (2018). Diffusion of innovation theory, principles, and practice. *Health Affairs, 37*(2), 183-190.

DePaul University (2021). Asset-Based Development Institute. https://resources. depaul.edu/abcd-institute/Pages/default.aspx

Educators Who Tell the Truth. Myles Horton – Educator, Activist: 1905-1990. https://www.americanswhotellthetruth.org/portraits/myles-horton

Elliott, P.W. (2011). *Participatory Action Research: Challenges, Complications, and Opportunities.* Saskatoon, Canada: University of Saskatchewan.

Eykeland, O. (2012). Action research – applied research, intervention research, collaborative research, practitioner research, or praxis research? *International Journal of Action Research, 8*(1), 9-44.

Fisher, K., Geenen, J., Jurcevic, M., McClintock, K., & Davis, G. (2009). Applying asset-based community development as a strategy for CSR: A Canadian perspective on a win-win for stakeholders and SMEs. *Business Ethics: A European Review, 18*(1), 66-82.

Freire, P. (1971). *Pedagogy of the Oppressed.* NY: Seabury Press.

Freire, P. (2000). *Pedagogy of the Oppressed* (30th anniversary ed.). NY: Continuum.

Fuimaono, R.S. (2012). The asset-based community development (ABCD) approach in action: An analysis of the work of two NGOs in Samoa. Available at. https:// mro.massey.ac.nz/xmlui/bitstream/handle/10179/3427/02_whole.pdf

Glassman, M., & Erdem, G. (2014). Participatory action research and its meanings: Vivencia, praxis, conscientization. *Adult Education Quarterly, 64*(3), 206-2021.

Greenwood, J., & Guner, N. (2008). *Social Change*. Madrid: Department of Economics Universidad Carlos III de Madrid.

Grundy, S. (1988). Three modes of action research. In S. Kemmis & R. McTaggert (Eds.), *The Action Research Reader* (3rd Edition). Geelong, Victoria, Australia: Deakin University Press.

Hall, B. (n.d.). In from the cold: Reflections on participatory action research from 1970-2005. Canada: University of Victoria. Available at: https://chairerp. uqam.ca/fichier/document/Publications/In From the Cold Reflections on Participatory Research from 1970-2005.pdf

Harrison, R., Blickem, C., Lamb, J., Kirk, S., & Vassilev, I. (2019) Asset-based community development: Narratives, practice, and conditions of possibility-A qualitative study with community practitioners. *SAGE Open, 9*(1). ISSN 2158-2440

Harwood Institute for Public Innovation and Community Conversations (2016). *Hands Up Mallee: Community Conversation Guide*. Available at: https://static1. squarespace.com/static/59fabd9490bcce30df85b49f/t/59fc3b1c652deadb10b09 9be/1509702442792/Community+Conversation+Guide.pdf

Holkup, A.P., Tripp-Reimer, T., Salois, M.E., & Weinert, C. (2004). Community based participatory research: An approach to intervention research with a native American community. *ANS Adv Sci., 27*(3), 162-175.

Holliman, R. (2017). Supporting excellence in engaged research. *Journal of Science Communication 16*(5), 1-10.

Horton, M., Kohl, H, & Kohl, J. (1997). *The Long Haul): An Autobiography*. NY: Teachers College Press.

International Association for Community Development (2009, November). What are Asset-Based Approaches to Community Development? Available at: http://csl.ubc.ca/files/2010/04/What-Are-Asset-Based-Approaches-to-Community-Development.pdf

Irish Universities Association. (2017, January). *Engaged Research: Society and Higher Education Addressing Grand Societal Challenges Together*. Available at: http://research.ie/assets/uploads/2017/07/FINAL-JAN-16 ER-Report-2016-Jan-v2.pdf

Israel, B.A, Coombe, C.M, Cheezum, R.R., et al. (2010). Community based participatory research: A capacity building approach for policy advocacy aiming at eliminating health disparities. *American Journal of Public Health, 100*(11), 2094-2102.

Israel, B.A., Eng, E., Schulz, A.J., & Parker, E.A. (2012). *Methods for Community-Based Participatory Research for Health* (2nd Edition). San Francisco, CA: John Wiley & Sons, Inc.

James, P. (n.d). Engaged research. Institute for Culture and Society. Sidney: Western Sidney University. Available at https://www.westernsydney.edu.au/_data/assets/pdf_file/0009/1149876/Engaged_Research.pdf

Johnson Butterfield, A.K., & Chisanga, B. (2008). Community development. In T. Mizrahi & L. Davis (Eds.). *Encyclopedia of Social Work*, Volume I (pp. 375-381). NY: Oxford University Press.

Kebede, W., Getu, M. & Negeri, D. (2011). *Insights from Participatory Development Approaches in Ethiopia: Analysis of Testimonies and Field Practices.* Addis Ababa University/School of Social Work: Eclipse Printing Press.

Keim, S. (2011). *Social Networks and Family Formation Processes: Young Adults' Decision Making about Parenthood.* Deutsche Nationalbibliothek: Springer.

Kemmis, S., & McTaggert, R. (1990). *The Action Research Planner.* Geelong, Australia: Deakin University Press

Koshy, E., Koshy, V., & Waterman, H. (2011). *Action Research in Healthcare.* Thousand Oaks, CA: Sage. [Chapter 1 What is action research? Available at: https://www.sagepub.com/sites/default/files/upm-binaries/36584_01_Koshy_et_al_Ch_01.pdf

Koshy, V. (2005). *Action Research for Improving Practice: A Practical Guide.* Thousand Oaks, CA: Sage. Available at: https://dl.uswr.ac.ir/bitstream/Hannan/132060/1/Valsa_Koshy_Action_Research_for_Improving_Practice_A_Practical_Guide__2005.pdf

Kretzmann, J.P., & McKnight, J.L. (1993). *Building Communities from the Inside Out: A Path toward Finding and Mobilizing a Community's Assets.* Chicago, IL: ACTA Publications.

Larsen, K.A., Sewpaul, V., & Hole, O.G. (Eds.) (2014). *Participation in Community Work: International Perspectives.* NY: Routledge.

Luckett, T., Walters, S., & von Kotze, A. (2017). Re-membering practices of popular education in the struggle for an alternative South Africa. *Interface: A Journal for and about Social Movements, 9*(1), 256-280. Available at: http://www.interfacejournal.net/wordpress/wp-content/uploads/2017/07/Interface-9-1-Luckett-Walters-von-Kotze.pdf

MacDonald, C. (2012). Understanding participatory action research: A qualitative research methodology option. *Canadian Journal of Action Research, 13*(2), 34-50. Available at: file:///C:/Users/billb/Downloads/37-Article%20Text-89-1-10-20120913.pdf

Marrow, A.J. (1969) *The Practical Theorist: The Life and Work of Kurt Lewin.* NY: Basic Books.

Masters, J. (1995). The history of action research. In I. Hughes (Ed.) *Action Research Electronic Reader.* The University of Sydney. Available at: http://www.iopp.ru/pub/21sept06_M2.doc

McKay, J., & Marshall, P. (n.d.) Action research: A guide to process and procedure. Available at: https://www.researchgate.net/publication/235942689_Action_Research_A_Guide_to_Process_and_Procedure

McKernan, J. (1991). *Curriculum Action Research. A Handbook of Methods and Resources for the Reflective Practitioner.* London: Kogan Page.

Midgley, J. (1995). *Social Development: The Developmental Perspective in Social Welfare.* Thousand Oaks, CA: Sage.

Minkler, M., & Wallerstein, N. (Eds.). (2008). *Community-Based Participatory Research for Health: From Process to Outcomes* (2nd Edition). San Francisco, CA: Jossey-Bass.

Minkler, M., Garcia, A., Rubin, V., & Wallerstein, N. (2012). *Community Based Participatory Research: A Strategy for Building Health Communities and Promoting Health through Policy Change.* The University of California, Berkeley School of Public Health.

Missingham, B. (2013). Participatory learning and popular education strategies for water education. *Journal of Contemporary Water Research & Education, 150,* 34-40.

Mitchell, C.J. (1969). *Social Networks in Urban Situations: Analysis of Personal Relationships in Central African Towns.* Manchester: Manchester University Press.

Mohamed, A.I.A., Mohamed, M.O., & Barom, M.N.B. (2020). A critical analysis of social development: Features, definitions, dimensions and frameworks. *Asian Social Science, 16(1),* 14-21. Available at: https://www.researchgate.net/publication/338286793_A_Critical_Analysis_of_Social_Development_Features_Definitions_Dimensions_and_Frameworks

Mohatt, N.V., & Beehler, S. (n.d.). Application of community engaged and community based participatory research to support military families. Available at: https://www.nap.edu/resource/25380/Mohatt%20%20and%20Beehler%20Application%20of%20Community%20Engaged%20and%20Community%20Based%20Participatory%20Research.pdf

Nahar, S. (2014). *Text Analysis of Social Development as a Concept.* Master of Social Work Thesis, University of Texas. Available at: https://rc.library.uta.edu/uta-ir/bitstream/handle/10106/24942/Nahar_uta_2502M_12925.pdf?sequence=1&isAllowed=y

National Institute of Health. (2011). *Principles of Community Engagement* (2nd Edition). NIH Publication No. 11-7782. Washington, DC: National Institute of Health. Available at: https://www.atsdr.cdc.gov/communityengagement/pdf/PCE_Report_508_FINAL.pdf

Nurture Development (n.d.). Asset Based Development in Practice. Available at: https://www.nurturedevelopment.org/asset-based-community-development/

O'Brien, R. (2001). Um exame da abordagem metodológica da pesquisa açáo [*An Overview of the Methodological Approach of Action Research*]. In Roberto Richardson (Ed.), Teoria e Prática da Pesquisa Ação [*Theory and Practice of Action Research*]. João Pessoa, Brazil: Universidade Federal da Paraíba. (English version) Available at: https://www.web.ca/~robrien/papers/arfinal.html

Pain, R., Whitman, G., & Milledge, D. (n.d.). *Participatory Action Research Toolkit: An Introduction to Using PAR as an Approach to Learning, Research and Action*. Available at: http://communitylearningpartnership.org/wp-content/uploads/2017/01/PARtoolkit.pdf

Pasick, R., Oliva, G., Goldstein, E., & Nguyen, T. (2010). *Community-Engaged Research with Community-Based Organizations: A Resource Manual for UCSF Researchers*. From the Series: UCSF Clinical and Translational Science Institute (CTSI) Resource Manuals and Guides to Community-Engaged Research, P. Fleisher (Ed.), Published by Clinical Translational Science Institute Community Engagement Program, University of California San Francisco. Available at: https://accelerate.ucsf.edu/files/CE/manual_for_researchers_agencies.pdf

Preradovic´, N.M. (2015). Service learning. Available at: https://www.researchgate.net/profile/Nives_Mikelic_Preradovic/publication/304196465_Service-Learning/links/5774db3708aeb9427e24ae53/Service-Learning.pdf

Rogers, M.E. (2003). *Diffusion of Innovation* (5th Edition). NY: Free Press.

Schwendimann, B. (2014). Concept mapping. In R. Gunstone (Ed.), *Encyclopedia of Science Education*]. Available at: https://www.researchgate.net/publication/276420008_Concept_Mapping

Simeon, A., Butterfield, A.K., & Moxley, D.P. (2019). Locality-based social development: A theoretical perspective for social work. In M. Payne & E.R. Hall (Eds.), *Routledge Handbook of Social Work Theory* (pp. 294-307). Oxford: Routledge.

Spetch, H. (1986). Social support, social networks, social exchange and social work practice. *Social Service Review, 60*(2), 218-240.

Streck, D.R. (2016). Participatory research methodologies and popular education: Reflections on quality criteria. *Interface - Communication, Health, Education, 20*(58), 537-547. Available at: https://scielosp.org/article/icse/2016.v20n58/537-547/en/

Susman, I.G., & Evered, D.R. (1978). An assessment of the scientific merits of action research. *Administrative Science Quarterly, 23*(4), 582-603.

Tekin, K.A., & Kotaman, H. (2013). The epistemological perspectives on action research. *Journal of Educational and Action Research, 3*(1), 81-91.

Wallerstein, N., & Duran, B. (2003). The conceptual, historical and practice roots of community based participatory research and related participatory traditions. In M. Minkler & N. Wallerstein (Eds.), *Community Based Participatory Research in Health* (pp. 27-52). San Francisco: Jossey-Bass. Available at: https://www.researchgate.net/publication/306452424 The theoretical historical and practice roots of CBPR?channel=doi&linkId=57be083708aed246b0f721f2&showFulltext=true

Wallerstein, N., & Duran, B. (2010). Community-based participatory research contributions to intervention research: The intersection of science and practice to improve health equity. *American Journal of Public Health, 100*, S40-S46. doi:10.2105/AJPH.2009.184036

Wallerstein, N., Oetzel, J., Duran, B., Tafoya, G., Belone, L., & Rae, R. (2008). What predicts outcomes in CBPR? In M. Minkler & N. Wallerstein (Eds.), *Community Based Participatory Research for Health: Process to Outcomes* (2nd Edition), (pp. 371-392). San Francisco, CA: Jossey-Bass.

Waterman, H., Tillen, D., Dickson, R., & de Koning, K. (2001). Action research: A systematic review and guidance for assessment. *Health Technology Assessment, 5*(23). Available at: https://njl-admin.nihr.ac.uk/document/download/2004475

Willcoxon, N. (2019). *Engaged Scholarship: A History and Present Dilemmas.* Available at: https://democracyandorganizing.org/wp-content/uploads/2019/05/Wilcoxin-Engaged-Scholarship-History-and-Present-Dilemmas.pdf

Yeneabat, M., & Butterfield, A.K. (2012). 'We Can't Eat a Road': Asset Based Community Development and The Gedam Sefer Community Partnership in Ethiopia. *Journal of Community Practice, 20*(1/2), 134-153.

CHAPTER 2

DEVELOPMENT ISSUES IN ETHIOPIA: PROSPECTS FOR ENGAGED RESEARCH

Wassie Kebede

Development is a broad agenda and trying to provide a full description of it in such a brief chapter is difficult. Pearson cited in Abuiyada (2018, p.115) defines development as "an improvement qualitative, quantitative or both-in the use of available resources. It is a hybrid term for a myriad of strategies adopted for socio-economic and environmental transformation from current status to desired ones." The Food and Agriculture Organization [FAO] of the United Nations (Bellù, 2011, p. 2) defines development in terms of as an "event consisting a new stage in changing situation. Development usually means improvement either in the general situation of the system, or in some of its constituent elements." Development is multi-dimensional and entails social, political and human development as well as economic development. Human capital building is central to a development endeavor.

This chapter discusses development issues in Ethiopia and relates its agenda of development to prospects for social work engaged research. Since the last decade, Ethiopia has become one of the fastest economically growing country in the world with the average Gross

Domestic Product growth rate of about 10% of per annum. Ethiopia aims to become a lower-middle income country by 2025 (Shiferaw, 2017). Poverty declined from 55.3% in 2000 to 33.5% 2011. The present guiding economic and social development framework is the Growth and Transformation Plan (GTP-II), a macro development plan to be phased out in June 2020. Despite its quick economic growth, Ethiopia experiences many constraints including low human development (education and health), unsafe water use in rural areas, lack of resilience to drought, poor market access to farmers, weak urban planning and land management, and limited safety-net for urban areas (World Bank Group, 2017). The country remains one of the least developed countries in human development. Education continues to lag with close to half of Ethiopians unable to read or write. There are significant barriers to gender equality and women's economic empowerment. Unemployment remains high in Ethiopia. Industrialization has become the ambition of Ethiopia to reach its goals of becoming a low-middle income country and addressing the economic and human development challenges listed above (UNDP, 2018). Social protection remains a priority policy issue in Ethiopia. "The current government of Ethiopia (1991-present) views social protection as a means to make other investments more effective, efficient and to support economic growth" (Lemma & Cochrane, 2019, p.15). However, incoherence within the social protection policy, its strategy and implementation plans remain a challenge.

Social work as a professional field of study and practice is new in Ethiopia. The links between development and social work are yet to be examined. The contribution of social work engaged research to development in general and community/social development in particular are areas meriting closer scrutiny. This may be similar or different depending on the state of social work education and professional practice in other developing countries. Nonetheless, this chapter outlines the issues in Ethiopia as a developing country, with the hope that readers in other parts of the world can draw conclusions about their own policy context and the state of development of social work in their countries and apply this to the situation in their countries.

This chapter describes three important areas of development concern. The first section presents an overview of Ethiopia's development agenda, summarizing development polices developed and endorsed by the government since 1993. The second section describes current areas of positive development (i.e., economic growth, education, health, social protection) as well as development challenges (i.e., corruption, political instability and ethnic violence, migration, unemployment). The last section summarizes engaged research in the Ethiopian policy context. Some policies such as social protection, HIV/AIDS, education and training, national youth policy, and national policy for women are tied to some of the engaged research reports presented in Chapters 3-11. These include engaged research efforts with Muslim women, student engagement in campus-based community policing, women and economic development, leprosy stigma and discrimination, and so on.

Ethiopia's Development Agenda

Ethiopia is reported to be one of the fastest growing economies in Sub-Saharan Africa, with an annual economic growth rate of 10% for more than a decade. Since 2010, the country has launched two ambitious growth and transformation plans – GTP I [2010/11-2014/15] and GTP II [2015/16-2019/20] – with the intent to "...attain a lower-middle-income status by 2020" (Shiferaw, 2017, p.1), although GTP II shifted the target date to 2025. The economic plans preceding GTP II were "directed towards achieving the Millennium Development Goals (MDGs)" (Haile, 2015, p.19). GTP II targeted sustainable economic growth, consistent with major features of the United Nations Sustainable Development Goals (SDG) for 2030. GTP II has four objectives: "achieve an annual real GDP growth rate of 11%..., develop the domestic engineering and fabrication capacity..., solidify the ongoing public mobilization... and organized participation and deepen the hegemony of developmental political economy" (National Planning Commission, 2016, p. 80).

Both GTP I and II, as national macro-economic policies, have emphasized economic growth-related agendas. However, there are a number of other governmental policies and strategies (see Table 2.1) designed to address other aspects of development. These policies and strategies identify many of the issues that need to be addressed to bring about social and economic development in Ethiopia. These issues are wide ranging and include empowerment, housing, health (including HIV/AIDS), education, income, social welfare, political stability, human rights, science and technology, and gender equality.

Table 2A: Selected Policies and Strategies and their Development Objectives

Name of Policy/ Strategy	Publication Year	Objectives and Focus Areas
National Social Protection Policy	2014	a) Protect the poor and vulnerable individuals, households, and communities. b) Establish social insurance system. c) Increase access to equitable and quality health, education and social welfare services. d) Expand and guarantee employment for the vulnerable to unemployment. e) Enhance employment guarantee for the segments of society under social problems. f) Ensure that the society at all levels play roles for the implementation of the policy.
Urban Housing Strategy of Ethiopia	2013	a) Guide the government intervention and participation of stakeholders in the sector. b) Integrate and coordinate efforts to enable access to housing by the poor and middle-income level households. c) Integrate the sector with employment creation. d) Encourage saving and arrange financial schemes.
Ethiopia's Agriculture Sector Policy and Investment Framework	2010	a) To contribute to Ethiopia's achievement of middle-income status by 2020. b) Aims to sustainably increase rural incomes and national food security.

National Employment Policy and Strategy	2009	a) Enhancing social welfare. b) Accelerating economic growth. c) Achieving political stability.
National Youth Policy	2004	To bring about the active participation of youth in the building of democratic system and good governance as well as in the economic, social and cultural activities in an organized manner and to enable them to fairly benefit from the results.
Policy on HIV/AIDS	1998	To provide an enabling environment for the prevention and control of HIV/AIDS in the country.
Ethiopian Education and Training Policy	1994	a) Develop the physical and mental potential and the problem-solving capacity of individuals. b) Bring up citizens who can take care of and utilize resources wisely, who are trained in various skills, by raising the private and social benefits of education. c) Bring up citizens who respect human rights, stand for the well-being of people, as well as for equality, justice and peace. d) Bring up citizen who differentiate harmful practices from useful ones, who seek and stand for truth, appreciate aesthetics and show positive attitude towards the development and dissemination of science and technology in society. e) Cultivate the cognitive, creative, productive and appreciative potential of citizens by appropriately relating education to environment and societal needs.
National Policy on Ethiopian Women	1993	a) Facilitating conditions to the speeding of equality between men and women. b) Facilitating the necessary condition whereby rural women can have access to basic social services and to ways and means of lightening their workload. c) Eliminating, step by step, prejudices as well as customary and other practices that are based on the idea of male supremacy and enabling women to hold public office and to participate in the decision-making process at all levels.

Author

Ethiopia today is a whirlpool of prospects and challenges. On the one hand, the country is registering enormous positive changes in its Gross National Product (GNP); physical infrastructure; peaceful relations internationally, especially with neighboring countries; educational enrolment rates; and protection of women and child rights, at least in the public arena. On the other hand, the country still suffers from internal political and ethnic instabilities, significant rural-urban and cross-border migration, poverty across the country as well as in specific urban and rural areas, poor quality education, gender-based violence, unemployment, human rights violations, urban displacement induced by development, health disparities, corruption and embezzlement, and a low income for the majority of citizens.

Positive Accounts of Development

There are significant positive changes in four areas: economic growth, education, health, and social protection. These areas are important in their own right and are influential in assessing other development sectors.

Economic Growth

In general, Africa's economic growth is improving, rising from 1.4% in 2017 to 3.5% in 2018 and it is projected to accelerate to 4% in 2019 and 4.1% in 2020 (Africa Development Bank, 2019). After decades of stagnation, the Ethiopian economy has shown rapid growth since the mid-2000s, surpassing the global average (Seid, Taffesse & Alie, 2016; Zewdu, 2015). Between 2012 and 2016 the Ethiopian economy grew an average of 9.5% (School of International relations and Public Affairs, Fudan University, 2017, p.6). Poverty has declined from 55.3% in 2000 to 33.5% in 2011 (The World Bank Group, 2016a). Ethiopia's economic growth is attributable to three key factors: a strong political will for development, central government capacity, and improving infrastructure, all of which have attracted foreign investors. In addition, Ethiopian labor costs are cheaper than those of many Asian countries.

According to Shiferaw (2017), from 1980 to 2014 agriculture was Ethiopia's leading economic sector, representing an average of 51% of the total economy, followed by the service sector (38%) and industry and manufacturing (11%). GTP II declared that agriculture would remain the major source of accelerated economic growth and development during its implementation period (i.e., 2015/16-2019/20). However, the plan also called for manufacturing and industry to be developed to assume economic leadership (National Planning Commission, 2017). Currently, Ethiopia's approach to macro-economic planning and transformation has adapted features of Asian models of economic development, particularly the focus on "shifting labor from agriculture to industry" (Fudan Report, 2017, p.6).

Education

Whenever there is regime change in Ethiopia, the policy on education changes to fit to the political ideology of the ruling system. For example, in 1975 the socialist government nationalized all private schools and created an education policy that emphasized the expansion of public schools to rural communities. Education was seen not only as a means for development, but also as a way to inculcate Marxist-Leninist ideology. Primary schools grew from 3,196 in 1974/75 to 7,900 in 1985/86 and enrolment increased from 957,300 in 1974/75 to 2,450,000 in 1985/86 [http://memory.loc.gov/frd/etsave/et_02 07.html]. In 1994, the Ethiopian Peoples Liberation Front government, which came to power around that time, adopted the Education and Training Policy (Ministry of Education, 1994), which emphasized the need for vocational and skills training to create self-employment for the high school graduates (Lasonen, Kemppainen & Raheem, 2005; Yeneayehu, 2011). Central to the government's efforts, Education Sector Development Programs (ESDP) are designed to interpret and aid in the implementation of the Education and Training Policy.

There have been five ESDPs since 1996/1997. Each iteration has had specific priorities and objectives that have both built on the prior educational plans and have identified new initiatives (Ministry of Education, 1996, 2002, 2005, 2010, 2015). All five ESDPs share an emphasis on quality, the creation of good citizenship, and capacity building of the education sector at various levels. ESDP V, the current plan, focuses on five priority areas: ensuring quality of education, creating good citizenship, capacity building of educational institutions, special support for persons with disabilities (special needs), and supporting students at various level to share common values and to embrace diversity (Ministry of Education, 2015). Although the government has articulated equity in school enrolment as one of the priority areas in all of the ESDP documents, the Japan International Cooperation Agency [JICA] (2012) reported that girls' enrolment and graduation from the first cycle (grade 1-4) lags behind that of boys. Girls, compared to boys, more often repeated in the primary grades.

Teferra et al. (2018) in the Ethiopian Education Roadmap (2018-2030) documented the overall educational achievements during the five ESDP periods. There have been successes in school enrolment, quality of education, expansion of school infrastructure, and alignment of the education sector with the country's GTP II and SDG 2030 strategies. Particularly remarkable achievements have been registered in expanded school enrolment and numbers of school as well as decreased dropout rates at the primary school levels (grade 1-6).

Health

The current health policy, which has been operational for just over 26 years, was enacted in 1993 when the country was led by a transitional government. The health policy's main priority areas include: propagating health self-awareness through Information Education Communication (IEC), controlling communicable diseases, promoting occupational health, developing health infrastructures, facilitating curative and rehabilitative health services {including mental health), integrating traditional and modern medicine, promoting health research, strengthening medical and medical equipment supplies, and developing required human resources in the health sector. The health sector, like the education sector, has a series of Health Sector Development Programs (HSDPs), consisting of five plans (Ministry of Health, 2005, 2006, 2010, 2015). The most recent plan period (2015/16-2019/20) changed the name to Health Sector Transformation Plan (HSTP), consisting of 15 strategic objectives under four perspectives (See Table 2B).

Table 2B: Perspectives and Strategic Objectives of HSTP

Perspective	Strategic Objectives
Community	Improve health status
	Enhance community ownership
Financial stewardship	Improve efficiency and effectiveness
Internal process	Improve equitable access to quality health services
	Improve health emergency risk management
	Enhance good governance
	Improve Regulatory System
	Improve supply chain and logistics management
	Improve community participation & engagement
	Improve resource mobilization
	Improve research and evidence for decision-making
Learning and Growth	Enhance use of technology & innovation
	Improve development & management of HRH
	Improve health infrastructure
	Enhance policy and procedures

Source: Ministry of Health (2015), Health Sector Transformation Plan (HSTP)

Universal health coverage, defined by The World Health Organization as "the provision of preventive, curative and rehabilitative health services without causing financial hardship when getting these services" (Hallalo, 2018, p. 2) is the primary goal. Community health insurance and social health insurance are two initiatives, in addition to other efforts made by government, to bring public health services to a satisfactory and sustainable level.

The Health Extension Program (HEP) was introduced in 2003 and has become the main vehicle for achieving universal primary health care coverage (Workie & Rarnana, 2013). The HEP "is a defined package of basic and essential promotive, preventive and basic curative health services targeting households" (Woldemariam, 2016, p. 8). HEP services provided are free and available to everyone. To cover the entire country, which has a population of 100,000 million, over 35,000 health extension workers have been trained and deployed and over 15,000 health outposts established. Partly due to the roles played by health extension workers

> between 2005 and 2011, under 5 mortality rate decreased from 123 per 1000 live birth to 88 per 1000 live birth, the contraceptive prevalence rate increased from 15 percent to 29 percent, …the total fertility rate decreased from 5.4 to 4.8 and use of insecticide-treated nets increased from 1.3 percent to 42 percent (Workie & Ramana, 2013, p. v).

As a quality improvement strategy for its health services, Ethiopia introduced the Water, Sanitation, and Hygiene (WASH) program in all health facilities in 2014, and the Clean and Safe Health (CASH) program, which is designed to reduce health care infections and make hospitals safer. Relatively speaking, Ethiopia's accomplishments in the health sector, especially in primary health care coverage, are remarkable, though much remains to be done to improve the quality of services at all levels.

Social Protection

Social protection is broadly defined as "the combination of institutions, laws, regulations and interventions that are involved in implementing social protection" (Hinds, 2014, p. 1). Social protection includes child and family benefits, maternity protection, unemployment support, employment injury benefits, sickness benefits, health protection, old-age benefits, disability benefits, and survivors' benefits. Social protection is at the center of the 2030 SDG agenda of developing and implementing nationally appropriate social protection systems. Accordingly, "[s]ocial protection is fundamental to achieving the SDGs, to promoting social justice and to realizing the human right to social security for all" (International Labour Organization, 2017, p. 2). Today, social protection provides support for about eight million Ethiopians, nearly 8% of the country's total population (Ayliffe, 2018).

Ethiopia's social protection landscape is composed of surface structures (i.e., explicit government laws, policies, strategies, and programs) and underlying structures (i.e., ideological, cultural, and practical influences). The surface structures include national policies about such issues such as education, health, nutrition, water, HIV/AIDS, and developmental social welfare as well as legislation on cooperatives, small-scale and micro enterprises and micro-finance institutions. The underlying structures of the country's social protection landscape include "tradition and culture; drought and famine, dynamics of interaction among key actors, the mainstream paradigm of development, the poverty reduction agenda of the ruling party; and Ethiopia's constrained fiscal space" (Hailu & Northcut, 2012, p. 829).

Ethiopia's first Growth and Transformation Plan (GTP I; 2010/11-2014/15) articulated the necessity of welfare services for the elderly and for persons with disabilities and emphasized strengthening Social Security services for various groups (Ministry of Finance and Economic Development, 2010). The second phase, GTP II (2015/16-2019/20), characterizes social welfare responses as "creating opportunities for the disabled, the elderly and vulnerable population groups to participate and equitably benefit from the political, economic, and social activities of the country and to increase citizen's social security service coverage" (National Planning Commission, 2016, p. 59).

Ethiopia enacted the National Social Protection Policy in 2014 to improve the safety and security of the country's vulnerable groups. The policy focuses on enhancing the knowledge, skills, and employment opportunities of citizens to increase their incomes and asset-building capabilities, protect citizens from exclusion, and ensure their rights and needs are met by reducing their vulnerability to risks that emanate from economic and social structural imbalances (Ministry of Labour and Social Affairs, 2014). The policy's target groups are expansive, including children under difficult circumstances, vulnerable pregnant and lactating women, vulnerable people with disability, elderly with no care and support, victims of social problems (beggars, commercial sex workers, drug and medicine addicts), and citizens affected by HIV and AIDS. Also included are those vulnerable to violence and abuse and natural and man-made risks, unemployed citizens, those without formal insurance coverage, victims of human trafficking and repatriated emigrants.

Social protection in Ethiopia is inseparable from agriculture, as agriculture is the livelihood for over 80% of the population. Promising returns from agriculture foster overall food security, promote the welfare of society, and cushion against unexpected shocks not only in rural areas but also in cities. Difficulties in smallholder farming, which is an important source of food security, can cause "vulnerability to poverty, food insecurity, and their often-fatal consequences-chronic malnutrition, premature mortality and recurrent famine" (Devereux & Guenther, 2009, p. 2). Accordingly, the government has put agriculture, particularly small landholders, at the center of its efforts not only for social protection, but also for economic growth.

Social protection programs in Ethiopia not only enhance consumption capacities, asset accumulation, and citizens' participation, but also increase household food security and the number of meals to which children have access. Such programs also improve livestock production. The Productive Safety-Net Program (PSNP), which was established in 2005, consists of four components: public work and temporary direct support, direct support, risk management and livelihood support. The PSNP has increased the amount of time children spend in school by reducing the burden on them to help family members with farming activities (Zewdu, 2015).

In addition to such individual- and household-level benefits of social protection, the government envisages social protection as "a key pillar in the climate change and disaster risk management" (Slater & Ulrichs, 2017, p. 8). Finally, social accountability – "the obligation of power holders to take responsibility for their actions" – is an integral part of social protection services, according to Ackerman (as cited in Ayliffe, 2018, p. 9). To foster social accountability in the social protection arena, the government has decentralized its institutional arrangements to *woreda* (district) councils, *kebele* (ward) councils, *kebele* cabinet, development army, mass organizations, and traditional civil society organizations. The term development army refers to organized groups at the *kebele* level that provide voluntary support to farmers in their activities related to crop production, soil protection, forestry, health services and social safety-net.

Challenges to Development

In contrast to the achievements that Ethiopia has registered in the development sphere, a variety of challenges cripple development initiatives. Although the challenges are numerous in type and character, four challenges – corruption, political and ethnic instabilities, migration, and unemployment – are multi-faceted and include economic, political, social, and cultural aspects.

Corruption

According to Vito Tanzi, corruption is the "intentional non-compliance with the arm's-length principle aimed at deriving some advantage for oneself or for related individuals from this behaviour" (as cited in Begovic, 2005, p. 2). The arm's-length principle equates the absence of bias in the economic, political and social culture of a society with the absence of corruption. The U.K.'s Department for International Development [DFID] (2015, p. 12) defines corruption as "the misuse of resources or power for private gain." Similarly, Liu (2016) defines corruption as the abuse of public office for private use.

Scholars have suggested various causes and consequences of corruption. Causes generally are categorized in relation to individual factors, organizational factors and social factors (Gorai, 2015; Pathak, Singh, Belwal & Smith, 2007). Individual factors refer to human greed, disregard for values, low income and urgent necessity of life, over ambition and belief on materialistic world, rationalization for wrongdoing, external pressure from bosses and families, opportunity and exposure to public resources and lack of professional integrity. Organizational factors refer to lack of good leadership, absence of good organizational culture, lack of proper system, weakness management/

control system, cover up of corruption and lack of transparency and accountability. Social factors refer to erosion of values, disregard for rule of law, influence by societal culture, lack of public awareness, lack of good role models, weak societal laws, apathy/impatience, negative tribalism/nepotism, and bad governance/political patronage. In developing countries corruption often is attributed to a lack of loyalty to the community, wider discretionary power coupled with low wages, administrative delays and read-tape, a slackening of moral and ethical values, and the cumulative effects working within corrupted systems. For example, Mulunesh Abebe (2018) reports that women smallholder farmers are tired of corruption in their locality. Her qualitative interviews note the idiomatic expression of a woman who said "as short and tall [individuals] do not walk alike, poor and rich [persons] are not treated equally at court. The Supreme Court is the most corrupted [institution]" (pp. 151.152).

Corruption can produce huge transaction costs, disable free-market economics and maximize government intervention/regulation, violate the rule of law, and increase basic business uncertainty (Begovic, 2005). The consequences of corruption can affect the community as a whole, not just the individuals involved. The Amharic saying *sishom yalbela seshar yichochewal* can be translated as he who does not eat (take a bribe) when he is appointed shall regret it when he is dismissed. This saying illustrates the expectation of, and approval accorded to corruption in Ethiopia. Ayferam, Bayeh, and Muchie's (2015) study, *Causes and Consequences of Corruption in Ethiopia: The Case of Ambo Town*, described corruption as directly linked to economic and social poverty. The low salaries of public officials were considered to be an economic cause of corruption, whereas poverty was cited as a social cause.

Plummer (2012) analyzed nine sectors (i.e., health, education, rural water supply, justice, construction, land, telecommunication, and mining) and found corruption present in each. Yet this list of key sectors where corruption was found is not exhaustive; corruption is also common in other government, private, and non-governmental organization (NGO) sectors. Cognizant of the rampant nature of corruption, the Ethiopian government established an Ethics and Anti-Corruption Commission in 2005 under the Proclamation no.433/2005 and revised the duties and responsibilities of the Commission in 2015 under Proclamation no. 883/2015 (Federal Democratic Republic of Ethiopia, 2015). Though the government claims it is trying its best to stop corruption, the problem remains immense at all levels of government. Apart from economic corruption, there is also deep-rooted political corruption. Public service in Ethiopia is highly politicized, making it vulnerable to political corruption. Membership in ethnically divided political parties, which share state power, provides an advantage in employment, education, access to land, or assuming power in government offices. As a result, corruption in Ethiopia is a systematic as well as a systemic problem. Corruption is systematic when it "permeates the entire society to the point of being accepted as a means of conducting everyday transaction" (Gebeye, 2015, p. 81). Although the country's revised anti-corruption law strictly criminalizes major forms of corruption, such as active and passive bribery, money laundering, or civil servants accepting gifts or hospitality that jeopardize their decision making, the legal anti-corruption framework is rarely enforced.

Political Instability and Ethnic Violence

Ethiopia has been politically volatile since the 1950s. Political instability is directly linked to ethnic violence that periodically arises because of political, social, economic and linguistic grievances. Political instability and ethnic violence affect the country's development path. The rural-urban political divide has been one of the main factors contributing to political instability in Ethiopia. The Ethiopian People's Revolutionary Democratic Front (EPRDF), which has ruled the country for almost three decades, has been systematically biased towards rural areas and denied or given less emphasis to urban communities. Furthermore, different political factions based in the country and abroad have exacerbated existing political cracks. The contested 2005 national election resulted in the revision of some laws and the enactment of others. Conditions for the civil society "in the post-election period [2005] have deteriorated alarmingly" (Smith, 2007, p. 6) as a result of the revised Civil Society Law that sanctioned funding strategies and spaces of engagement of NGOs. The 2019 law was replaced by a new law, which re-instated the previous freedom for NGOs to solicit their major share of funds from abroad.

Ethiopia's socio-political image is paradoxical. On the one hand, the country's economic growth exceeds that of many African countries over the last decade. On the other hand, the country is accused of unfair economic distribution and receives a lower rating in its Human Development Index. Ethiopia contributes to regional security and stability in East Africa, but also reportedly has directed security forces to brutalize its own citizenry. The Ethiopian government has been accused of using "state security forces (police and intelligence in particular) as instruments of the party to preserve the existing power structure" and crushing all opposition groups including journalist, protesters and opposition party members (van Veen, 2016, p. 8). Change, however, appears to be occurring. A reformist group came to power in March 2018 and started to change many of the previous government's brutal practices and human rights violations. As a result of this political transformation, progress is being made towards creating a more free and democratic society based on the local philosophical concept called *medemer* (synergy), coined by Prime Minster Abiy Ahmed .

Theoretically, diversity is a well-accepted concept. Adamu (2013, p. 17) defines diversity as "differences between individuals on any attribute that may lead to the perception that another person is different from the self." Though there are various forms of diversity, ethnic and linguistic diversity are pronounced in Ethiopia and have been used for political ends. Ethnic diversity not only magnifies individual differences, but also group differences. Ethnic federalism, one of the principles introduced by the government in the 1990s, widened such group differences. As the result, ethnic conflict has intensified (Taye, 2017) and affects the country's social development agenda. In order to minimize ethnic-based political tensions, Prime Minister Abiy Ahmed and his reformist group allowed all opposition parties to come to the negotiation table leaving their stiff struggles, including those over arms. All opposition parties subsequently called competitor parties, accepted the offer to come the table for peaceful negotiations, and thereby start their power struggles in democratic ways. Another critical measure taken by the Prime Minister to lessen ethic tension was traditional reconciliation strategies using elders, tribal leaders, religious leaders and other renowned persons to mediate between intra-ethnic and enter-ethnic groups to make peace. Furthermore, the establishment of a National Council for Boundary Demarcation and Reconciliation Commission started operations to identify causes and suggest recommendations to resolve boundary tensions between regions in Ethiopia.

Migration

Migration is a global phenomenon that has existed since antiquity. Human migration is the movement of people from one place to another to secure a place to live. It can occur within the sovereign territory of a country or across borders. Both types of migration have advantages as well as disadvantages. For example, families and countries of origin can benefit from remittances sent home by migrants. Migration also can serve as a strategy to reduce unemployment. But migration can have disadvantages, some which include loss of skilled labor and loss of investments in training in the source country, and loss of use of skills in the host country when immigrants take jobs below their level of qualification (Ciuciu, 2018). Migration has social as well as economic effects for both sending and receiving countries. Social effects include changes in family composition, family separation, and the abandonment of older people and children, among others. In addition, there are other outcomes in the realms of education and health.

Migration can be categorized according to several different dimensions. Focusing on political boundaries results in migration being considered internal or international. By movement patterns, migration can be defined in several ways. Step Migration means moving from a small settlement and going to a larger settlement in the urban hierarchy over the years. Circular Migration is the cyclical movement between origin and destination settlements, typically for employment, including seasonal migration driven by seasonal labor demand, and Return Migration, a one-time emigration and return after an extended stay outside the destination. Chain migration occurs after a small number of groups move to a host destination and are followed by others in the community. Highlighting the decision-making aspects of migration results in its characterization as either voluntary or involuntary (World Economic Forum, 2017).

All of these forms of migration have been taking place in Ethiopia. Rural-urban migration is the commonest form of migration in the country. For some, migrating from rural to urban areas is a strategy to escape poverty (Fransen & Kuschminder, 2009). Still others migrate to urban areas to access better education, jobs, or business opportunities. Migration also is seen by rural households/families as a form of investment with the anticipation that migrant family members will be sources of remittance. Population pressure and food insecurity in rural areas push residents to migrate to urban centers. Melesse and Nachimuthu (2017, p. 39) argue that "[e]nvironmental degradation, lower agricultural productivity, inadequate social services, demographic pressure, land shortages in rural areas [are] identified as the major push factors of migration."

There are also pull factors in urban and semi-urban areas that attract rural migrants. The anticipation having a decent life in an urban area is one of the main pull factors. A chain of relationships can act as a pull factor, wherein rural residents whose family members have already migrated to urban areas are more tempted to migrate than those without such networks. According to The World Bank (2010, p. 25), "social networks influence the patterns of internal movement. Most of the migrants move to areas where they already know people or where they have information about the place." Rural-urban migration exposes children to a number of risks including sexual harassment, domestic labor and other forms of child exploitation. In Ethiopia, the majority of child domestic workers have left poor rural families to migrate to urban areas. One study found that the mean age at which children, mostly females, became domestic workers was 15 and their weekly average working hours was 53, over 13 hours more than the legally allowable weekly working hours for adults (Population Council, 2018).

International migration is another challenge being experienced by Ethiopia. This form of migration largely is illegal. Major destinations of international (and illegal) migrants are the Arab Gulf countries, Southern Africa (mainly South Africa), and the European countries. Legal international migrants have destinations on almost every continent, with the main ones being North America and Europe. However, in recent years many legal migrants also have settled in East Asian countries and China, especially for the purpose of education and business/trade.

Political upheavals, until recently, and economic aspirations have contributed to international migration. As Muhamed (2016) notes, cross-border migration may be influenced by personal, communal, social environment, economic, political, and technological factors. His study of the history of youth migration to Arab countries reported that key drivers of migration were unemployment, abject poverty, misconceptions and attitudes about job creation versus employment by government, avoidance of family pressure to marry, and absence of entrepreneurship support. These drivers are partly economic and partly socio-cultural. Migrants to South Africa from the Southern part of Ethiopia report poverty, unemployment and family pressure, peer pressure, population growth, and land shortage as push factors in their migration decision. They also acknowledge that deception by human traffickers/smugglers influenced their decisions. They expected high incomes in the destination country as well as job opportunities (Abire & Sagar, 2016). Migration brings various negative consequences for Ethiopian migrants, their families and the sending and receiving communities. Rural-urban internal migration, for example, creates population pressure in urban areas, which, in turn, can result in migrants experiencing food insecurity, congestion/overcrowding, violence, prostitution, and disease. Migration also puts pressure on urban health services, schools and food costs (Melesse & Nachimuthu, 2017). Miheretu's (2011) study of a northern Ethiopian town reports that migrants had problems with housing, food, social services, and employment, and they also experienced culture shock.

Young female migrants to Middle Eastern countries have faced a number of negative consequences. Female migrants may experience violations of their human rights, "including beating, indentured labor, not receiving food, not receiving payment, sexual harassment, verbal abuse and restricted movement" (Maastricht Graduate School of Governance, 2014). The challenges faced by international migrants are similar to those reported by the internal migrants. Both groups experience sexual harassment and other forms of abuse, though the intensity of maltreatment may be different.

Unemployment

Unemployment is one of the commonest indicators of economic and social dysfunction. If the unemployment rate is high compared to the proportion of the total active labor force, a nation is economically dysfunctional. A nation with a high unemployment rate is exposed to various social challenges such as crime, drug abuse, and labor migration.

The working age population can be divided into two groups, those in the labor force and those not in the labor force. Those not in the labor force can be further separated into those not looking for a job due to various reasons, those who are retired, and those permanently unable to work because of disabilities or other health factors. Among those in the labor force, two groups include those employed, either full-time or part-time, and the unemployed. An individual is unemployed, according to the International Labour Organization's guideline, if "the person (a) is not working, (b) currently available for work and (c) seeking work" (as cited in Byrne & Strobl, 2001, p. 1). According to the Reserve Bank of Australia (n.d.), unemployment occurs when a person is willing to work but is unable to find a paid job.

Causes of unemployment may vary from one country to another as well as over time within a given nation. A primary reason for unemployment is a disparity between job supply and employment demand. A mismatch between the skills required by existing jobs and those possessed by employment seekers is a critical challenge in developing countries. This problem, coupled with corruption, jeopardizes the employment opportunities of the labor force. Unemployment is more severe among young people in developing countries, and youth unemployment is a global problem. Ayhan (2016, p. 263) notes that the "youth unemployment rate is approximately three times bigger than the adult one, 4 out of every 10 unemployed persons globally are young people." In developing countries youth unemployment represents a threat to economic, social and political stability (Msigwa & Kipesha, 2013). Economically, it leads to labor instability; increased welfare cost; and unused investments in general education and specialized training, including higher education.

Since work determines other aspect of a person's life, entering to the job market is crucial. In Ethiopia, 52% of the population is in the labor force. Due to high fertility and declining mortality, Ethiopia has experienced rapid population growth, which contributes to high labor competition and adds to the unemployment rate. Unfortunately, since the latest census occurred in 1997, there is no updated comprehensive data regarding the actual employment or unemployment rates in comparison to population growth in Ethiopia. Accordingly,

> Unemployment and underemployment continue to be serious social problems in Ethiopia despite some improvements in recent years. This is mainly a result of rapid population and labor force growth and limited employment generation capacity of the modern industrial sector of the economy (Ministry of Labour and Social Affairs, 2009, p. 7).

Although accelerated economic growth and government efforts to reduce unemployment have been commendable, the unemployment rate remains high in Ethiopia's urban centers. The World Bank Group (2016b, p. 29) notes that "in Addis Ababa the unemployment rate is 24%. ...unemployment rates are particularly high for those who are with secondary education but no college degrees." Nayak (2014) reports that nearly 37.5% of urban Ethiopian youth were unemployed, whereas the unemployment rate of their counterparts in rural Ethiopia is only 7.2%. Regardless of age, women are more likely than men to be unemployed. Abera's (2013) research on female-male unemployment among those ages 20-24 and found the unemployment rate for females to be 38.7% compared 23.2% for males in 2005. Factors contributing to youth unemployment are low absorption capacity of the formal economic sector, both private and public, a slow rate of employment creation, skill shortages, and lack of entrepreneurship among youth. At the national level, the causes of high unemployment include poor economic performance, low educational attainment, rapid population growth, lack of entrepreneurship, mismatch between skills and position requirements, and inadequate training.

Unemployment has adverse effects on the individual, family, community and country. A study conducted in Ambo town and its vicinity by Fila, Mansingh and Legesse (2016) identifies numerous consequences of unemployment. Among them are migration, drug addiction, gang fights, prostitution, physical and sexual abuse, depression and other mental health problems, and conflict in the family. Dale's (2014) study of unemployed youth from poor families in Addis Ababa found that these youth have much free time but few ways to fill it, as they cannot afford many of the activities attractive to young people. This, in turn, led to depression and loneliness. Members of the Ethiopian government are aware that unemployment may lead youth to engage in unhealthy behaviors, including protests and demonstrations against the administration at the local and national levels. In his interview with the BBC on July 11, 2017, Negeri Lencho, the former Information Minister, stated that the protests in Oromia and other regions throughout 2014-2017 were the result of grievances of young graduates who could not find jobs (*Ezega News*, November 1, 2017).

Conclusion

A review of Ethiopia's development agenda and its challenges, current areas of positive development, and describing the importance of engaged research in addressing policies and interventions is the major focus of this chapter. The chapter discusses development policies and related issues in Ethiopia. It links development prospects to engaged research. In terms of development constraints, Ethiopia experiences many challenges including low human development, unsafe water uses in rural areas, lack of resilience to drought, poor market access by farmers, weak urban planning including poor land management, and a limited safety-net for its growing urban population. There are also positive development outcomes in economic growth, education, health, and social protection. Analyzing engaged research in relation to the development and policy contexts in Ethiopia provides an insight for readers to review similar matters in the context of other countries. Analyzing the links between policies and development can help gauge the direction of engaged research, and thereby influence the direction of existing policies and their development agendas.

References

Abera, B. (2013). *Socio-Economic and Demographic Determinants of Unemployment in Ethiopia.* (Master's thesis). Addis Ababa: Addis Ababa University. Available at http://etd.aau.edu.et/bitstream/handle/123456789/3119/Berhan%20Abera.pdf?sequence=1&isAllowed=y

Abire, G.B., & Sagar, Y.G. (2016). The determinant factors of illegal migration to South Africa and its impacts on the society in case of Gombora district, Hadya Zone in Ethiopia: A Bayesian approach. *Journal of Mathematics, 12(3),* 51-65.

Abuiyada, R. (2018). Traditional development theories have failed to address the needs of the majority of people at grassroots levels with reference to GAD. *International Journal of Business and Social Sciences, 9*(9), 115-119.

Adamu, Y.A. (2013). Diversity in Ethiopia: A historical overview of political challenges. *International Journal of Community Diversity, 12*(3), 17-27.

Africa Development Bank (2019). African Economic Outlook 2019. Available at https://www.afdb.org/fileadmin/uploads/afdb/Documents/Publications/2019AEO/AEO_2019-EN.pdf

Ayferam, G., Bayeh, E., & Muchie, Z. (2015). Causes and consequences of corruption in Ethiopia: The case of Ambo town. *Journal of Education Administration and Management, 2(1),* 072-079.

Ayhan, F. (2016). Youth unemployment as a growing global threat. *Actual Problems of Economics 7(181),* 262-269.

Ayliffe, T. (2018). *Social Accountability in the Delivery of Social Protection: Ethiopia Case Study.* Orpington, UK. Available at: https://www.developmentpathways.co.uk/wp-content/uploads/2018/05/Social-Accountability-in-the-Delivery-of-Social-Protection-Ethiopia-Case-Study.pdf

Begovic, B. (2005). *Corruption: Concepts, Types, Causes and Consequences.* Buenos Aires - Argentina: Centre for Liberal Democracy Studies. Retrieved from https://www.cadal.org/documents/documento_26_english.pdf.

Beyene, A. (2018). *Agricultural Transformation in Ethiopia: State Policy snd Smallholder Farming.* 7 Uppsala, Sweden: Nordic Africa Institute. Available at http://nai.diva-portal.org/smash/get/diva2:1256803/FULLTEXT01.pdf

Byrne, D., & Strobl, E. (2001). *Defining Unemployment in Developing Countries: The Case of Trinidad and Tobago.* England: University of Nottingham: Centre for Research in Economic Development and International Trade.

Ciuciu, M.M. (2018). Advantages and disadvantages of labour migration. *The Annals of the University of Oradea: Economic Sciences, Tom XXVII,* (1), 38-46. Available at http://steconomiceuoradea.ro/anale/volume/2018/n1/3.pdf

Dale, B.B. (2014). *Unemployment Experience of Youth in Addis Ababa*. (Master's thesis). International Institute of Social Studies: The Hague. Available at https://www.academia.edu/36399835/Unemployment_Experience_of_Youth_in_Addis_Ababa

Department for International Development [DFID]. (2015, January). *Why Corruption Matters: Understanding Causes, Effects and How to Address Them*. London, UK. Available at https://www.gov.uk/government/publications/why-corruption-matters-understanding-causes-effects-and-how-to-address-them

Devereux, S., & Guenther, B. (2009, January). Agriculture and social protection in Ethiopia. FAC Working Paper No. SP03. Available at https://www.researchgate.net/publication/238106113_Agriculture_and_Social_Protection_in_Ethiopia

Ezega News. (2017, November 11). Unemployment main causes for protects in Ethiopia-Negeri Lencho. Available at https://www.ezega.com/News/NewsDetails/4918/Unemployment-Main-Cause-for-Protests-in-Ethiopia-Negeri-Lencho

Bellù, L.G. (2011). *Development and Development paradigms: A (reasoned) Review of Prevailing Visions*. United Nations: Food and Agricultural Organization [FAO]. Available at http://www.fao.org/3/a-ap255e.pdf

Federal Democratic Republic of Ethiopia (2015). Revised Federal Ethics and Anti-corruption Commission Establishment (Amendment) Proclamation. Retrieved from https://chilot.files.wordpress.com/2017/04/proclamation-no-883-2015-revised-federal-ethics-and-anti-corruption-commission.pdf

Fila, T.D., Mansingh, P.J., & Legesse, W. (2016). Consequences of youth unemployment: The case of Ambo town, Oromia, Ethiopia. *International Journal of Research in Applied, Natural and Social Sciences, 4*(10), 70-76.

Fransen, S., & Kuschminder, K. (2009*). Migration in Ethiopia: History, currents trends and future prospects*. Paper Series, Migration and Development Profiles. Maastricht Graduate School of Governance. Maastricht University.

Gebeye, A.B. (2015). The legal regime of corruption in Ethiopia: An assessment from international law perspective. *Oromia Law Journal 4(1)*, 73-124.

Gorai. M.G. (2015). *Foundational understanding of corruption*. Available at https://chs.uonbi.ac.ke/sites/default/files/chs/chs/CHS%20-%2017-06-2016%20-CONCEPT%20OF%20CORRUPTION.pdf

Haile, T.G. (2015). Comparative analysis for the SDPRP, PASDEP and GTP of the FDR of Ethiopia. *Global Journal of Business, Economics and Management, 5(1)*, 13-24.

Hailu, D., & Northcut, T. (2012). Ethiopia's social protection landscape: Its surface and underlying structures. *International Social Work, 56(6)*, 828-846.

Hallalo, A.H. (2018). Achieving universal health coverage through health financing reform: Ethiopian showcase. *Health Economics & Outcome Research, 4(1)*, 1-5.

Hinds, R. (2014). Defining social protection systems: Helpdesk Research report. Available at https://gsdrc.org/docs/open/hdq1085.pdf

International Labour Organization (2017). *World Social Protection Report: Universal Social Protection to Achieve the Sustainable Development Goals.* Geneva: International Labour Office.

Japan International Cooperation Agency (2012). *Basic Education Analysis Report.* Available at http://open_jicareport.jica.go.jp/pdf/12083135.pdf

Lasonen, J., Kemppainen, R., & Raheem, K. (2005). *Education and Training in Ethiopia: An Evaluation of Approaching EFA Goals.* Finland: Jyväskylä University Press.

Lemma, D.M., & Cochrane, L. (2019). Policy coherence and social protection in Ethiopia: Ensuring no one is left behind. *Societies 2019, 9*(1), 19: doi:10.3390/soc9010019.

Liu, X. (2016). A literature review on the definition of corruption and factors affecting the risk of corruption. *Open Journal of Social Sciences, 4*, 171-177.

Maastricht Graduate School of Governance. (2014). *Shattered Dreams and Return of Vulnerability: Challenges of Ethiopian Female Migrants to the Middle East.* IS Academy Policy Brief, No. 8. Available at https://migration.unu.edu/publications/policy-briefs/shattered-dreams-and-return-of-vulnerability-challenges-of-ethiopian-female-migration-to-the-middle-east.html

Melesse, B., & Nachimuthu, K. (2017). A review on causes and consequences of rural-urban migration in Ethiopia. *International Journal of Scientific and Research Publications, 7(4)*, 37-42.

Miheretu, A.B. (2011). *Causes and Consequences of Rural-Urban Migration: The Case of Woldiya Town, North Ethiopia.* (Master's thesis). Addis Ababa: University of South Africa. Available at http://uir.unisa.ac.za/bitstream/handle/10500/4756/dissertation_miheretu_ba.pdf?sequence=1

Ministry of Education (1994, April). *Federal Democratic Republic Government of Ethiopia: Education and training policy.* Addis Ababa, Ethiopia.

Ministry of Education (1996). *Education sector development program I (ESDP I) 1996/97-2001/02.* Addis Ababa, Ethiopia.

Ministry of Education (2002). *Education sector development program II (ESDP II) 2002/03-2004/05.* Addis Ababa, Ethiopia.

Ministry of Education (2005, August). *Education sector development program III (ESDP III) 2005/06-2010/11: Program action plan.* Addis Ababa, Ethiopia.

Ministry of Education (2010, August). *Education sector development program IV (ESDP IV) 2010/11-2014/15: Program action plan.* Addis Ababa, Ethiopia.

Ministry of Education (2015). *Education sector development program V (ESDP V): Program action Plan.* Addis Ababa, Ethiopia.

Ministry of Finance and Economic Development (2010, November 10). *Federal Democratic Republic of Ethiopia: Growth and Transformation Plan 2010/11-2014/15.* Addis Ababa, Ethiopia.

Ministry of Health, Planning and Programing Department (2005). *Health sector development plan (HSDP-III) 2005/06-2009/10.* Addis Ababa, Ethiopia

Ministry of Health (2006, May 1). *Ethiopia health sector development program (HSDP-II) 2002/03-004/05: Report of the final evaluation of HSDP-II (Volume I).* Addis Ababa, Ethiopia.

Ministry of Health (2010, October). *Health sector development program (HSDP-IV) 2010/11-2014/15.* Addis Ababa, Ethiopia.

Ministry of Health (2015, October). *Health sector transformation plan (HSTP) 2015/16-2019/20.* Addis Ababa, Ethiopia.

Ministry of Labour and Social Affairs (2009, November). *National employment policy and strategy of Ethiopia.* Addis Ababa, Ethiopia.

Ministry of Labour and Social Affairs (2014, November). *The Federal Democratic Republic of Ethiopia: National social Protection policy.* Addis Ababa, Ethiopia.

Msigwa, R., & Kipesha, F.E. (2013). Determinants of youth unemployment in developing countries: Evidences from Tanzania. *Journal of Economics and Sustainable Development, 4*(4), 67-76.

Muhamed, E.S. (2016). *Migration of Ethiopian Youth to the Middle East and its Impacts on the Migrants' Sending Community: Raya-Mehoni Town.* (Master's thesis). Trondheim: Norwegian University of Science and Technology. Available at https://www.semanticscholar.org/paper/Migration-of-Ethiopian-youth-to-the-Middle-East-and-Muhamed/dc4ee9360450d599606fc3c84beb440709ac9cfe

Mulunesh Abebe (2018). Women farmers: l and rights in the context of constraining cultural norms. In A. Beyene. (Ed.). *Agricultural transformation in Ethiopia: State Policy and Smallholder Farming* (pp. 143-159). Uppsala, Sweden: Zed Books.

National Planning Commission (2016, May). *Federal Democratic Republic of Ethiopia: Growth and Transformation Plan II (GTP II) 2015/16-2019/20.* Addis Ababa, Ethiopia.

National Planning Commission (2017, June). *Federal Democratic Republic of Ethiopia: The 2017 Voluntary National Reviews on SDGs of Ethiopia: Government*

Commitments, National Ownership and Performance Trends. Addis Ababa, Ethiopia.

Nayak, K.B. (2014). Unemployment in Ethiopia: A call for an action. *International Journal of Management and Social Sciences Research, 3*(4), 34-40.

Pathak, D.R., Singh, G., Belwal, R., & Smith, R.F.L. (2007). Governance and corruption: Developments and issues in Ethiopia. *Information and Communication technology-Africa, (6),* 1-27

Plummer, J. (Ed) (2012). *Diagnosing corruption in Ethiopia: Perceptions, Realities and the Way Forward for Key Sectors.* Washington DC: The World Bank.

Population Council (2018). Migration and child domestic work: Evidence from Ethiopia. Available at https://www.popcouncil.org/uploads/pdfs/2018PGY MigrationCDW-Ethiopia.pdf

Reserve Bank of Australia (n.d.). Unemployment: Its measurement and types. Retrieved from https://www.rba.gov.au/education/resources/explainers/pdf/ unemployment-its-measurement-and-types.pdf?v=2019-02-03-09-26-45

School of International Relations and Public Affairs, Fudan University (2017, November). *Development and Industrialization in Ethiopia: Reflection from China's experience.* Available at http://www.sirpa.fudan.edu.cn/wp-content/ uploads/2018/01/Development-and-Industrialization-in-Ethiopia-Reflections-from-China%E2%80%99s-Experience.pdf

Seid, Y., Tafesse, S.A., & Ali, S.N. (2016). Ethiopia an agrarian economy in transition. Retrieved from file:///C:/My%20Files%201/root/Article%20writing/ Edited%20Book/Wassie/Ethiopia%20development%20context/Yaried.pdf

Shiferaw, A. (2017). Productive capacity and economic growth in Ethiopia. CDP Background Paper No. 34 (T/ESA/2017/CDP/34). Available at https:// www.semanticscholar.org/paper/Productive-Capacity-and-Economic-Growth-in-Ethiopia-Shiferaw/565d12d2affadd55b8db7efd14f0d93bea0d 7ff7

Slater, R. & Ulrichs, M. (2017). How is social protection in building resilience in Ethiopia? Policy Brief. Available at https://www.odi.org/sites/odi.org.uk/files/ resource-documents/11306.pdf

Smith, L. (2007). *Political Violence and Democratic Uncertainty in Ethiopia: Special Report.* Washington DC: United States Institute of Peace.

Taye, A.B. (2017). Ethnic federalism and conflict in Ethiopia. *African Journal on Conflict Resolutions, 17(2),* 41-66.

Teferra, T., Asgedom, A., Oumer, J., W/hanna, T. Dalelo, A. & Assefa B. (2018. July). *Ethiopian Education Development Roadmap (2018)2030): An Integrated Executive*

Summary. Available at https://planipolis.iiep.unesco.org/sites/planipolis/files/ressources/ethiopia_education_development_roadmap_2018-2030.pdf

The World Bank (2010, August 24). *The Ethiopian Urban Migration Study 2008: The Characteristics, Motives and Outcomes of Migrants to Addis Ababa*. Available at http://documents.worldbank.org/curated/en/207921468022733336/The-Ethiopian-urban-migration-study-2008-the-characteristics-motives-and-outcomes-to-immigrants-to-Addis-Ababa

The World Bank Group (2016a). *Ethiopia's Great Run: The Growth Acceleration and How to Pace It*. Washington D.C: The World Bank.

The World Bank Group (2016b, February 03). *5th Ethiopian Economic Update: Why so Idle? Wages and Employment in a Crowded Labour Market*. Available at http://documents.worldbank.org/curated/en/463121480932724605/5th-Ethiopia-economic-update-why-so-idle-wages-and-employment-in-a-crowded-labor-market-draft-for-public-launch

UNDP (2018). *National Human Development Report 2018: Ethiopia. Industrialization with a human face*. Available at http://hdr.undp.org/en/content/national-human-development-report-2018-ethiopia

van Veen, E. (2016). *Perpetuating Power: Ethiopia's Political Settlement and the Organization of Security*. The Hague: The Clingendael Institute.

Woldemariam, T.A. (2016). Ethiopia on the path towards universal health coverage (UHC). Available at https://www.birmingham.ac.uk/Documents/college-social-sciences/social-policy/hsmc-library/Priorities2016/Addis-Tamire-Woldemariam.pdf

Workie, W.N., & Romana, G. (2013). *The Health Extension Program in Ethiopia: UNICO Studies Series 10*. Washington DC: The World Bank.

World Bank Group (2017). *Country Partnership Framework for the Democratic Republic of Ethiopia 2018-2019*. Report No. 119576-ET. Available at http://documents.worldbank.org/curated/en/202771504883944180/pdf/119576-revised-Ethiopia-Country-Partnership-Web.pdf

World Economic Forum. (2017). *Migration and its impact on cities*. Geneva: Switzerland.

Yeneayehu, D. (2011). Ethiopian education policy analysis: Using Foucault's Genealogy. Available at https://www.academia.edu/11891083/Ethiopian_Education_Policy_Analysis_Using_Foucault_s_Genealogy

Zewdu, A.T. (2015, May 15). *The Effects of Ethiopia's Safety-Net Program on Livestock Holdings of Rural Households*. (Master's thesis). Oslo: University of Oslo. Available at https://pdfs.semanticscholar.org/0c9f/52355300c467a90c3af72be3d754be2fa686.pdf

CHAPTER 3

KHAIRAT MUSLIM WOMEN EMPOWERMENT

Yania Seid-Mekiye

This study seeks to understand the way in which Muslim female students perceive women's status in Islam and how they experience gender inequalities in the name of Islam. This was deemed as important for the participants for their future communication with other Muslim women when their organization started actual work. In addition, the action research participants developed the objectives of the Khairat Muslim Women Empowerment Organization (KMWEO). Once I met study participants, we agreed that before dealing with the future clients of the organization, the study should explore their perception of the women's status in Islam and how they experience gender inequalities. The participants were seven Muslim female students at Addis Ababa University Institute of Technology Campus, who intend to establish KMWEO. Female students were selected as study participants, because my intent was to use the study as a preliminary study on gender and Islam as my future area of scholarship. Focus group discussions were used to collect data and the study participants were engaged in the overall action research process. The women perceive that in Muslim families, Islam is understood on the way that legalizes gender inequality and women's disadvantaged position. After this discussion, KMWEO objectives were developed. This engaged research process helped me to focus on gender and Islam as the future area of my scholarship. For participants, this engaged research became the base for establishing their objective of starting a new organization. For me and for the participants, it was challenging to clearly articulate the findings. The limitation of this research on the women's status in Islam and Muslim families is that it was focused only on student perceptions. Therefore, further research is needed to help to strengthen the KMWEO activities.

Introduction

The term empowerment refers to a process that increases the assets and capabilities of individuals or groups to make purposive choices and to transform those into desired actions and outcomes (Kundu & Chakraborty, 2012). Empowerment is a central value within social work practice, and it relates to other core values and capabilities, like self-determination, self-control, and personal agency. Women's empowerment is a process through which women can enjoy greater control over material and intellectual assets that enable them to have greater autonomy over themselves, in household decision making and the use and availability of economic resources (Kundu & Chakraborty, 2012; Wahab & Khatun, 2015).

Gender inequality and the socio-economic disadvantage of women have been long-standing issues negatively affecting women globally. Women's quest for justice and equality with men in matters of education, socio-economic standing, marital relations and self-dignity, and interpretation of religion are factors influencing the need for women's empowerment. However, many prevailing interpretations of Islam relegate women to an inferior status, subjected to men due to gender inequality exercised in the name of Islam. Many Muslim men and some Muslim women agree that men may claim superiority in the name of Islam, and they consider the current inferior position of

Muslim women and their confinement as a diminished status supported by Islam (Wadud, 1999).

Contrary to the current condition of Muslim women and perception of Muslims, during the lifetime of the Prophet, women contributed to the social and economic life of their societies, enjoying social power, visibility and freedom. They were quite active throughout the early decades after the coming of Islam. However, gradually the status that women enjoyed at the beginning of Islam was undermined and Muslim women were "restricted behind closed doors" (Ali, 2003, p.83). Gradual restrictions placed on women's public role, their exclusion from the major domains of activity in society, and the controls imposed on them were the combined outcome of the worst features of misogyny, with Islam interpreted in the most negative way possible for women (Ali, 2003; Wadud, 1999). The majority of Muslim women also accept the status ascribed to them in the name of Islam (Esposito, 1998).

Ethiopian women, in general, experience gender inequality in education, work, and income, and political participation. Although some non-governmental organizations (NGOs) are making efforts to redress gender inequality in general, most are working on improving women's socio-economic problems. While this may help to empower women, it may not be sufficient to help to fulfill their own needs. There are women like Muslim women and others, who cannot easily access social support; they keep suffering degradation in their daily lives, as well as a diminished status as human beings. This, in turn, results in the persistence of gender inequality in education, reduced economic opportunity, and limited resource sharing, and decision-making. Despite efforts by government and NGOs to alter gender inequality, Ethiopia has been unable to bring about gender parity. Thus, the Khairat Muslim Women Empowerment Organization (KMWEO) came about to help Muslim women use their assets and also create new assets to empower themselves. Despite founding this organization, little is known about how the Muslim female students who intended to start KMWEO understand Muslim women in Islam and the gender inequality that women face in Muslim families. The main objective of this study is to understand the perception of Muslim female students on women's status in Islam and in Muslim families. There are two research questions in this study. How do the female students perceive women's status in the Quran and the Muslim family? What should be the objectives of the organization that students would establish?

Framing the Engaged Research

This section discusses the concept of empowerment, women in Islam, Muslim women scholars' views on family headship versus maintenance, polygamy in Islam in comparison with monogamy, and a Muslim feminist perspective on women's status in Muslim society.

Empowerment of Women

Women's empowerment is a contemporary issue for developing countries like Ethiopia. Empowerment is a means for sustainable development. Women must be empowered in order to be active and responsible citizens of a given nation, to benefit from lawful activities, and to protect themselves from any kind of discrimination and violence. The empowerment of women is defined as follows:

> Women Empowerment can be considered as a change in the context of a woman's life that enables her increased capacity to lead a fulfilling human life, characterized by external qualities such as health, mobility, education and awareness, status in family, participation in decision making and level of material security, as well as internal qualities such as self-awareness and self-confidence (Wahab & Khatun, 2015, p. 1).

Challenging long-standing traditions those make women subordinate to patriarchy and the difficult situation women in developing countries face helps to ensure the empowerment of women (Kundu

& Chakraborty, 2012). In Ethiopia, one of the means for women's empowerment is education, which in this case, helped female students understand the current condition of Muslim women and fuelled their intention to establish an organization to facilitate community support. Education can expand consciousness about societal arrangements that create oppression either through deprivation or the commission of actual acts designed to degrade women in ways that diminish their control over themselves and their health, family life, economic activities, work, sexuality, or relationships within extended networks of kinship. That women could empower themselves in relationship to other women reveals how empowerment itself can be relational, a product of women helping other women through social support.

Women in Islam

Islam has assigned a position of dignity and honor to women, which is essential for peace, comfort, happiness, continuation of the species and progress. The Qur'an, according to Khan (2008), holds that men and women complement each other and are a means of mutual fulfillment. The Qur'an says: "They are a garment for you, and you are a garment for them" [2:188]. Islam teaches that the faculties and capacities bestowed by God upon the human being are a divine bounty and must be beneficently employed. The Qur'an says: "Allah brought you forth from the wombs of your mothers, when you knew nothing, and gave you ears and eyes and hearts that you may employ them beneficently" [16:79].

From the perspective of the Qur'anic passages, one can understand that no man is superior to a woman by gender alone. The Qur'an states that God created humans, male and female, from the same *nafs*so that they may find tranquility, mercy, and affection with each other. Male and female believers are each other's *walis* (protectors, guardians) (Wadud, 1999). Divine will contemplates a relationship of harmony, consultation, and cooperation, as opposed to conflict and domination, between the two genders (Al-hibri, 2000).

Figure 3A: Relationship of Allah with Men and Women in the Qur'an and in Society

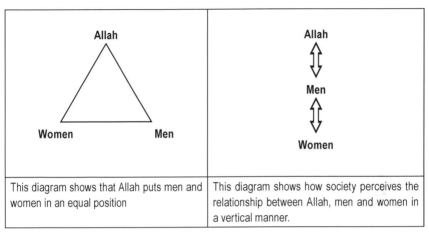

This diagram shows that Allah puts men and women in an equal position	This diagram shows how society perceives the relationship between Allah, men and women in a vertical manner.

Author.

Figure 3A depicts the analysis of Wadud (2006a) on Allah, self (women) and other relations (men) drawn in the form of triangle, with Allah on a vertical line in relation with the other two which are supposed to be found at the two tips of the horizontal line of a triangle. Wadud indicates that in the Muslim family, the triangle shows vertical relations with Allah at the top, men in the middle and women at the bottom. Her assessment is that the patriarchal relationship between men and women in Muslim society is against the very nature of Islam.

In the name of Islam, women hold inferior positions in socio-economic and political spheres. Al-hibri (2000) argues that this non-Qur'anic logic provides the underpinnings of a patriarchal world, with most Muslim jurists like the societies in which they live, uncritically upholding the central thesis of patriarchy that males are superior to females. This central patriarchal assumption has distorted their understanding of Qur'anic text and led them to develop oppressive patriarchal jurisprudence.

Just because men may be better at a given task than women in general, this does not mean that males are inherently superior (Badawi, 1995). This is an error made by many feminists who assume that liberation may be achieved by adopting or abolishing male roles (Al-Mannai, 2010). Even elite and educated women appear to be unaware generally of rights granted to them centuries ago by the *Shari'a*, or Islamic law (Kamaruzaman, 1986, as cited in Al-Mannai, 2010).

Muslim Women Scholars' Views on Family Headship versus Maintenance

Muslim women authors such as Al-hibri (2000), Barlas (2002), and Wadud (1999; 2006b) denounce the concept of husbands' headship of the family, which is well established and commonly practiced amongst Muslims. They do not agree with a concept in which the husband automatically obtains the right of family leadership. This violates not only the spirit of feminism but also stands in sharp contradiction to the Islamic perspective of egalitarianism between men and women (Mir-Hosseini, 2006). As they see it, men have no privilege to act as the head of a family (Barlas, 2002). To be a head or leader of the family, a man must fulfill his expected role, otherwise his headship or leadership role as a privilege or authority cannot last long as claimed. Instead, it is sustained as far as the man fulfills the criteria. Existing social factors and attitudes are unconscious factors in the interpretation of social issues in the Islamic texts. When circumstances change, attitudes are modified to fit the situation with various cultural patterns actively influencing the interpretation of the text (Roald, 2001).

Polygamy or Monogamy?

Though polygamy continues to be permitted, the number of wives is restricted to a maximum of four, and guidelines are provided for the just and equal treatment of co-wives (Esposito, 1998). According to Badawi (1995), Mejia (2007), Dagher (1995) there is only one verse in the Qur'an [4:3] which explicitly mentions polygamy and restricts its practice in the life of Muslims. In this verse, the terms of the number of wives permitted and the requirement of justice between them was revealed after the battle of *Uhud* in which dozens of Muslims were martyred leaving behind widows and orphans.

> If you fear that you shall not be able to deal justly with the orphans, marry women of your choice, two, or three, or four; but if you fear that you shall not be able to deal justly (with them). Then only one…That will be more suitable, to prevent you from doing injustice (Qur'an [4:3], Yusuf Ali translation, 1993, p. 179).

This Qur'anic verse was revealed in the context of war (Mernissi, 1991). Polygamy in this context allowed for widows and orphans to be assimilated into existing families, thus allowing for financial and emotional support (Hassouneh-Phillips, 2001). This provides a moral, practical, and humane solution to the problem of widows and orphans who are likely more vulnerable in the absence of a husband/father figure to look after their needs (Badawi, 1995; Mejia, 2007; Dagher, 1995). Wadud (1999) indicates that this verse is concerned with justice: dealing justly, justice to orphans and wives, and the just management of funds. "While modern day polygamy has strayed far from this original context [in the Quran], Muslim men's right to marry up to four wives remains largely undisputed" (Hassouneh-Phillips, 2001, p. 738).

Muslim Feminist Perspective on Women's Status in Muslim Society

Three perspectives exemplify the diversity of approaches to gender equality in Muslim societies (Ladbury & Khan, 2008). Azza Karam (as cited in Ladbury & Khan, 2008) distinguishes between secularists, Muslim feminists, and Islamists. In the 1990s, the Muslim Feminist Perspective came to exist with the emergence of postcolonial and postmodern feminism that embraced multiple forms or expressions of Feminism. "The Muslim feminist viewpoint provides the religious and cultural sensitivities which are missing in Western feminist theory, while allowing women in predominantly-Muslim states to become the authors and subjects of their own narratives" (Tickner, 1992, p. 3). In contrast to the secularist position, Muslim feminists argue that no meaningful change can occur in Muslim societies unless it derives its legitimacy from the Qur'an's teachings (Barlas, 2002). Muslim feminists see equality and social justice at the heart of Islam since the Qur'an allows for gender equality in all spheres of life.

The Qur'an was revealed into an existing patriarchy and has been interpreted by adherents of patriarchies ever since" (Barlas, 2002, p. xi). In addition, Islamic texts, like other sacred texts, are open to variant meanings and this has allowed different interpreters from the 7th century onwards, to give meaning to words, phrases and verses according to their ideological stance and the beliefs related to those stances. Wadud (1999) puts forth the argument that the dominant, patriarchal interpretations of Islam have fostered the myth of women's inferiority in several ways. They have used sayings attributed to the Prophet Muhammed, including disputed sayings, to undermine the intent and teachings of the Qur'an. They have taken Qur'anic verses out of context and read them literally, ignoring the fact that the Qur'an often uses symbolic language to portray deep truths.

In short, Muslim feminists explain the sexual inequality and oppression that women in Muslim societies experience largely in terms of the misogynist readings of the Qur'an and other sacred texts by male religious leaders. Male religious leaders first reflected, and through their interpretations further institutionalized, the patriarchal culture of their day (Ladbury & Khan, 2008). Therefore, this study addresses the impact of Islam on the mind and heart of the ones who seek to engage in community support. The Muslim female students I agreed to discuss self-perception as Muslims and women and wanted to establish the KMWEO as a vehicle for championing women's empowerment.

Research Methods

As the engaged researcher, my philosophical stance was in line with a constructivist philosophical stance, which is characterized by a belief in a socially constructed, subjectively-based reality, and the problem or issue influenced by culture and history (O'Brien, 2001). This action research focuses on exploring the reality of the study participants with their full engagement in the process of knowledge production for future action.

Engagement

The engagement process began by searching for Muslim women who would discuss about women in Islam and Muslim families. The participants were chosen on the basis of obtaining their perceptions, opinions, and attitudes (Kleiber, 2004). Snowball sampling was used. I found a man who was working with certain group of women who were trying to organize Muslim women. However, this man informed me of other women who were trying to get together and gave me the cellphone of one of them. These women were Muslim female students in Addis Ababa University. To the lady whom I called for the first time, I introduced myself, my area of interest and what I needed. I wanted to know if she was a part of a group on campus who were interested in forming an association that will work with Muslim women. She told me that she and the six female students intended to establish an association to work with Muslim women. We fixed a date to meet and I asked her to come with her friends.

Five students joined me, and we agreed to contact two additional Muslim female students who were interested in the Muslim women support organization initiative. I introduced my area of interest and explained why I needed Muslim women in the action research process. There was a discussion on what to do in the future organization, their intentions and the background of their efforts. They brainstormed about Muslim women in Ethiopia. The women came to know each other and illuminated their perspectives on the issues they faced, shared support, and came together to champion change through KMWEO.

The women started with identification and communication, followed by inviting additional Muslim female students to participate. After the first meeting, they decided the topic, selected issues to be discussed, and helped determine the method of engaged research. This was supported by Roberts and Dick (2003), who indicate that there are short- and long-term benefits when practitioners and participants make choices about the way action research is undertaken, data captured, analyzed, reflected upon, and findings used for a given purpose. "Emancipation will be increased when the participants are most involved in decisions and when their content and process knowledge is most privileged and utilized" (Roberts & Dick, 2003, p. 486). This identified engagement method helped to achieve the objectives of the action research.

The Action Research Process

In the acting stage, all action research group members met with me to formulate research questions, decide on data collection methods, and fix a time and place convenient for all of us. For two days, we discussed the issues identified during our first meeting. The women listed out the three methods, a questionnaire, interviews, and focus group discussion. We agreed to use Focus Group Discussion (FGD), a method that brings together a small number of 7-12 individuals for an average of an hour to an hour and a half to discuss the topic of inquiry. I explained that I would be taking notes on the issues that came up during our conversations and writing the research questions identified by the women. I would write a draft of my notes together with one of the participants and read them for the whole group.

During the FGDs, I took notes, the content of which served as data. The women freely discussed and expressed their opinions. Discussion proved a major strength since the students shared their opinions, attitudes, and beliefs with one another. As facilitator as well as a participant of the group, I took a less structured approach to posing questions so that the women students could moderate or be directly involved in discussion based on their own perspectives. This less-structured approach offered more opportunity for discovery and conversation (Kleiber, 2004). During discussion, the facilitator and one of the participants took notes, and both the facilitator and participants took turns in aiding the discussion and offering perspectives about the issues they faced. At the end of the session, the women drew conclusions from their discussion.

Data collection took place for three days, morning and afternoon. Session 1 began by establishing rapport, followed by activities to identify the study topic, propose the research questions, determine the method of data collection and fix a time for the next meeting. Session 2 focused on women in Islam and Muslim families with particular focus on the husband-wife relationship in the verse 4:34 of the Qur'an, as well as Muslim understanding of the verse and actual practice. In Session 3, we discussed polygamy in Islam and actual practice in Muslim families. In these three sessions, research questions, forwarded both by the participants and the researcher, guided the dialogue. In Session 4, we discussed on the objectives of the organization that the women wanted to establish, and in Session 5, all group members reflected on their perception of women's status in Islam and gender inequality in Muslim families.

I used Smith's (2012) recommendation for four stages of data analysis such as reading the data multiple times, taking notes (coding), categorizing notes into promising themes, looking for relationships between and among themes and clustering them together in writing up the report. The findings were categorized in two sessions and were presented as the major themes of Muslim women's status in Islam and Muslim families. This included a comparison between women in Islam and their actual condition. The second theme was an overview of the objectives of KMWEO. In session 6, the participants commented on and edited the analysis of our discussions. At the end of report writing, the group set a time to contact Muslim women to explore their perceptions, and as a first step, give training based on the gaps identified through their reflections.

Findings and Analysis

The findings are presented first on women's status in Islam and Muslim families with particular emphasis on their perception, and second on the objectives of the organization that is supposed to be established.

Women status in Islam and in Muslim families discusses women's role in Islam and in the family; verse 4:34 of the Quran and women in the Muslim family, and finally polygamy in Islam and in Muslim families. The finding about the objective of the Khairat Muslim Women Empowerment Organization present the view that participants have on the Muslim women's status in Islam and Muslim families, and their desire for community support service through the organization.

Perception of Women's Status in Islam and in the Muslim Family

Theoretically, Islam obliges Muslims to live in equitable and just relationship, whereas practically, patriarchy dominates the women's status in Muslim family relationships through inequitable gender relationships. Under this major theme, three issues are emerged: (1) women's role in Islam and gender role in Muslim families; (2) verse 4:34 of the Qur'an and marital relationships in Muslim families; and (3) Muslim female students' perception about polygamy in Islam and its actual practice in Muslim families.

Participants believe that Muslim women had higher status in Islam when comparing early Islamic times to the current situation. Especially in the first century of Islam, women enjoyed rights, freedom and protection, but women's rights deteriorated after the Islamic Prophet and his immediate followers passed away. However, the students perceive that the experience of Muslim women at present in Muslim families is not always similar to the actual description of women's role in Islam, in the early Islam as well as the current global expectations of women's position. There was a group discussion on the level of respect that mothers provide in Islam. Participants' perceive that in Islam, women as mothers are given more respect than the fathers. Participants indicated that there is no idea of a superiority-inferiority connotation in Islam. This is similar to Al-hibri's (2000) argument that in the perspective of the Qur'anic passages, no man is superior to woman by virtue of his gender alone. This perception of the participants is similar with one *Hadith* which is mentioned by Al-Mannai (2010):

> In an authentic *Hadith*, a man came to the Prophet and asked him: "Who is the one most worthy of my care?" The Prophet replied, "Your mother". The man asked, "Then Whom?" He replied, "Your mother." The man further asked, "Then whom?" He replied, "Your mother." The man asked, "Then whom?" And in this fourth time the Prophet replied, "Then your father" (Al-Mannai, 2010, p. 83).

FGD participants also discussed about the role of women as expected in Islam and the reality in the family. The women students are aware that the role of women in Islam focuses on the private sphere despite restrictions to participate in the public sphere. However, they look at it from a different perspective. For instance, there was a question posted, "Do not you think the role of women in Islam restricts them at home?" The women indicated that Islamic recommendation for staying at home do not restrict women, rather, it is she who is best for her child so that she is recommended to stay at home until the child gets strong. Her place at home shows the extent to which the woman is important for the continuation of a responsible generation. Even if she is educated, prioritizing the welfare of her children is preferred, even if it is a must for her, and possible in Islam, to participate in public.

In addition to the above, argument participants believe that compared to mothers' public role for a while, it is better not to lose two or three children as the future generation. This perception implies that the role of human creation from the Islamic perspective is very communal. However, gender relations became a problem when the value of a private role of women is undermined. In real life, it is mostly the public role of men that is given recognition. Thus, based on the ideal Islamic teaching or because of existing gender relations when women stay at home, it legitimizes the latter by means of help from the former.

Consequently, Islamic teaching serves as a pretext to strengthen gender inequality.

In public, Muslim women can attend the university. She can educate herself which is even a responsibility/right given to her. The women mentioned Ayesha, the wife of the Prophet as an example of the educational status of women in Islam. She was playing the scholarship role through her contribution of reserving /compiling / 2260 Hadith (the doings and the sayings which serve for further understanding of Quran, shaping the practice and behavior of the Muslim society) of the Prophet. This is similar with the arguments by Ali (2003) and Badawi (1995) that women can participate in any work while being within the framework of Islam. However, the gender inequality practices observed in Muslim families is the distorted implementation of Qur'anic duties and the Hadith as well as women's lack of awareness of their rights. Qur'an and the Hadith are mostly used by Muslims to perpetuate systemic gender inequality and gender discrimination within family relations such as expecting women to be submissive and connecting it with getting a reward in the hereafter.

Verse 4:34 of the Qur'an and Muslim Marital Relationships

In line with women's rights in the marital relations, the group discussed the issue of women's obedience and men's protective role mentioned in the Qur'an 4:34 verses that inequalities prevail in the Muslim marital relationships. Participants positively considered the idea of Quranic verse 4:34 as the expression of men as protectors and maintainers of the family so that consequently, women are supposed to be obedient to maintain tranquility. However, in the real life the group members, they question the way in which men fulfill their responsibilities of being protectors and maintainers, since this depends on their personality and their level of commitment to their religious order. Gender relations are based on this verse when men perceive their responsibility as a superiority that is also considered as religious order. This, in turn is used to legitimize and perpetuate the existing gender inequalities and patriarchal relations. Similarly, Wadud (2006a) indicates that Allah, self (women) and other relations (men) in the form of triangle as the former is on a vertical lines relation with the two whereas the latter two supposed to be found at the two tips of horizontal line of a triangle (See Figure 1). However, in the Muslim families the relation is supposed to have vertical relations such as Allah at the top, men at the middle and then women. As Wadud (2006) indicates, the patriarchal relationship between men and women in Muslim society are against the very nature of Islam.

Group members also viewed this Qur'anic verse as showing the way for dealing with conflict between husband and wife if there is infidelity on the part of the wife. Accordingly, this verse should not generalize to every possible relationship between male and female human creatures. They thought that most of the time, men use one literal meaning of this verse as it is comfortable for them to perpetuate gender inequality. In society, the points from verse 4:34 are picked up due to the socialization of men's minds to implement the Qur'anic intention on man-woman or husband-wife relations that benefit existing unjust gender relations. Similar to the view of Wadud (1999), the Qur'anic idea of human relationships was mentioned by the women students as the ideal society. The meaning of this verse is the expression of neither a biological nor inherent, but valuable obligation for men to create a better society by bettering their relationships with women.

Group members were asked whether they perceive that overprotection discourages a woman, makes her an object, and causes her not to use her full potential. They replied that people who lack understanding of the rights and protections that Islam provides for women perceive that Islam makes women an object. If a woman needs individual freedom, Islam may discourage her since the Islamic perspective of freedom is assumed to value family rights over the rights of an individual. If a woman needs respect of herself in the way that Islam provides, she can enjoy relative rights. Therefore, the idea of women's objectivity is from a non-Muslim perspective, not from a Muslim women's perspective. One participant stated that:

> We Muslim women in modern day have a problem of accepting the reality. We have a natural difference as compared to men. You know things would be unacceptable when they are treated from Islamic perspective. Islam has positive discrimination due to the natural difference of men and women, not to discourage and objectify women…

In line with the above argument, participants indicate that overprotection of women in Islam is not discouraging, but rather it facilitates conditions for her contributions to the family and the community at large. The women who know Islam should not be discouraged. Rather discouragement comes only from those who are ignorant. Islam makes life easy for women and if she needs, she can use her capacity to do whatever is meaningful for herself, family and community.

Polygamy in Islam and its Actual Practice in Muslim Families

The five out of seven participants agree with the theory of polygamy in the Quran. As they explained, polygamy is important because the number of male deaths is higher than that of women, so women are higher in number and these extra women need a husband. Therefore, to protect women from adultery and from any other abuse and assault, polygamy is allowed. Muslim men marry more than one woman and are interested to marry a virgin woman, a woman who does not have a child, and a woman for their own interest. However, the women students indicate that especially in families that do not understand Islam, polygamy is practiced for men's purpose and that interest perpetuates gender inequality.

Group members observed that in most Ethiopian Muslim families, men marry more than one woman to fulfill their sexual desires or to make women a protector of their property. This is mainly observed in the rural areas where most Muslim men do not care about women's rights. As one member stated,

> In Islam polygamy is not a must; it is not encouraged
> but just permitted since it has no spiritual significance.
> So, overusing "*halal*" makes or may lead to a *harem*.
> If *halal* creates a problem, then it should be cancelled.

For instance, fathers have a responsibility for the appropriate raising of children, but if the polygamous marriage is a problem for the appropriate nurturance of children, then it should not be practiced. Qur'an permission is not the problem. The problem is the actual practice of polygamy in Muslim families reflects the existing gender relations. In most families, women are economically dependent on family members when they live with their parents, and also when a woman gets married, first wives remain dependent on the husbands. Either the first wife or the new coming women challenge the husband because of their economic status. The women students recommended that men should marry more than one wife only to address socio-economic conditions in society, instead of for fulfilling their sexual desires.

The perception of the women regarding polygamous men is different and contextual, depending on the reasons for their husband's second marriage. Three participants indicate that if their husbands are very righteous and need a second marriage in order to support a vulnerable woman, they can accept it. For instance, if the case is to allow a single woman to get married and protected under the institution of marriage or to support a widow or divorced woman who has children and are in need of support, then the second marriage will be accepted. The problem is Muslim men, even the religious ones, are not practicing polygamy in line what is indicated in the Qur'an.

The students agree that it is difficult to accept polygamous marriage in line with the existing reality of the Muslim family. Similarly, Ahmed (1993) indicates that the fact that a man is allowed in extraordinary circumstances to marry up to four wives must be seen in context. It is quite clear that the ideal marriage in Islam is one wife, and the Qur'an emphasizes and indeed advocates it (Wadud, 1999). However, there are situations in times of war or famine or social upheaval when it is better that a woman is safely and honorably married than having to fend for herself as a destitute or prostitute. It is, therefore, the spirit that must be understood, not the letter of the law (Ahmed, 1993; Wadud, 1999; Dagher, 1995).

In conclusion, the group members perceived that the Muslim families that they have experienced are mostly living with practices perpetuating gender inequalities. From a gender perspective, the men in the Muslim families use Islam for their own interest. In the actual condition of most Muslim families, there is a problem of understanding Islam and there is a mixing of Islam and culture so that practicing gender inequality in the name of Islam is common. Apart from men's misuse of Islam, most Muslim women do not understand their status and role which is similar with the statement of Esposito (1998) who indicated that reflecting the realities and values of patriarchal society; women remain subordinate to the men of their family and community. The Muslim female students are interested in and intend to establish an organization for Muslim women's empowerment to challenge gender inequality in the name of Islam.

The Intent for Establishing Khairat Muslim Women Empowerment Organization

Due to individual, familial and community-related perceptions, Muslim women experience problems that derive from themselves, family members and community. Muslim women need service providers who understand their concerns and also challenge some of their viewpoints which hinder their empowerment and problem-solving capacity. The discussion of women's status in Islam and in Muslim families led the group to formulate the objectives of the Khairat Muslim Women's Empowerment Organization. The objectives were formulated based on the assessment of the needs of women as well as their priorities for solving their problems. One of the objectives is building the capacity of women through the provision of training and helping them help themselves. The training would focus on socio-economic, health and spiritual issues. It would also include creating goal-oriented female students, making efforts to help Muslim women solve and trying to solve their socio-economic problems, helping women become aware of their health issues, creating self-confident women aware and conscious of their environment, and helping Muslim women be active participants in their overall development. In regard to creating goal-oriented female students, educational gaps in elementary enrollment are narrowing between non-Muslim girls and Muslim girls, and between Muslim girls and boys. However, at the level of high school and tertiary education, the success of Muslim girls is much lower than that of non-Muslim girls, and their attrition rate is high. Considering the Muslim societal condition and the context of the country, the women prioritized enhancing Muslim women's educational access and success.

Much of oppressive Muslim practices are not based on the religion but on the socio-political and economic aspect of families and societies. Therefore, the intent of the KMWEO will emphasize the awareness of Muslim women and girls on their status and rights, as well as their duties in Islam in the context of present socio-economic problems. As the founders of KMWEO, I and study participants intend to share our experiences and ideas on how to solve socio-economic problems. Considering the awareness of women's health, KMWEO will focus mainly on uneducated Muslim women who are at home. When women lack educational access and success, their awareness of health and childcare will be much less than that of educated women. In collaboration with other organizations working on health issues, KMWEO will work to improve women's awareness of transmitted diseases and their causes and so that women can be protected before being infected. Since they are part of the problem, Muslim men will also be considered.

Similar with Abdullah (1998), as the findings indicate, Ethiopian Muslim women have their own dignity and independent personality as opposed to their current disadvantaged and dormant conditions as Muslim and as women. Society in general and Muslim women in particular needs some kind of consciousness-raising about themselves, their environment and its influence on their life. Muslims in general also need awareness about the current condition of Muslim society in Ethiopia in general and Muslim women in particular. In terms of women's participation in development, the first challenge is raising women's awareness and facilitating empowerment to solve socio-economic problems. Once women's problems are solved, this directly or indirectly affects the socio-economic development of the family. Second, the participation of women in development is related to their ability to influence their family members to contribute more for the familial, societal and national development. When Muslim women are supportive of the male members of the family, they serve as positive stimuli for the efforts of men. As such, KMWEO will encourage the indirect participation of women in development as facilitators of the social development activities of men family members. The rationale for this principle is that when Muslim have children who need daily and continual support from their mothers, it would be difficult for these mothers to engage in public activities including their own job. Thirdly, when women get empowered through training on women in Islam and women status in the Muslim societies, they can be champions of their own development which has been hindered in the name of Islam.

Strengths, Challenges, and Lessons Learned

My engagement with Muslim students was harmonious and based on our mutual understanding as Muslim women. Thus, the data was collected with honesty which in turn has positive implications for the trustworthiness of data as well as findings. The discussions helped identify the role of Muslim women students, and the issues to be given priority while starting work in KMWEO. Participants reported that the discussion increased their knowledge, made their views multidimensional, and served as a refresher course that would be used in day-to-day communication with future KMWEO clients. The FGDs helped them understand how some Muslims perceptions are different while all are Muslims.

In addition, the trust developed between the researcher and the study participants led the researcher to help in developing the KMWEO objectives. The study participants' perception of the status of women in Islam, families and communities was very helpful to challenge patriarchal notions in Muslim families. This in turn, serves as a means for women's empowerment. Although the majority of Muslim women are disadvantaged from worldly benefits in the name of Islam, and also lack recognition of their rights as indicated in the Qur'an, the women students shed some light on ways to the future empowerment of Muslim women and the protection of their rights. They confirmed that their discussion helped them know each other in their future community support activities in their organization. There were discussions in three specific areas that indicate women's status in Islam and Muslim families, and KMWEO objectives were developed. The overall process helped me as the engaged researcher to focus on gender and Islam as the future area of my scholarship.

In addition, the study achieved its purpose of helping the women come to know each other on the status of women in Islam and in Muslim families. Although not possible in this early stage of engaged research, future and ongoing efforts can include the practical aspect of empowerment of the Muslim women in line with the views of the group. The engaged research shows the strong side of the women to be champions of change in promoting Muslim women's empowerment and achieving gender equality. These inner qualities, as well as diversities among them aided them in thinking about the community in which they live, forged their resolve to provide support as much as possible.

In my early graduate education, I focused on gender studies, and after enrolling in doctoral education, I have been interested in research on Muslim women. My intent to conduct research with Muslim women is supported by Adamu (1999) who indicates that despite social gender inequality, Islam is a religion which embraces all aspects of Muslim women's lives and shapes their experiences. Any attempts to exclude religious concerns from a priority in research and practice will likely exclude Muslim women as participants in knowledge building in social work and makes unfinished business of the empowerment process. Thus, connecting Islam with gender issues will help address Muslim women's concerns. With this inspiration in mind, I sought to find Muslim women who could discuss their concerns together and hopefully achieve the establishment of KMWEO.

When I was planning for conducting a research with Muslim women, I had no clue on the issues to be addressed. However, the project conducted with Muslim female students helped me to identify and fix a research area and the topic of the dissertation. During the action research, we discussed the participant's perception of women's right in Islam and actual practice in the marital relationship. Though I did not conduct action research in my dissertation research, I conducted research on the marital experiences of Muslim women. In short, the idea for my doctoral dissertation emanated directly from the perspectives of the Muslim women students on verse 4:34 of the Quran and marital relationship in Muslim family. I was interested to study the views of married Muslim women about their experience of marital relationships in conjunction with the verses on women in Islam. Since the women students in this study did not have marital relationships, they thought it was important to know common views applicable to times when they would be working with married Muslim women.

This engaged research helped me to become more aware of the reality in Ethiopian Muslim families and how it is not always similar, albeit the intention of Islamic scriptures. Based on this experience, I have conducted further research on gender and Islam in Ethiopia with particular focus on marital relationships. This research focuses on educated women's experiences of marital relationship as well as their perception about gender and Islam in Ethiopia. Overall, this engaged research project opened a door for me to deal with Muslim women's issues in Ethiopia.

Conclusion

This study deals with women in Islam and Muslim families from the perspective of female Muslim students who intend to establish an organization to support the empowerment of Muslim women. The objectives for the Khairat Muslim Women Empowerment Organization

(KMWEO) were developed during the FGDs as part of this engaged research. This action research process helped Muslim women students to come to common ground and an understanding of women's status in Islam and in the Muslim family, as a first step in developing future activities related to empowerment of Muslim women. Their common understanding helped them know each other for their future community support activities in their organization. Coming to a common understanding of women's status in Islam and the actual conditions that women face in Muslim families moved study participants forward to maximize their efforts to achieve their goal of becoming champions of change for Muslim women. Thus, in addition to KMWEO's initiation to empower Muslim women, further research is required on how to combat the negative efforts of gender relations that are legalized in the name of Islam in Muslim families. This engaged research helped me be more aware of the reality in Ethiopian Muslim families and how it is not always similar, albeit the intention of Islamic scriptures. Based on this experience, I have conducted further research on gender and Islam in Ethiopia with particular focus on marital relationships. This research focused on the educated women experiences of marital relationship as well as their perception about gender and Islam in Ethiopia.

References

Abdullah, N.B. (1998). *I Appeal to your Sense of Shame my Muslim Sister…Will You Not Respond?* Mecca: Al-Haramain Foundation.

Adamu, F. (1999). A doble-edged sword: Challenging women's oppression within Muslim society in Northern Nigeria. *Gender and Development, 7*(1), 56-61.

Adnan, G. (2004). *Women and the Glorious Qur'an: An Analytical Study of Women-related Verses of Sura An-Nisa'a.* Göttingen: Germany: Universitätsverlag Göttingen.

Ahmed, A.S. (1993). *Living Islam, from Samarkand to Stornoway.* London: BBC Books Limited.

Al-hibri, A.Y. (2000). An introduction to Muslim women's rights. In G. Webb (Ed.), *Windows of Faith: Muslim Women Scholar-Activists in North America* (pp. 51-71). NY: Syracuse University Press.

Ali, K. (2006). *Sexual Ethics and Islam: Feminist Reflections on Qur'an, Hadith, and Jurisprudence.* Oxford: Oneworld Publications.

Ali, W. (2003). Muslim women: Between cliché and reality. *Diogenes 50*(3), 77–87.

Ali, Y. (1993). *The Meaning of the Holy Qur'an.* Brentwood, MD: Amana Corporation.

Al-Mannai, S.S. (2010). The misinterpretation of women's status in the Muslim world. *Digest of Middle East Studies, 19*(1), 82-91.

Badawi, J. (1995). *Gender Equity in Islam: Basic Principles.* Indianapolis: American Trust Publication.

Barlas, A. (2002). *"Believing Women" in Islam: Unreading Patriarchal Interpretations of the Qur'an.* Austin: University of Texas Press.

Dagher, H. (1995). *The Position of Women in Islam.* Villach, Austria: Light of Life.

Esposito, J. (1998). Introduction: Women in Islam and Muslim societies. In Y.Y. Hadded & J.L. Esposito, (Eds.), *Islam, Gender and Social Change* (p. ix-xxviii). NY: Oxford University Press.

Hassouneh-Phillips, D. (2001). Polygamy and wife abuse: A qualitative study of Muslim women in America. *Health Care for Women International, 22,* 735–748.

Khan, M. Z. (2008). *Women in Islam.* London, UK: Islam International Publications.

King, A. (2009). Islam, women and violence: *Feminist Theology, 17*(3), 292-328.

Kleiber, B. P. (2004). Focus groups: More than a method of qualitative inquiry. In K. deMarrais, & S.D. Lapan, (Eds.). *Foundations for Research: Methods of Inquiry in Education and the Social Sciences* (pp. 87-102). Mahwah, New Jersey: Lawrence Erlbaum Associates.

Kundu, S., &Chakraborty, A. (2012). An empirical analysis of women empowerment within Muslim community in Murshidabad district of West Bengal, India. *Research on Humanities and Social Sciences, 2 (6),* 1-11.

Ladbury, S., &Khan, S. (2008). Increased religiosity among women in Muslim majority countries. Issues Paper. *Social Development Direct.* Retrieved January 17, 2018 from http://www.gsdrc.org/docs/open/eirs1.pdf

Mejia, M.P. (2007). Gender jihad: Muslim women, Islamic jurisprudence, and women's rights. *Kritike, 1(1),* 1-24.

Mernissi, F. (1991). *The Veil and the Male Elite: A Feminist Interpretation of Women's Rights in Islam.* NY: Perseus Books.

Mir-Hosseini, Z. (2006). Muslim women's quest for equality: Between Islamic law and feminism. *Critical inquiry, 32,*629-645.

O'Brien, R. (2001). An overview of the methodological approach of action research. In R. Richardson (Ed.), *Theory and Practice of Action Research.* João Pessoa, Brazil: Universidade Federal da Paraíba. Available at http://www.web.ca/~robrien/papers/arfinal.html

Roald, A. (2001). *Women in Islam: The Western Experience.* London: Routledge

Roberts, G., & Dick, B. (2003). Emancipatory design choices for action research practitioners. *Journal of Community & Applied Social Psychology, 13,* 486–495.

Tucker, J. (2008). *Women, family, and gender in Islamic law.* Cambridge: Cambridge University Press.

Wadud, A. (1999). *Qur'an and Woman: Reading the Sacred Text from a Woman's Perspective.* NY: Oxford University Press.

Wadud, A. (2006a). *Inside the Gender Jihad: Women's Reform in Islam.* England, Oxford: Oneworld Publications.

Wadud, A. (2006b). Islam beyond patriarchy through gender inclusive Qur'anic analysis. *Wanted: Equality and Justice in the Muslim Family,* 95-116.

Wahab, A. &, Khatun, M. (2015). A sociological study on empowerment of Muslim women in Darrang District of Assam. *IOSR Journal of Humanities and Social Science, 20(10),* 19-24.

CHAPTER 4

WOMEN AND ECONOMIC DEVELOPMENT

Abiot Simeon

This action research promotes women's economic empowerment through microenterprise community development. Women are typically paid less and have less secure employment than men. Women are largely relegated to more vulnerable forms of employment with no or little financial security or social benefits. This study attempts to improve the income of a women's group through exploration of their performance and a future microenterprise work plan. It focuses on one microenterprise group of 37 members. Participatory action research was used to explore group performance and their future plans in the Hadiya Development Association. The Nominal Group Technique (NGT) originated as participatory social planning techniques for conducting challenging group meetings (Delbecq, Van de Ven, & Gustafson, 1975). It is a well-known approach for structuring group meetings (Dowling & Louis, 2000). The NGT facilitates productive group decision-making processes and has been implemented in several fields and situations since its development (Potter, Gordon & Hamer, 2004). NGT was used to collect data from the women in terms of their past accomplishments and challenges and their future plans. Through use of NGT, I was able to help participants generate many creative new ideas. Every member was able to express their ideas, thereby minimizing the influence of more powerful or influential participants. In this process, the women's group engaged in analyzing their microenterprise work in relationship to their future livelihoods. Results show that microenterprise is a strategy which can foster economic empowerment and help women to improve their living standard and family survival. Challenges that women experience in their microenterprise work are shortage of loans and working capital, lack of adequate working space, accessibility of raw material, inadequate bookkeeping and financial management skills, and inconvenient infrastructures and technologies. Ongoing challenges include minimal community support, lack of previous experience, frequent change in places to work, and seasonal market fluctuations. This participatory study promotes women's economic self-sufficiency and future actions for sustaining their microenterprise work.

Introduction

Globally the share of women in paid employment has continued to increase slowly and reached 41% in 2008 (United Nations, 2010). In Southern Asia, Northern Africa and Western Asia, only 20% of those employed outside of agriculture are women. Women are over-represented in informal employment and are largely relegated to more vulnerable forms of employment. In Ethiopia, where the agricultural sector predominates, women are mostly employed in agriculture and in jobs with no or little financial security or social benefits. Women face the challenge of extreme poverty and gender inequality, factors which in turn compromise employment possibilities, and result in inadequate income.

Microenterprise is a viable mechanism for advancing economic opportunities for women in developing countries. Microenterprises are particularly important for women since they offer a more flexible and less restrictive form of employment. Women are more likely than men to spend their income on household consumptions and family needs. Thus, assistance to women has a multiplier effect that improves the welfare of the whole family. In this regard, microenterprise helps women expand business activities, contribute to household income, and promote food security, children's education, and health. Microfinance programs promote lending and saving practices that can foster a livable wage, and as a result, support women's movement out of poverty. Small businesses allow poor people to increase their income and accumulate assets. The strategy also offers opportunities to gain knowledge, make decisions, control working conditions, build household assets, and fulfill personal goals (Sherraden, Sanders, & Sherraden, 2004). Microenterprise work can stimulate skills development, produce personal satisfaction, and increase self-esteem.

The role of microenterprise in employment and income generation is increasingly recognized as one strategy for addressing unemployment, especially for women. It is a major playing field for policymakers and donors to enhance economic growth and alleviate poverty by promoting economic development, job creation, self-sufficiency, and the opportunity to develop talents and skills to improve financial wellbeing. Microfinance organizations and donors have components of financial support and envision that lending will translate into self-employment opportunities and home-based businesses. These organizations provide access to loans that increase women's resources and reduce their overall vulnerability. Financial assistance helps poor women to increase income, build feasible businesses projects, and reduce their vulnerability to external distress. It enables women to become economic agents of change and self-empowerment.

In Ethiopia, the strategy of women-operated microenterprises is an important vehicle for creating job opportunities and economic empowerment. The Ethiopian national strategies give emphasis to the development of micro and small enterprises. According to Federal Democratic Republic of Ethiopia (2016), micro and small enterprises can influence job creation, entrepreneurship expansion, industrial development, and economic growth. It creates employment opportunities and income generation (Ministry of Urban Development and Construction, 2013). The approach demands low level training and a small amount of capital, thereby making entry at the local level accessible for women and their families (Nega & Hussein, 2016).

This engaged research focused on women's group in Hossana town under Hadiya Development Association Program (HDAP). The Women's Group began in 2009 with initial financial support from HDAP. The group is comprised of 37 members, both married and unmarried women. They have their own office and meet regularly. After taking initial entrepreneurship training, they organized themselves into small business clusters. The project facilitator supervises their activities and supports regular weekly savings. It explores the accomplishments, challenges, and future plans of the Women's Group. Women's are fully involved in the process of research. They are the source of information and participate in the analysis of the result. The women play the primary role in prioritizing their microenterprise works of action. The researcher facilitated group discussions by applying the nominal group technique, and organized, and compiled the final research results. This engaged action research addressed how women can work together to advance their economic well-being using a microenterprise perspective.

Framing the Engaged Research

Self-employment's as a strategy for economic development was publicized initially by the International Labour Organization in 1972 through the investigation of unemployment within urban low-income countries (Raheim, 1996). Poor people organize in groups and start small `reasons: to expand economic advantage and available assets, overcome insufficient opportunity and inequity, and utilize available resources and achieve autonomy (Sherraden, Sanders, & Sherraden, 2004). Small business can create employment opportunities for the entrepreneur and family members as well as others, provide services for local consumers or users, and provide an outlet for creative entrepreneurial activity (Carter & Jones-Evans, 2006). In developing countries, the economic condition of women is low, and the majority of micro-enterprise work carried out by them and has role in economic self-sufficiency and local economic development (Sharma, Dua, & Hatwal, 2012). Microenterprise can reduce poverty, enhance women's involvement in social and economic development, and fulfill household consumption expenditures (Asian Development Bank, 1997). Small business helps women to be self-employed, generate income, and support their family's livelihood (International Labour Organization, 2003). Microenterprise's self-employment positively influences the accumulation of assets, improves child schooling, results in skills and experience, builds support networks, and increases income (Schreiner, 1999). Microenterprise creates wealth and promotes social, economic, and human development.

Financial access is a vital part for the growth and development of a small business strategy. Micro credit organizations make loans and start or strengthen small business among the poorest. These organizations are mostly non-governmental organizations (NGOs) that depend on external funding sources and organize the poor and provide credit opportunity as a human right strategy (Elahi & Rahman, 2006). They mainly provide financial support to the poor who can engage in microenterprise to improve their livelihoods (Nawai & Shariff, 2010). These organizations mediate economic self-sufficiency by lending small amounts of money to poor people to improve their livelihoods (Dixon, Ritchie, & Siwale, 2006).

Even if the grants offered by microcredit organizations are very small and for a short period of time, the funding is a stimulus for the subsequent development of an income base, perhaps enough to help people leave poverty. In Birkenmaier and Tyuse (2005), services and loan accessibility from microcredit financial organizations can build assets, reduce poverty, increase financial stability, and empower families' economic development. These programs can create self-employment opportunities for poor people and enable them to achieve economic self-sufficiency (Servon & Bates, 1998). The majority of world population consists of women and many live under the poverty line (Mohanty, 2004). Microenterprise can serve as an important economic development strategy for poor women. Compared to men, women rely on petty trades and services for income, employment, and self-sufficiency, and have priority access for micro credit and micro finance services (Lodhi, Luqman, Javed, & Asif, 2006).

The challenges of microenterprise work are diverse. According to Moyo (2003), critical factors for successful microenterprise work are a supportive policy environment, clear vision and mission, and capacity building. Other challenges include self-motivation, inadequacies of loan sanctions, and effective marketing (Mohanty, 2004). From the study on dairy industry microenterprise work in Kenya, women had constraints in accessing credit facilities because of high interest rates and lack of collateral and limited marketing skills (Wanga, Mutuka, & Olubandwa, 2009). Microcredit institutions face the problem of repayments sufficient to earn interest and justify further loan services. Still other challenges involve the inadequacy of loans, short repayment periods and earnings to support repayment (Nawai & Shariff, 2010).

Constraints also include a lack of relevant laws and administrative procedures, inadequate collateral, limited access to organizational credit, high transaction costs, exclusion from participatory processes, lack of market information, and insufficiency of skill development opportunities (Asian Development Bank, 1997). According to Yoshino and Taghizadeh-Hesary (2016), slow small and medium enterprise growth occurs because of limited financial access, lack of databases, low research and development expenditures, undeveloped sales channels, and low levels of financial inclusion. In addition, microenterprises work is inherent with difficulties in credit access, shortage of raw materials, low demand and shortage of customers, inadequate working space, limited supply of equipment access, and limited electricity and water supplies (Siebel, 1996 cited in Adekunle, 2011). Lack of consistent data, inconsistent funding, increased competition, and difficulty in reaching market can also reduce the effectiveness of microenterprise (Servon, 2006).

The Ethiopian government has been focusing microenterprise to increase women's income and reduce unemployment and poverty. The women encountered challenges for their maximum economic benefit efficiency. The challenges are lack of financial access, training opportunities, technology access, market information access, infrastructure access, raw materials access, and market linkage opportunities (Lemma, 2017). Bekele and Worku (2008) found that women's businesses in Ethiopia are constrained in terms of financial loan access, managerial and technical skills, and incompetency in transforming gained profits into assets. According to Federal Democratic Republic of Ethiopia (2016), microenterprise workers also face the following constrains: rent seeking behavior, low level of entrepreneurial competency, low technology and skill capability, and finance and market for the product. Women entrepreneurs in Ethiopia often experience severe barriers in terms of technical skills, raw materials, technological input, infrastructural development, access to water and facilities as well as finance (Nega & Hussein, 2016). Consequently, women's microenterprise work is fertile ground for engaged research. It is important to engage women's groups working in microenterprise to help them understand their performance, critically reflect on their challenges, and facilitate future planning.

Research Methods

Engagement

The women's group was formed by Hadiya Development Association project with initial financial assistance. The group organized with members who are highly exposed to poverty and have no income. After taking training on microenterprise work, members organized themselves into various small business activities. The members save every week and are supervised by a program facilitator. The group explored their issues through self-reflective inquiry. I facilitated a collective action research process and the women participated actively in the process of data collection, analysis, and prioritization of pooled information. The researcher facilitated group discussion, organized, and compiled the final research results. The facilitator welcomed the members, explained the procedures, ensured all members participation, recorded ideas on flip chart, and helped members to vote and rank recorded ideas against the initial question. Members reflected on their microenterprise performances and challenges as a learning experience. There was a continuous dialogue and discussions between me and the group members through meeting process. This process identified local needs, assessed resources, and discussed ways to improve their microenterprise. The data on group's microenterprise achievements, challenges, and next plans were collected through nominal group strategies. All women group participated, identified, and prioritized listed information regarding their microenterprise accomplishments and challenges.

The nominal group techniques can be used with small groups as well as with a larger number of participants. The strategy allows participants to identify the priority concerns of the group (Witkin & Altschuld, 1995). NGT allows each participant to share equally and prevents one person or a few from dominating the discussion. This engaged process created an opportunity for participants to pool their knowledge and judgments. This highly structured method encouraged more passive group members to participate and resulted in a set of prioritized ideas. Participants arrived at decisions acknowledged by all members as being a genuine product of group dialogue. In summary, the nominal group technique offered a way for the facilitator to involve all participants, even those who were more passive, and brought all participants into the process of generating ideas. Moreover, it structured a process that allowed participants to offer innovative ideas and solutions.

Implementation

As a data collection tool, NGT has a structured variation of the participants working on their own within the group and then moving into group discussion of the ideas they generate. NGT melds individual and group work. In the process of information gathering, I posed several questions to respondents and individual members that helped those members generate their ideas. Then as the facilitator, I asked all group members to prioritize their ideas or suggestions. The NGT process proceeded in a step-by-step process.

In <u>Step 1: Presentation of the Issue</u>, I introduced microenterprise work, assigned participants into 5 nominal groups (two groups having eight members and three groups with seven members), and familiarized participants with meeting and discussion structures. The group members were given a formal introduction about the importance of every task and each member's contribution as productive participants. Each group facilitator presented the questions to their respective group members in written form and read them aloud to make sure each person fully understood the questions. Spontaneous side discussions were prohibited, but the facilitator allowed for short moments in which group members could interact so as to foster clarification and verification. <u>Step 2: Working Alone / Individual Brainstorming,</u> was for generating individual lists of ideas stimulated by the questions I posed to the group. The group members were then asked to quietly and individually record their ideas in short sentences or phrases. Each person generated ideas from their previous microenterprise experiences and accomplishments and wrote them down on paper. Each group facilitator encouraged members to write down as many ideas as possible about how they achieved success in microenterprise.

In <u>Step 3: Gathering Ideas / Documentation,</u> <u>each group created a </u>list of ideas addressing microenterprise accomplishments. A round robin process of offering ideas without discussion resulted in a comprehensive list of accomplishments. Each person provided one idea at a time and the facilitator wrote an idea exactly as stated by participants on flip chart paper, which was visible to the entire group. Then the facilitator proceeded to ask for another idea from the next group member. This process proceeded until all members' ideas had been written and documented. The facilitator used only a few of the participants own words. Participants were permitted to revise an earlier contribution and to develop new ideas for their own lists. In <u>Step 4: Discuss and Clarify Ideas / Review of Ideas</u>, I worked with participants to clarify and reduce any duplication. The list of ideas on accomplishments of women's microenterprise work was edited and condensed when ideas were combined. Flip chart sheets were hung up next to each other, so that all of the participants and group members could see them at the same time. A letter was assigned to each discrete contribution on the flip chart sheets. To facilitate discussion, each item on the flip charts had a unique letter. I led the groups in discussion of each idea, one by one, to clarify each idea, add to it if possible, or meld it with another idea. No argument about the merits, validity, or worth of any idea was allowed at this point. The final clear and concise list of the women's microenterprise accomplishments were posted for all to see.

In Step 5: Developing Priorities / Ranking, I helped identify the most preferred ideas. Using the compiled list generated in Step 4, I asked each group member to select five to ten most important items from the group list, in order of importance, and write them on index cards. Accordingly, each group member identified the most five important earlier accomplishments of their microenterprise work. Next, each member ranked the five ideas selected, with the most important receiving a rank of 5, and the least important receiving a rank of 1.

In Step 6: Voting on Ideas was the process to identify each group's most preferred ideas of achievement. I created a tally sheet on the flip chart with numbers down the left-hand side of the chart, which corresponded to the ideas from the round-robin. I collected all cards from the participants and asked one group member to read the idea number and number of points allocated to each one. Simultaneously, I recorded and then added the scores on the tally sheet. The ideas that were the most highly rated by the group were the most favored group actions or ideas in response to the question posed. After the preliminary vote was taken, group members were able to discuss why certain ideas received too many or too few votes. The person that submitted the idea was able to clarify their position if others were confused about it and were possibly able to sway others to their side if they provided a convincing argument. Then, I counted up the number of votes for each idea. The final lists of accomplishments, challenges, and future plans from the five NGT groups were 47, 61, and 53 respectively. Avoiding duplications and melding similar ideas reduced the total lists into 36, 46, and 40 ideas correspondingly.

Step 7: Analysis and Discussion of the Implication of the Results resulted in a final vote through which the participants would decide how many of the final ideas on their previous microenterprise deeds would be transformed into action. After finishing their ideas on achievements and success of their microenterprise work, participants took a break and participated in two similar NGT sessions that listed the group's most important challenges and future plans for microenterprise work. The participants were actively involved in the analysis of their own situation and future planning. Women's Group data was gathered through nominal group discussions, and triangulated through member feedback, discussions, and prioritization. In this sense, the women became their own researchers. I helped participants refine the information gathered through their consensus. The refined data was prepared in written form and processed with the Women's Group for validation and confirmation.

Findings

The Hadiya Development Association, the mediating organization in this project, used small business as a strategy of community development. Participants were women between 25 – 60 years old, with an average age of 33. Forty percent are illiterate and 60% are able to read and write. From the participants 40% are married, 34% are divorced, and 26% are widowed, with an average family size of four children. Microenterprise women participants went through series stages of Nominal Group activities, generated, and listed out information regarding their previous accomplishments, challenges, and plans. Women have had much success in their microenterprise work. Their most valued achievements include employment and earned income, increased saving capacity, the provision of lower-cost goods to poor people and covering their living expenses. They also prioritized their ability to pay educational fees and provide school uniforms for their children, being able to start traditional group saving associations, starting their microenterprise work, and paying their house rent. The Women's Group accomplishments are presented in Table 4A.

Table 4A: Accomplishments of the Women's Group

1	Earning income
2	Providing employment
3	Capable of saving
4	Services to poor people / Providing lower-cost goods/
5	Covering living expense cost
6	Buying uniform for their children and paying their school fees
7	Establishing *Equibs* / Local community saving systems or associations /
8	Fulfilling necessary materials for microenterprise work
9	Starting microenterprise work
10	Affording house rent
11	Expansion of previous miniature business
12	Job or employment creation
13	Life standard improvement
14	Family survival
15	Economic empowerment
16	Resisting current economic crises
17	Affording health treatment expense
18	Managing family members
19	Children school success
20	Development of team spirit /habit of working together /
21	Developing the feeling of independency
22	Interpersonal skills development
23	Knowledge about microenterprise development
24	Getting profit
25	Life standard improvement
26	Mental satisfaction
27	Well established saving system
28	Social networks among each other
29	Achievement of change through working together
30	Developing practice of helping each other
31	Promise for living
32	Opportunity of loan service from their own saving
33	Entrepreneurship skill development
34	Selling their products daily
35	Providing their products to shops and other restaurants
36	Regular meeting for discussions

Source: Author.

The women faced several obstacles in their microenterprise work. The greatest challenges include starting microenterprise without making market and demand assessment, frequent, seasonal, and unpredictable market fluctuations, unsecure health insurance, and the health conditions of the women. Other major challenges include limitations in bookkeeping and financial management skills, lack of workspace, and poor transport infrastructure for moving products. A few members did not start saving, and frequent changes in the market resulted in a loss of customers. The microenterprise challenges are presented in Table 4B.

Table 4B: Microenterprise Challenges of the Women's Group

1	Starting microenterprise work without making market and demand assessment
2	Unpredicted seasonal fluctuation
3	Market fluctuation
4	Unsecured health insurance
5	Global economic crisis
6	Group members health conditions
7	Lack of earlier experiences on microenterprise work
8	Insufficiency of bookkeeping and marketing skills
9	Inadequate financial management and micro entrepreneur business skills
10	Lack of working facilities
11	Poor transport infrastructures
12	Unavailability of conducive marketplace and environment
13	High price for input raw material
14	Lack of enough working space
16	Inconsistency of raw materials supply
17	Non supportive conditions of neighbors and others towards their business
18	High payment for medical treatment
19	Long distance to reach marketplace
20	Shortage /insufficient / of loan service
21	Unable to compete with others /with rich merchants/
22	Shortage of working capital
23	Working in very narrow working space
24	Income fluctuations

25	Lack of community supports
26	Absence of additional credit and initial capital
27	Absence of legal service
29	Inadequate pre-training on financial management and bookkeeping skills
30	Sudden raising up of raw materials prices and day-to-day inflation
32	Few took initial money and didn't start saving
33	Few left the group and didn't spend their money on microenterprise work
34	Loss of capital because of frequent price fluctuation
35	Inability to pay house rent in high business market areas
36	Loss of customers because of frequent changes of their working place
37	Lack of getting additional financial support
38	Low quality products because of unfavorable weather condition
39	Income /customers/ minimization during summer times
40	Absence of additional supports
41	High rate of taxation
42	Absence of cash at hand
43	Influence of others or high competition
44	Absence of working protection
45	Discrepancy between incomes and expenses
46	Inability to pay house rent during summertime

Source: Author

The women have multiple and varied future plans. Their priorities include revising the overall microenterprise work, assessing the community's needs and demands, and making a market analysis so that they engage in businesses that fill a niche in the community. They prioritize training on financial management and using modern technology in their work. The list of future plans of are presented in Table 4C.

Table 4C: Future Plans of the Women's Group

1	Revising the overall microenterprise work
2	Assessing communities needs and demands
3	Making market analysis
4	Taking training on financial management and bookkeeping skills
5	Working appropriate types of microenterprise work which fit to the area

6	Expansion of microenterprise work
7	Incorporating modern technological equipment
8	Experience sharing with successful groups who engaged in similar activities
9	Awareness training for neighbors and other peoples
10	Selecting profitable kinds of work and engage
11	Developing strategies to enhance capital
12	Buying crops when it is cheap and selling back when expensive
13	Involving stakeholders including kebele government administrative unit
14	Searching further assistance and funds
15	Shifting to more profitable kinds of microenterprise work
16	Looking free house rent or in low price at highly business area
17	Applying unused skills among the members
18	Selling products to nearby towns
19	Bringing materials from other places and selling with profit
20	Being a role model for non-microenterprise women
21	Becoming totally independent
22	Getting wider working space of land and start dairy farm
23	Working productive kinds of microenterprise work
24	Working more than one kind of small business
25	Implementing daily market information seriously
26	Strengthening networks
27	Looking for working space free from renting
28	Selecting profitable marketplaces and profitable businesses
29	Working different types of business
31	Involvement in appropriate types of microenterprise work
33	Engaging on microenterprise based on market assessment, training, and coaching
34	Getting support and taking training on expansion of microenterprise work
36	Being conscious of timely profitable microenterprise work and price fluctuation
37	Negotiating with local officials for getting working space priority
38	Promoting, teaching, and engaging others in microenterprise work
39	Adding new members to the group
40	Starting up new kinds of profitable local businesses

Source: Author

At the end of the engaged research, participants held a discussion with Hadiya Development Association Program on the implementation of the results. The organization accepted and agreed with their results.

The Women's Group prepared a final list of past performance and their plans for future microenterprise work. Both HDAP and the Women's Group started working on a plan of action that aligned with their findings to maintain microenterprise performance and enhance members' livelihoods. The final future plans that the participants prioritized and ranked are listed in Table 4D.

Table 4D: Prioritized and Ranked Future Plans

1	Assessing community immediate demand
2	Making market assessment.
3	Selecting the right types of profitable microenterprise work which fit the local area.
4	Taking training on bookkeeping and financial management skills
5	Assessing group's skills and applying unused skills.
6	Experience sharing with successful microenterprise groups.
7	Applying modern technological equipment.
8	Making strong networks with stakeholders and local officials.
9	Adding new members to the group.
10	Searching further assistance and funds

Source: Author

Strengths, Challenges, and Lessons Learned

The women participated in training, obtained initial working capital, and started microenterprise work under supervision and support from the Hadiya Development Association Program. Working under the umbrella of the mediating organization helped the Women's Group. They received advice and support from attending regular meetings for experience sharing and discussion of their work and had their own permanent office. This enhanced their social capital and created a forum for learning from each other and solving common problems. Microenterprise can change the lives of participants and move families above the level of survival. It broadens the opportunity for credit access and resources and creates employment options. The women use their microenterprise income for daily living expenses including house rent and health expenses, children uniform and school fees, and they develop feeling of independency.

Although women gain benefits from microenterprise work, they faced multi-dimensional challenges. These includes shortages of working capital, frequent price fluctuations, repeated changing of their working place as the result a reduction in customers, and inability to expand their work because of loan inaccessibility. The women have reserved potential for entrepreneurship, but they were not able to get startup capital and more ideal market locations. Nonetheless, microenterprise serves as an anti-poverty strategy and promotes economic empowerment. Microenterprise strengthens human capital, social capital and financial capital as microentrepreneurs meet together in regular gatherings and save money for future needs and investment. Social workers who are involved at the local level can understand the practice of women's economic empowerment through mediating organizations. Microenterprise is an economic development approach that should be practiced and supported by social work in developing countries such as Ethiopia. Social workers should develop practice knowledge to advance the actions of microentrepreneurs to fight poverty and support social change.

Influence on the Author's Scholarly Direction

The engaged research offered me practical insight into the local community settings and situations and prospects of social development strategies and interventions. Grassroots community engagement can help social workers understand indigenous skills and local knowledge and outside interventions such as those undertaken by local development organizations. My involvement with the Women's Group advanced my understanding and insight into local people's knowledge, skills, and the way in which they use limited resources for social betterment.

Before my engaged research experience, I completed a comprehensive literature review on community development in a doctorial course entitled, Knowledge Building for Social Work and Social Development. This action research project helped me refine my understanding of the literature and gain a more realistic and detailed understanding of social development from the perspective of women microentrepreneurs. I came to understand microenterprise as one way that social development organizations can bring about change in the lives of extremely poor women.

As I worked with the Women's Group, I was astonished by the programmatic function of the mediating organization, and this drove the direction of my scholarship towards community and social development practice. When I conducted my review of models of community development, I was unsure about whether community development practice could serve as a focus for my dissertation. My engagement with the women's microenterprise work gave me a clue that I might study locality-based social development from an organizational perspective. The engaged research also guided my understanding of local social development and the nexus between organizational social development and social work. As a result, my dissertation studied the founding, early development, stabilization, and institutionalization of a locality-based social development organization, and I came to understand the connection between local level social development and social work (Simeon, 2016).

Recommendations for Advancing Engaged Research

Engaged research provides support to participants for utilizing their own knowledge and skills to advance their well-being. Engaged research participants can have full participation and decision-making role. They are the source of information and knowledge. Participants can play cooperative roles in exploring the information deeply. They build social relations and strengthen working cooperation and cohesiveness through the mutual sharing.

Engaged research strategy can be used for training. The trainees would have an opportunity to share their ideas and a primary agent of the training process. in determining and focusing on their concerns and pursuing specific training and strategic planning for the future. This strategy expands trainees' equal participation on the agenda and maximizes the learning opportunities for the trainees. The trainer collaborates with the participants and gives ownerships rather than imposing upon the trainees. Engaged research strategies can be applied by researchers when the intent is to gather information with member's full participation and hear their voice. Researchers and participants can work collaboratively in sorting out the most pressing social issues and problems and engage in the prioritization of interventions strategies.

The organization could undertake engaged research to address their local community concern. It can make partnerships with the community and explore their immediate needs and priorities so that improve their social, economic, and political conditions through generating knowledge from inside. Community members take responsibility and ownerships in investigating their concern. It gives focus on collaboration, community voice, and negotiation. Mobilizing change on community issues which is critical for their advancement and development. Development organizations in Ethiopia have been working to reduce poverty and empower society. The government organizes supports various development agencies, organize peoples in groups, and create livelihood strategy. These mediating organizations can apply engaged research process for both assessing the achievement or implementation of their project and evaluation of its accomplishments. The steps used to gather sufficient information from the beneficiaries and assist for supervising the attainments of goals.

References

Adekunle, B. (2011). Determinants of microenterprise performance in Nigeria. *International Small Business Journal, 29*(4), 360–373.

Asian Development Bank. (1997). *Microenterprise development: Not by credit alone.* Manila, Philippines: Asian Development Bank. Available at http://citeseerx.ist. psu.edu/viewdoc/download?doi=10.1.1.202.4644&rep=rep1&type=pdf

Bekele, E., & Worku, Z. (2008). Women entrepreneurship in micro, small and medium enterprises: The case of Ethiopia. *Journal of International Women's Studies, 10*(2):3-19. Available at https://vc.bridgew.edu/jiws/vol10/iss2/2/

Birkenmaier, J., & Tyuse, S.W. (2005). Affordable financial services and credit for the poor. *Journal of Community Practice, 13*(1), 69-85.

Carter, S., & Jones-Evans, D. (Eds.). (2006). *Enterprise and small business: Principles, practice and policy* (2nd Ed.). Harlow, England: Pearson Education Limited.

Delbecq, A.L., Van de Ven, A.H., & Gustafson, D.H. (1975). *Group techniques for program planning: A guide to nominal group and Delphi processes.* Glenview, IL: Scott, Foresman and Co.

Dixon, R., Ritchie, J., & Siwale, J. (2006). Microfinance: Accountability from the grassroots. *Accounting, Auditing & Accountability Journal, 19*(3), 405- 427.

Dowling, K.L., & Louis, R.D. S. (2000). Asynchronous implementation of the nominal group technique: Is it effective? *Decision Support Systems, 29* (3), 229–248.

Elahi, K.Q., & Rahman, M.L. (2006). Micro-credit and micro-finance: Functional and conceptual differences. *Development in Practice, 16*(5), 476-483.

Federal Democratic Republic of Ethiopia. (2016). *Growth and Transformation Plan II (GTP II) (2015/16-2019/20).* Addis Ababa, Ethiopia: National Planning Commission.

International Labour Organization. (2003). Ethiopian women entrepreneurs: Going for growth. Addis Ababa, Ethiopia: International Labour Organization

Lemma, Z.D. (2017). Challenges facing women micro and small-scale business enterprise owners in Jimma town. *International Journal of Scientific and Research Publications, 7*(6): 647-653

Lodhi, T.E., Luqman, M., Javed, S., &Asif, M. (2006). Utilization of micro-credit by the female community: A case study of Azad Jammu and Kashmir (Pakistan). *International Journal of Agriculture & Biology, 8*(2), 175-177.

Ministry of Urban Development and Construction. (2013). *Survey on Micro and Small Enterprises (MSES) in selected major cities of Ethiopia*. Addis Ababa, Ethiopia: Ministry of Urban Development and Construction.

Mohanty, A. (2004). Women in management of micro-enterprises: Problems and prospect. *Journal of Social Science, 8*(3), 245-251.

Moyo, T. (2003). Critical success factors for microenterprise development in Africa: An overview. *An International Journal of Holistic Mission Studies, 20*(3), 166-170.

Nawai, N., &Shariff, M.N.M. (2010). Determinants of repayment performance in microcredit programs: A review of literature. *International Journal of Business and Social Science, 1*(2), 152-161.

Nega, F., & Hussein, E. (2016). *Small and Medium Enterprise access to finance in Ethiopia: Synthesis of Demand and Supply*. Addis Ababa: Ethiopia: The Horn Economic and Social Policy Institute.

Potter, M., Gordon, S., & Hamer, P. (2004). The nominal group technique: A useful consensus methodology in physiotherapy research. *NZ Journal of Physiotherapy, 32*(2), 70- 75.

Raheim, S. (1996). Micro-enterprise as an approach for promoting economic development in social work: Lessons from the self-employment investment demonstration. International Social Work, *39*, 69-82.

Schreiner, M. (1999). Self-employment, microenterprise, and the poorest Americans. *Social Service Review, 73*(4), 496-523.

Servon, L.J. (2006). Microenterprise development in the United States: Current challenges and new directions. *Economic Development Quarterly, 20*(4), 351-367.

Servon, L.J., & Bates, T. (1998). Microenterprise as an exit route from poverty: Recommendations for programs and policy makers. *Journal of Urban Affairs, 20* (4), 419-441.

Sharma, A., Dua, S., & Hatwal, V. (2012). Micro enterprise development and rural women entrepreneurship: Way for economic empowerment. *Journal of Economics and Management,1*(6),114-127.

Sherraden, M.S., Sanders, C.K., & Sherraden, M. (2004). *Kitchen capitalism: Microenterprise in low-income households*. Albany, NY: State University of New York Press.

United Nations. (2010). *The Millennium Development Goals Report 2010*. NY: United Nations.

Simeon, A. (2016). *A case study of Mission for Community Development Project as a multifaceted urban social development organization in Addis Ababa Ethiopia*. [Unpublished Doctoral Dissertation]. Addis Ababa University.

Wanga, D.O., Mutuku, M.M., & Olubandwa, A.A. (2009). Value added milk products: Constraints to women in milk microenterprises in Kenya. *Journal of Development and Agricultural Economics, 1*(7), 144-149.

Witkin, B.R., & Altschuld, J.W. (1995). *Planning and conducting needs assessments: A practical guide.* Thousand Oaks, CA: Sage.

Yoshino, N., & Taghizadeh-Hesary, F. (2016). Major challenges facing small and medium-sized enterprises in Asia and solutions for mitigating them: ADBI working paper Series. Tokyo: ADB Institute.

CHAPTER 5

LEPROSY: STIGMA AND DISCRIMINATION IN AN ETHIOPIAN SUB-CITY

Getaneh Mehari, Getu Ambaye

Leprosy has been a public health problem in Ethiopia for centuries. In the remote past, leprosy was not associated with stigma and discrimination because of Biblical teaching related to the disease. The emergence of leper colonies since the dawn of the 20th century marked the beginning of segregation of people with leprosy. In Addis Ababa, institutional care of people infected by the disease started in 1933 with the foundation of a leper colony on the outskirts of the city. This study focuses on the stigma and discrimination as experienced by members of the lepers' community in Addis Ababa. The research is principally informed by the empowerment approach to social work practice and the principles of participatory action research. The methods used resemble Paulo Freire's (2000) dialogical process that promotes critical thinking and eventually leads to action and social change. The findings demonstrate that the members of the lepers' community clearly understand and explain

108

the causes of stigma and discrimination they have been experiencing since settling in the study area. Stigma and discrimination still prevail because of misconceptions about the biomedical characteristics of the disease. People exercise social exclusion, including marital exclusion, to avoid the stigma and discrimination associated with the disease. Having described the magnitude of their problems, participants of the inquiry group suggest mechanisms for mitigating the stigma, prejudices and discrimination related to leprosy. They also reflect on their collective socio-economic and political rights.

Introduction

Although leprosy was a public health problem in Ethiopia for centuries, it was not associated with stigma and discrimination. The establishment of the St. Anthony Leprosarium in 1901, the first leper colony in Ethiopia, marked the beginning of segregated institutional care. This was followed by the establishment of other leprosaria including the Princess Zenebework Leprosarium (PZL) which was opened in 1933 on the outskirts of Addis Ababa. The establishment of PZL attracted a large number of people with leprosy which, in turn, led to the emergence of leper communities in the surrounding area known as Zenebework or Gebre Kirstos Sefer. From then on, members of the leper community have been subjected to stigma and discrimination as misconceptions and beliefs related to the disease still prevail in Ethiopia. Although leprosy has been eradicated from other parts of the world, it continues to be a public health problem in Ethiopia. As stigma and discrimination related to HIV/AIDS have been at the top of the public health and media agenda, problems associated with leprosy seem to have been marginalized medically and politically.

Existing studies in Ethiopia focus mainly on the history of the disease (Melese, 2005; Pankhurst, 1984), and its biomedical dimension (Tadele, 1988). Only a few researchers have studied its social dimension (Mesfin, 1992; Yohannes, 1973). The research project we report explores the social dimension of the disease focusing on stigma and discrimination within the context of the leper community of Gebre Kirstos. Gebre Kirstos was a residential place isolated from the main city and inhabited by the leper community and other families of lower economic status. The population map has been changing considerably in the past two decades as more and more people settled in and around the area formerly isolated from the main city. Despite these changes, the members of the leper community encounter different levels of social ostracism in Gebre Kirstos and the wider society of the capital city.

We decided to conduct this study based on our previous research experience related to the leper community in the Gebre Girstos area. Getaneh conducted literature-based research in 2008 as a part of his engagement in the Bergen Summer Research School at the University of Bergen, Norway. In 2005, Getu worked as an assistant researcher and conducted a survey research that evaluated the impact of HIV/AIDS on community-based associations and community members including the leper community in Addis Ababa. When we agreed to collaborate on this research project, we conducted field work at a local leper community to gain insight into the current life conditions of the community and conducted an initial assessment of community life. As a result of the reconnaissance, we observed two situations. First, the members of the leper community were experiencing different forms of exclusion and discrimination. Second, they had a strong feeling of marginalization including exclusion from projects taking place in their sub-city that could produce benefits for people coping with the social consequences of leprosy.

This study explores leprosy-related stigma and discrimination. It also aims at engaging members of the leper community to rethink and re-examine their own situation and consider possible solutions for their problems. Our intentions were framed by certain circumstances. First, the study was a mini-action research to fulfill a requirement of a doctoral course on Action Research. Second, it was to be conducted as a preliminary project to inform potential dissertation work. As O'Brien (2001, p. 7) notes, action research can be carried out when the major concern of the study is "solving real problems. It can, however, be used by social scientists for preliminary or pilot research, especially when the situation is too ambiguous to frame a precise research question." Thus, we, as engaged co-researchers, agreed to conduct an action research as an initial social work inquiry which could be expanded in our future research with marginalized communities. The project employed Freire's methodological approach to dialogue, which is used to describe the situation of leprosy-related stigma and discrimination.

Framing the Engaged Research

For centuries, leprosy or Hansen's disease, has been a public health problem in many parts of the world. For example, leprosy was one of the major health problems in Norway in the 19th century (Idgens & Bjerkedal, 1973). Most Western European countries introduced the policy of complete segregation, which forced people with leprosy to lives in leper colonies or leprosaria. Norway was the first European country introducing the policy of complete segregation as a means of controlling the spread of the disease (International Leprosy Congress, 1994).

The history of leprosy in Ethiopia goes back to the ancient times. The prevalence of the disease has been high from time immemorial. The existence of leprosy in Ethiopia is well-documented by European travelers since the 16th century. According to Francisco Alvares, a Portuguese priest stayed in northern Ethiopia in the 16th century, there were many leprosy patients in the country. Europeans visited Ethiopia in the 19th and 20th centuries also reported that leprosy was a widely spread disease in many parts of the country including Gondar, Gojjam, and Shoa, and in towns such as Gore, Dessie and Harar (Pankhurst, 1984). Although leprosy was a public health problem since ancient times, it was not associated with stigma and discrimination. This was primarily because the Ethiopian Orthodox Church and its followers assisted leprosy patients in the name of Gebre Kirstos, a patron of lepers. The establishment of the St. Anthony Leprosarium in 1901, the first leper colony in Ethiopia, marked the beginning of segregated institutional care. The leprosarium was established in Harar with the support of Ras Mekonnen, the cousin of Emperor Menelik I. This was followed by the foundation of Princess Zenebework Leprosarium (PZL) in 1933 on the outskirts of Addis Ababa and the Kuyera Leprosarium in 1951 near Shashamane town (Pankhurst, 1984; Melese, 2005).

The establishment of PZL attracted large numbers of people with leprosy, which led to the emergence of leper communities in the surrounding area known as Gebre Kirstos or Zenebework, named after Gebre Kirstos Church located in the vicinity and Princess Zenebework Leprosarium respectively. The lepers' communities emerged as a result of the migration of leprosy patients in search of medical treatment and other services (Melese, 2005). Since the leprosaria could not provide lodging for their clients, the patients established villages in their vicinity. For example, Gebre Kirstos Sefer emerged near PZL as people with Hansen's disease moved to the areas where the leprosaria were located. These developments gave rise to the emergence of segregated camps as well as segregated villages of leprosy-affected people. In 1965, the PZL was transformed into a hospital known as ALERT, the All Africa Leprosy Rehabilitation and Training Centre.

Today, Gebre Kirstos is not a completely segregated leper village. Gebre Kirstos has been transformed from a segregated village of leprosy sufferers to a part of Addis Ababa inhabited by people with different socio-economic backgrounds. According to Melese (2005) the incorporation of Gebre Kirstos Sefer into the administrative structure of the city, the establishment of a military camp, and the construction of many houses were among the major causes of the transformation. These changes attracted numerous people to the area either to settle there permanently or to run small businesses.

Stigma and Discrimination

Leprosy is a health problem that affects the lives of many people in Ethiopia. The estimated number of leprosy sufferers in the country was 150,000 in 1955 (Price, 1969), 200,000 in 1962 (Yohannes, 1973), and 120,000 in 1983 (Tadele, 1988). Ethiopia is one the African countries with high prevalence rate of leprosy (Berhe, Haimanot, Tedla, & Taddesse, 1990) and thousands of newly-detected leprosy cases.

According to Sileshi (2015), the average number of new leprosy cases detected per year is around 5000 whereas a large number of new cases remain under-reported. Leprosy has a considerable effect in increasing the number of disabled people in Ethiopia. It is estimated that about 700 people in the country are disabled every year due to leprosy.

Leprosy is not only a bio-medical disease, but also a social disease since it is closely associated with stigma and discrimination. Rafferty (2005) points out that in order to achieve a complete cure, the social and psychological well-being of those inflicted by the disease must be considered. Stigma is one of the major factors that cause delay in seeking medical treatment, thereby hampering early detection and treatment, and hindering the achievements of leprosy control programs (Nicholls, Wiens, & Smith, 2003; International Leprosy Congress, 2002). In his anthropological study in India, Barrett (2005) argues that stigma and social discrimination are more severe than the disease itself. He further notes that social stigma leads to concealment of leprosy status which contributes to late detection and delayed treatment, and these factors accelerate the spread of the disease.

Stigma and discrimination are the main manifestations of social problems associated with leprosy. Goffman's (1963) discourse on stigma as a discrediting attribute or an undesired differentness from what is socially expected is the foundation for all modern definitions of the concept. Goffman (1963) indicated that stigma may be related to mental illness, physical deformities and what were perceived to be socially deviant qualities in which the person as a whole becomes deviant:

> While the stranger is present before us, evidence can arise of his possessing an attribute that makes him different from others... He is thus reduced in our minds from a whole and usual person to a tainted, discounted one. Such an attribute is a stigma, especially when its discrediting effect is very extensive... (pp. 11-12).

In medical anthropology, stigma is closely related to chronic illnesses and impairments since people with these conditions often can be marked as different or stigmatized (Shuttleworth & Kasnitz, 2004). Discrimination refers to negative acts resulting from stigma that serve to devalue and reduce the life chances of those who are stigmatized. Discrimination is defined by comparing it with the concept prejudice. Prejudice is a "theory of racial and other forms of inequality" whereas discrimination is "unequal treatment of a particular group or category" of people (Johnson 2000, p. 237).

Barrett (2005) studied leprosy-related social stigma and discrimination in India, where leprosy stigma is "highly contagious" and is consistent with Goffman's idea of "courtesy stigma." Leprosy stigma is not limited to people with leprosy; it also affects their families and relatives. Several Indian families send their relatives infected by the disease away to distant urban areas for fear of discrimination against the entire household and related social and economic losses. Options for the survival of lepers exiled as a result of stigma are very limited; their chance of getting employed is poor and they receive little or no family support. This situation leads to a cyclic nature of leprosy stigma and discrimination. The exiled "... must find subsidized living in an isolated colony or else live on the streets and beg in areas frequented by tourists and pilgrims" (Barrett. 2005, p. 217).

Gender and cross-generational dimensions of leprosy stigma are characterized by gender inequalities and the absence of protection. Women suffer from problems including physical and sexual abuse. Children suffer from stigma though they have never been diagnosed for leprosy because leprosy stigma is inherited (2005, p. 224). Other authors point out the deformity and disability effects of leprosy and the misconception and beliefs of society about the causes and transmission of the disease. The causes of stigma and discrimination are also related to incomplete and inaccurate knowledge and fear of the disease (Melak, 2008).

The Meaning of Community

There are different ways of conceptualizing the meaning of the term community. Community can be a geographic area or defined by shared interests or a common identity among individuals. Community can be based on religion, language, or ethnicity. Although related, the meanings of the terms group and community are quite different:

> The group is specialized; whereas the community is a global response to the totality of life, the group is relatively homogeneous; whereas the community is pluralistic and heterogeneous, although it must be homogeneous with regard to goals the exercise of social power; the group may be intimate, whereas the community extends friendship and communion and is inclusive (Lee, 2001, p. 354).

At the same time, not only are communities multidimensional, but as in this case, members of the leper community share many things that differentiate them from other communities in the vicinity and the wider context of Addis Ababa. Consequently, we have adopted Homan's (2008) definition of community as "a number of people who share a distinct location, benefit, interest, activity, or other characteristic that clearly identifies their communality and differentiates them from those not sharing it." (p. 98)

Marginalization in communities relates to the concept of empowerment. Empowerment is the process whereby social workers engage in a set of activities with the client, in this case the leper community, and work to reduce the powerlessness that has been created by negative judgments based on membership in a stigmatized group (Lee, 2008). Since one of the principal goals of engaged research is empowerment, this research involves not only identifying both internal and external power blocks but also finding ways to reduce these power blocks to bring about change in the context of the leper community. The following quotation has inspired us to apply participatory action research among the leper community: "Communities, like people, can experience power deficits and can be empowered... All communities are sustaining of life to certain degrees, and each one has its strength and weakness" (Lee, 1994, p. 265).

Research Methods

The Process of Action Research

The research method was informed by the major principles of action research. Action research is an approach of inquiry based on reflection, data gathering and practice. Action research is not confined to understanding the world; it also seeks to change and improve it. According to Baum and colleagues (2006), action research has the following major features: 1) it is mainly intended to instigating action; 2) it involves reducing and eliminating the power differences between researchers and study participants so that the later become co-researchers; and 3) it advocates for active engagement of participants in the entire process of the inquiry.

We, as co-researchers, considered different models of engaged research before embarking on the inquiry. The following two models can be considered in the process of action research. The first is Kemmis' model (cited in Hopkins, 1983) which sketches action research as a cyclical process consisting of four phases: planning, acting, observation and reflection. The process starts with planning for action followed by action, observation and reflection. The reflection phase will be followed by another round of the action research process: re-planning, acting, observing and reflection. The process continues until the problem is solved satisfactorily or the participant researchers gain basic insight. Susman's model (1983) elaborates the action research process in five steps. Unlike Kemmis' model that starts with planning, Susman's model begins with diagnosing which involves identifying a problem and is followed by four steps: action planning, taking a selected course of action, evaluating (examining the outcomes of the action) and agreeing upon learning, which focuses on identifying major findings which could be used to redefine the problem (Kemmis, cited in Hopkins, 1983).

The intention of this project was not to pass through every stage of action research as our purpose was to act as social change activists in order to elevate participants to the level of co-researchers and empower them through active engagement. Considering our purpose and circumstance, we concentrated on two major steps which coincide with the Friedman's (2006) action science procedures: 1) creating a community of inquiry embracing the researchers and selected representatives of the study community; and 2) working with the members of community. In our case, this meant understanding the current situation of leprosy-related stigma and discrimination and letting members of the community of inquiry rethink and redefine stigma and discrimination in their context and propose actions to be taken.

The research design is informed by techniques and procedures forwarded by proponents of participatory action research. As noted earlier, this engaged research project was informed by Friedman's (2006) notion of community of inquiry and the procedures outlined by him. According to Friedman (2006), a community of inquiry refers to a community of researchers and practitioners who redefine their roles and formulate common values, norms, terminologies and procedures. It is a special kind of community which plays the role of producing knowledge. In our case, the community of inquiry embraces two researchers and selected members of the lepers' community of Gebre Kirstos area. As researchers, we used the community of inquiry to produce knowledge about the situation of stigma and discrimination based on people's experiences and meanings. In so doing, we followed two stages to create a community of inquiry and engage the members of the community in the process of this research. These stages dealt with creating a community of inquiry and producing knowledge through a dialogical process.

In creating a community of inquiry, we maintained contact with officials of the Ethiopian National Association for Peoples Affected by Leprosy (ENAPAL) to establish connection with key persons from the leper community. ENAPAL officials assisted us in starting good relationships with the members of the leper community. Executive Committee members of Addis Ababa Region Ex-leprosy Patient Women Work Group assisted us in recruiting initial members of the community of inquiry. We employed snowball sampling to select more members to form an inquiry group that embraced participants from different social backgrounds. In this, we considered age, gender, educational background, and leprosy status, both leprosy free and leprosy-affected people. Finally, we came up with an inquiry group that embraced fifteen members, five females and ten males. We also explained the responsibilities and rights of the participants and the importance of establishing genuine collaboration to promote free discussion, engagement and active participation in the inquiry process.

Three Rounds of Engagement

Producing knowledge through the dialogical process includes three rounds of discussion followed by activities such as data collection, analysis, preparing a summary of findings, reflections, and modifications. During the first round, we initiated discussion on how people in the leper community experience stigma and discrimination, the meaning they attach to stigma and discrimination, and how they manage their lives in the wider urban setting. We also kept notes during the discussion, analyzing the information, and preparing summaries of the findings.

The activities carried out during the second round included presenting the summary of initial findings to the group, and encouraging reflection and further discussion on the issues, meanings and conflicting ideas that appeared in the previous discussion. We kept notes, gathered more information, and modified the previous points of discussion based on the reflections. Activities carried out during the third round consisted of presenting the second version of the findings for further reflection and discussion, encouraging the members of the group to give much attention to ways to improve the situation, developing a tentative action plan for future intervention, and closing the rounds of discussions by emphasizing our enthusiasm and commitment to work with them in the future.

Data Collection

A qualitative approach was employed to collect data from the members of the leper community. The principal method involved rounds of dialogue among members of the community of inquiry. The process of gathering the data was informed by the empowerment approach to social work practice, which is a kind of dialogue between the participants and researchers from which the reality emerges through construction and reconstruction and leads to action. Moreover, data related to the lived experiences of individuals were collected through interviews and small group discussions that were framed by guiding questions focusing on leprosy-related stigma and discrimination.

Some theoretical discussion seems important to identify the roles played by the researchers and the study participants in the context of action research. One of the typical features of action research is that the social roles played by the researcher and participants during the various stages of the cyclical process cannot be clearly differentiated. The roles in the relationships between the two parties can be partly distinguished based on the power effects of knowledge and action during interaction (Freire, 2000). The power effects of knowledge are evident, starting from defining the research question, all the way through the inquiry process and acting on the research result. In this regard, Heron and Reason (2006) identify three forms of roles: a same role inquiry, a counterpart role inquiry, and a mixed role inquiry, in which each of the two parties share different roles.

According to O'Brien (2001), action research is appropriate when practitioners want to draw better understanding about their previous or ongoing practices, when activists plan to foster social change, and when academics are invited to carry out action research to solve certain problems in organizational settings. In this study, we did not share the position of practitioners inspired to learn from their practice or that of academics who conduct action research to solve organizational problems. Instead, we take the position of social change activists or research catalysts whose major aim is promoting social change through empowering the members of the community of inquiry. We followed the principles of action research as outlined by O'Brien (2001). The principles include reflective critique which considers social reality as relative, sees participants as collaborators or co-researchers, and views the ideas of each person as equally important. We tried our best to make the process of the inquiry participatory by encouraging members of the inquiry group to express their ideas, views, opinions, values and experiences without frustration or reservation. We also valued ideas of each participant as equally important.

Data Analysis

Data analysis is an integral part of the entire process of this research. After a successive process of data analysis, we produced the written report giving due emphasis to subjective and contextual understandings, interpretations of the reality, and explanations of stigma and discrimination as experienced by members of the leper community. Throughout the intermittent meetings and discussions, our task was summarizing the interpretations and subjective understanding of study participants at each stage of the research. At each succeeding stage, we presented the summary points and facilitated discussions among the members of the inquiry group, then we went home and analyzed the data, moved back to the study site, presented the summary of findings, and gathered more reflections. We continued the dialogue, data collection, analysis and reflection until the last round of the process. Certain themes and categories emerged out of this cyclical process of data analysis and reflection. In the process, relationships were established between and among the themes or categories of data. The process of interpreting shared meanings and common understandings raised the collective consciousness of participants and inspired them to take collective actions to tackle leprosy-related stigma and discrimination.

Findings on Leprosy and Stigma and Discrimination in the Ethiopian Sub-city

The dialogical process carried out with the inquiry group focuses on issues related to the causes and consequences of leprosy-related stigma and discrimination, and the magnitude of stigma and discrimination during three political regimes. It also covers implications of leprosy-related stigma and discrimination, and mechanisms suggested by the members of the inquiry group to reduce the negative impacts of stigma and discrimination.

Causes of Stigma and Discrimination

The first cause was misunderstanding in the wider society about the disease, particularly about its means of transmission. Most participants reported that many people believe that the disease is transmitted easily through physical contact. There are also people who believe that leprosy is a hereditary disease. Some fear that the disease could be transmitted even through conversation and breathing. Poor interaction between the members of the leper community and other people, and a lack of attention to the promotion of public awareness were mentioned as factors aggravating the problem. Some of the participants complained that the attention given to leprosy, including media coverage, had declined. One member who was an active participant, complained bitterly, "Unlike the attention given to HIV/AIDS, nothing has been done about our problems. Leprosy is a forgotten and neglected agenda." Sharing this view, members of the inquiry group argued that government and media attention has been shifted to HIV/AIDS-related stigma and discrimination while the social problems related to leprosy have been neglected.

Members of the inquiry group claimed that, as compared to other people, they have a better level of awareness of the cause and means of transmission of the disease. The following points were clearly reflected by the members of the group. The disease is caused by bacterial infection; it is not a hereditary disease. Unlike HIV/AIDS ('the killer disease', as participants call it), leprosy is not transmitted through sexual intercourse. Leprosy is not easily transmitted through simple physical contact. Rather, the disease is transmitted to individuals who are exposed to the bacteria for a long time. Most participants argued that, in most cases, leprosy occurs on persons whose family members and relatives were not affected by the disease. One participant posed this question, "If the disease is transmitted from parents to children, how could persons who do not have leprosy have relatives infected by the disease?" Another participant added the following: "If the disease is inherited and transmitted from generation to generation, why do we give birth to healthy children?" Participants posed these kinds of critical questions frequently and claimed that the belief that leprosy is a hereditary disease is the major cause of stigma and discrimination.

The other factor that leads to stigma and discrimination is the physical deformity caused by the disease. Most of the participants admitted that late treatment, partial treatment, or lack of medical treatment lead to physical injuries and disfigurement. Physical deformity, in turn, exposes people with leprosy to stigma and social exclusion. People with observable physical deformity and disability could be easily identified and treated differently. Healthy persons descended from parents with leprosy are not instantly exposed to this kind of social problem. Discrimination against healthy persons who are associated with leper families emerges when their family status is disclosed.

Stigma and Discrimination in the Three Regimes

Participants discussed the situation of leprosy-related stigma and discrimination during the Imperial Period (1930-1974), the Derg Regime (1974-1991), and the current government. Older participants recalled their experiences when leper colonies expanded, and institutional segregation and social exclusion was widely practiced during the Imperial Period. Most people with leprosy were kept in the Princess Zenebework Leprosarium. Those who lived outside the leprosarium were isolated from participating in community-based organizations (CBOs) that embraced leprosy-free people. They were also excluded from formal and informal community meetings, cultural and religious festivals, and jobs in government institutions. One older participant affirmed the level of stigma and discrimination in those days:

We had a separate city bus, Number 7! Children used to ridicule us whenever they saw Number 7. It was common to hear harsh words uttered by children and teenagers. The most common statement was this one: '*Yeqomatoch atobus metach!*' ['The lepers' bus is coming!']. In those days, children and teenagers used to utter these words repeatedly whenever they saw the bus: *Yeqomatoch atobus metach! Yeqomatoch atobus metach! Yeqomatoch atobus metach!*

The problem of social exclusion and mistreatment involved the action of public agencies, as well as individuals and social groups. One participant also reported that sometimes people with leprosy were caught and sent without their consent to distant areas such as Ginde Beret, a district in Western Shewa Zone of Oromia Region. Moreover, mobility outside Gebre Kirstos was difficult for people with leprosy. In those days, people living around Gebre Kirstos used to say: "Do not mix my cattle with that of the lepers; do not buy milk from them." In this regard, Melese (2005) argues that the main source of such misconceptions and fear of leprosy was exaggerated information propagated by the elite of that time who were strongly influenced by Western discourses related to the disease. Leprosy was portrayed as a contagious disease that could be transmitted easily from person to person. Keeping people with leprosy in segregated places was considered as the only means of controlling the disease. A letter, written in 1949 by the municipality to the Princess Zenebework Leprosarium, reflects the level of misconception propagated by the elite:

It is identified that the inpatients of the leprosarium are engaged in breeding cows and supplying the city with milk. Notwithstanding its inconvenience to sanitary and public health works, the sufferers' activity obviously engenders the healthy ones. Therefore, prompting that is up to the administration of the leprosarium to restrain the sufferers from such kinds of activities and relations with the people living outside the premises of the village… from this time onwards, if the sufferers are found out supplying milk to residents living outside the premises of the leprosarium as usual, it is decided to put all the cows on the market and prohibit the sufferers from keeping cows once and for all (quoted in Mesele, 2005, p. 172).

An elderly woman explained the situation by recalling the practice of not only segregating people with leprosy but also their cows. She was the victim of this practice as she kept cows and delivered milk to people in the surrounding area. People believed that the disease could be transmitted through everything that belonged to people affected by leprosy.

The situation was much better during the Derg period. People affected by leprosy were able to live together with other people. They also started using public transportation with leprosy-free people. This could be partly because the Derg, a regime that declared itself a socialist government, took measures to protect marginalized groups, including people with leprosy, both in urban and rural areas. Marginalized social groups (e.g., artisans such as potters and tanners) in rural areas of the country were treated better during the Derg era because of government protection (Freeman, 2002).

The members of the inquiry group had different opinions on the level of stigma and discrimination in the current period as compared to that of the past two regimes. They agreed that the current situation is by far better than that of the Imperial Period. Some argued that the current period is also better than that of the Derg period, but others did not accept this view. Some reported that the current government has given much attention to people affected by leprosy, whereas others insisted that still the level of stigma and discrimination is strong. One young woman complained that "There are people who call our place *yeqomatoch sefer*' ('the lepers' neighborhood') even now. I myself and my friend quarreled in a city bus with a young man when he uttered *yeqomatoch sefer*' in his phone conversation." Another participant said:

The problem is not simple even nowadays. I think there is no one who likes us genuinely. Let alone eating together with us, people systematically move away from us when we travel by bus. They feel shame to sit together with us. I do not think that somebody else loves me, not at all!

Participants note that some people do not like to hear the name Gebre Kirstos or Zenebework, as these words have been closely associated with leprosy and the leper community. The problem is the public attitude towards the place as well as the community. As a result, the residents of Gebre Kirstos, including people with leprosy, healthy members of the leper community, and leprosy-free people settled in the area suffer from different levels of stigma and discrimination. This problem is reflected in a form of social ostracism related to marriage relations. A young woman shared her experience as follows:

The discrimination still exists. People do not like the name of the place-Gebre Kirstos. They dislike it! There are some people who move away when they identify our identity. They could be involved in a friendly discussion with one of us, however, they would interrupt the conversation and move away saying, 'Oh! You are from *yeqomatoch sefer!*'

Educated people who know that the disease does not transmit through heredity do not feel comfort with us [healthy ones]. For example, I was a college student. I used to change the name of my *sefer* when I talk with my classmates. I did not tell them the truth. I used to hear when they talk about stories like this: 'Mr. X was on the verge of holding a wedding to get married, however, the bride was found to be *qomata* [a person with leprosy]. So, the wedding was cancelled.'

I have been listening to these kinds of stories partly engaged in the conversation. Now, for example, I have a boyfriend. He lives far away from here [Gebre Kirstos]. We talk about these kinds of issues. I raise the topic indicating that I have heard about it on the radio show. My parents are disabled [because of the disease]. He does not know about the reality. I just discuss the issue with him without disclosing my identity. Sometimes I ask him, 'Does leprosy transmit through heredity?' He would say, 'No, it does not. But this kind of thing…it does not make me happy'. So, his attitude is not good. The people live here [at Gebre Kirstos] in harmony. People outside this place, including those who are educated, do not accept the reality.

This young woman used words such as "the place", "here", and "this place" to refer to Gebre Kirstos or Zenebework Sefer. Her story reveals that she has been moving between two worlds: her own community of Gebre Kirstos and the outside world. She is trying to maintain her relationship with her boyfriend, but she also is afraid of exclusion and rejection. She is not sure whether her relationship with her boyfriend will continue if she reveals her leprosy-related identity. The data presented and discussed here may not help us to compare the level of stigma and discrimination during the different regimes. However, the reflection of members of the inquiry group reveal an important point. Although the level of social exclusion has tended to decline, people with leprosy and their relatives are still subject to stigma and discrimination in Addis Ababa, the capital city of Ethiopia.

Exclusion, Isolating the Self, and in-Group Solidarity

One of the issues explored in this study was the implications of stigma and discrimination in the lives of people associated with the leper community. The influence of stigma and discrimination on the lives of members of the leper community varies from one context to another. For instance, the magnitude of stigma and discrimination within Gebre Kirstos area is less intense as compared to the situation in other parts of the city. In part, this is because Gebre Kirstos embraces people with leprosy and other residents who settled there in recent decades. Hence, people affected by the disease and leprosy-free people share the same physical space and interact in their day-to-day lives.

The level of social exclusion in the Gebre Kirstos area is declining because leprosy-free people have brought about attitudinal changes as they have learned from their observation and experiences living with individuals and families affected by the disease. Leprosy-affected and leprosy-free people live, work, eat and drink together. They are involved in community-based associations such as *idir, equb,* and *senbet-maheber* with leprosy-free people, and play leadership roles in such associations. They attend funeral ceremonies as well as other religious festivals together. Some members of the community narrated cases related to marriages taking place between a member of the leper community and leprosy-free people in Gebre Kirstos.

The reality in the wider society of the city is quite different. Stigma and discrimination outside Gebre Kirstos are severe and multidimensional. When they move to different parts of city, people with leprosy encounter mistreatment and exclusion. One young female participant described the situation as follows:

> We have no confidence to utter a single word about our identity when we move outside our place, since there is severe stigma and discrimination. I remember what happened to us in the recent past. It happened while we were at a bus station in the Kasanchis area in Addis Ababa, waiting for a bus. Other people were staring at us and asked, 'Who brings these people here? Where do these people come from?' It was a frustrating moment for all of us!

Leprosy-related stigma and discrimination affects both people with leprosy and healthy persons related to people affected by the disease.

Marital exclusion is a good example. Matrimonial exclusion is partly the result of misconceptions about the means of transmission of the disease. However, people also avoid such a marriage for social reasons, especially because of fear of stigma and social exclusion. The following story illustrates how healthy members of the leper community encounter challenging circumstances when making decisions related to marriage:

> The girl is free from the disease, but her parents are affected by it. She is an employee of a city bus company. A young and rich man fell in love with her. He dated her for some time. The man repeatedly tried to give her a ride when she was about to go home. She declined the request of the man telling him that they need time to know each other. She did not want to mention Zenebework or Gebre Kirstos (the names of her home place) as she feared that their relationship would come to an end. Finally, she decided to tell him the truth. One day, the girl disclosed the place of her residence when the man gave her a ride; his face was completely changed when she said, 'My home place is Zenebework!' She further asked him whether his intension was to marry her. He said: 'Yes.' Then she told him, 'I am not a real person to be your wife; I am a daughter of parents affected by leprosy.' The person did not say any word. He did not try to meet her again. That was the end of their relationship.

The story narrated above reveal that healthy individuals could encounter social exclusion just because they are related to Zenebework or Gebre Kirstos. The following story shows how two young women, descendants of healthy parents, suffer from social ostracism because a leprosy-infected relative stayed with their family for a couple of years. The names in the story as pseudonyms.

> Zewditu was a victim of leprosy-related social ostracism though she was a healthy young woman. Her parents

live in one of the sub-cities of Addis Ababa. They have seven children and all family members are not affected by the disease. The family was labelled as a 'leper-family' when Kebede, Zewditu's uncle, came to stay with the family. Initially, Kebede had no clearly observable signs of leprosy though he walked with a crutch. People in the neighborhood did not know about the cause of his disability, since it was reported that Kebede was an ex-soldier wounded in a battlefield. However, people in the neighborhood knew the cause of his disability when the signs of leprosy were clearly observed. Kebede died after he stayed with them for five years.

However, the new status of the family affected the marriage opportunities of Zewditu and her younger sister Tizita. Zewditu's boyfriend, an educated and well-to-do young man, cancelled the proposed marriage while preparations for the wedding were in progress. The man disappeared immediately after he was informed that she belonged to a leper family called '*betesebu kumitina alebet*' [it is a leper's family]. Tizita's attempts to get married were aborted for the same reason. The two sisters managed to get married after moving to other parts of the city where the story of their family is not known.

The cases presented above show two things. First, healthy persons related to people with leprosy or families who take leper victims into their homes experience similar social problems, but they use different coping mechanisms. The employee of the city bus company and other members of the leper community tend to look into options such as strengthening their in-group solidarity and searching for a marriage partner within the leper community. Second, leprosy is a disease that can spoil the status of individuals and families regardless of their residential place. Zewditu's family did not live in the neighborhood inhabited by leprosy-affected people, but in a sub-city located far away from Gebre Kirstos. However, they suffered from social exclusion because their family was labelled a leper family and they were considered as 'yeqomata zer' which literally means descendants of the leper. Zewditu and her sister moved away from the family leaving behind their spoiled name to get rid of their damaged social status

The members of the inquiry group have noted an increasing rate of endogamous marriage within the leper community. Despite this trend, some individuals marry outsiders and live outside Geber Kirstos. Most of these people encounter a different aspect of social problems and tension. One participant mentioned the case of a recent bride, a daughter of leprosy-infected parents, who was living with her husband in one of the sub-cities of Addis Ababa. As her husband knows the health status of his parents-in-law, he does not allow her to visit them. As a result, she had to come to Gebre Kirstos secretly to attend the funeral of her father who died some years ago.

Members of the leper community who enter into marriage with outsiders face lifelong challenges that require living in harmony in the world outside Gebre Kirstos and maintaining their social bonds with the leper community. The first requires dealing with conflicts not only with their marriage partner, an outsider to the leper community, but also managing potentially fragile and delicate relationships with the parents, relatives and friends of their spouse. This is a difficult attempt in the social context that labels such a marriage tie as 'kibre nek'.

Kibre-nek is an Amharic phrase. The term 'kibr' literally means prestige. 'Kibre-nek' refers to something, in this case marriage with people associated with leprosy, which spoils the prestige and status of individuals, families and relatives. An Amharic film entitled Kibre-nek, a widely watched movie in Ethiopia, portrays the complexity of social problems related to such kinds of marriages. Binyam, one of the major characters, is the well-educated young man and a son of wealthy and prestigious parents. Juliana is a beautiful and educated young woman working in a company. Juliana does not know her mother, but her father is disabled and disfigured as a result of leprosy. She did not tell Binyam about the reality. Rather, she told him that she lost her parents when she was a child and was raised by missionaries. Binyam introduces her to his parents and informs them about his plan to marry her. In the meantime, Binyam's parents are informed about Juliana's father who came to the city for medical treatment. Binyam's mother had a heart attack when she heard the story and stayed in a hospital for several days. Binyam was shocked when Juliana's friend told him the truth, and he stopped his relations with Juliana. His father instructed him to go away and Binyam left his parents' house. Finally, after many ups and downs, Binyam decided to marry Juliana but was isolated from his parents. The movie depicts the social dimension of leprosy in the context of the Ethiopian capital city. The battle for social prestige seems the major factor that leads to stigma and discrimination rather than fear of leprosy as a bio-medical problem.

The participants of the study did not exclusively blame others for the social problems related to leprosy but pointed out their own perceptions and practices that aggravate these issues. Some of the members of the inquiry group reported the prevalence of perceived stigma and discrimination among members of their own community. A 57-years old man expressed his own perceptions and the avoidance practices resulted from his expectations of perceived stigma and discrimination:

> We also aggravate the level of stigma and discrimination. Partly there is a problem with us. For example, I isolate myself by moving away from others... We stigmatize ourselves. I used to do that during the Derg period. When tea was served during meetings, I used to say, 'I do not like tea' to avoid exposing my leprosy affected hand which is in fact deformed. I used to take a chair around the corner in a hotel. We have an assumed fear... fear of exclusion. Of course, there is change nowadays.

This quotation reveals that leprosy-related stigma and discrimination force people affected by the disease to feel that they are stigmatized by other people. Expressions such as 'I think no one likes us!' reflects the feeling of exclusion which is shared by many people affected by the disease. Consequently, they tend to isolate themselves from public places, social gatherings and interactions just because they perceive that other people consider them as mutilated, dangerous, and inferior. A 30-years-old woman who is disfigured by the disease portrayed her lived experiences and feelings in this way:

> We, the disabled ones, face challenges when we go to town… People are not happy when they see our hands. We could cover our feet but not our hands. So, we often prefer to stay and live here [at Gebre Kirstos area] together… I came [from a rural village] to this place when I got sick. I have no problem when I go there to visit my family in my home village. Everybody knows about me, but they do not bother about that [about the disease]. Some of them come here to visit me. Those who live here in Addis Ababa also come and visit me. The problem comes when we go to the town, outside Gebre Kirstos. We could cover our feet, but not our hands, face…we cannot do that! Some people insult and ridicule us. We feel something bad at that time. We can do nothing, however, as God gives us the disease.
>
> There is no problem in our place here in Gebre Kirstos area. If people talk bad things about us here, we could say 'this is our place! Go away if you like!'… We all live here together; the health center is located here; we live happy here as we are many. The problem is when we go away from this place. We do not feel good whenever we find ourselves elsewhere. We do not feel good when we go to visit our relatives; they could love us; they could respect us. Whatsoever, I do not feel good when I move in the city as I have something bad in my mind. My mind has never been cleansed from the bad feelings. Our marriage, our life, our happiness is here in our village, not elsewhere!

This woman's lived experience shows the level of psychological and social trauma resulting from her experience of stigma and discrimination. She has experienced more discrimination here in the city than in her home village in a rural area. She has developed a negative attitude towards the society outside Gebre Kirstos because of her experience of social exclusion and mistreatment. Her feeling of exclusion and disgrace in the wider city context has pushed her and other members of the leper community to look inwards and strengthen their group solidarity. They portray the city society as a threat to their wellbeing. They feel secure in their own village and community. Most of the young and leprosy-free members of the community also share this attitude. As a result, most of them tend to strengthen their social lies in their community. In response, they are inclined to in-group marriage. The words of the young women, "Our marriage, our life, our happiness is here in our village!" reveals this reality.

The members of the inquiry group also talked about the prevalence of institutional discrimination. Most of them argue that the government discriminates against them. Some thought that the government discrimination is reflected by the absence of development schemes such as road construction in Gebre Kirstos area. As one of the participants reported:

> Not only we ourselves, but also our *sefer* (neighborhood) is discriminated against. Now the government is constructing roads in many places in the city even in Sebeta (a town to the south of the city). As you can see our place is muddy! Even government discriminates against us...We have been forgotten regarding development schemes.

Institutional discrimination, according to the participants, is also prevalent in the health institutions. Doctors and other medical professionals do not give attention to the disease and the problems of people affected by leprosy. They mistreat people with leprosy and discriminate against people who suffer from the disease. One participant believes that the leprosy budget has been merged with that of tuberculosis. The media also discriminates against people with leprosy by ignoring their problems. Another participant complained, "The media does not talk about our problem." Stigma and discrimination are also related to job opportunities. People affected by leprosy, especially those who have observable physical marks and body deformities, suffer more in this regard. One member stated that several years ago, his wife was competing for a vacancy, and she passed the written exam. However, during the interview, she was rejected because the interviewers observed signs of the disease.

Strengths, Challenges, and Lessons Learned

The major strengths of this engaged research are the advantages and strengths of a collaborative approach. Essentially, the very nature of action research is collaborative. The collaboration of the co-authors created opportunities for sharing their knowledge, skills and techniques involved in the process of engaged research. During the implementation process, we shared the major tasks while we engaged participants in the project. The project recognizes the unique strengths that each person brings in working with existing communities through collective engagement. At the different stages of the research process, we tried to make the discussion more participatory by encouraging the participants to express their ideas, views and experiences freely. More importantly, as a result of our prior experiences of the study site and community, we managed to win the trust of the community members and conduct the engaged research successfully.

The engaged research is strengths-based and action-oriented, which is congruent with the basic values of social work. The various defining attributes of the profession are social change, problem solving, and empowerment, the application of theories for interventions, human rights and social justice. Social work is essentially an intervention-oriented profession. Knowledge of the multifaceted problems faced by the leper community is relevant for evidence-based social work practice. According to Walsh (2006), evidence-based practice is the process of utilizing a variety of sources in the professional literature to select interventions that are most likely to promote client change or improvement. In this regard, action research is essentially a means of improving and enhancing practice.

One important lesson learned is related to community-based social work practice. Understanding the main functions and membership criteria of community-based organizations (CBOs) in Ethiopia is vital for social work practice with vulnerable groups. These associations, regarded as wellsprings of social capital and people-based knowledge, have immense potential for problem-solving and decision-making in community settings. Voluntary indigenous associations such as *iddir*, *equb*, and *senbet-maheber* serve as means to establish stable patterns of relationships between members, provide socio-economic support and assistance in times of crisis, and address community concerns in difficult times.

The values of such CBOs are congruent with the values and principles of participatory action research. They are vital for community level approach to social work practice in terms of making community assessments and organizing, empowering and mobilizing communities, groups and organizations to fostering social change and economic transformation. In this context, community-based organizations such as *iddir* should take part in awareness promotion activities related to leprosy. The way that CBOs are established is conducive for undertaking the empowerment approach to social work practice. Midgley (2010) notes that developmental social work practice can be applied to work with vulnerable people such as the stigmatized and the marginalized leper community. Lee (2001, p. 5) defines the empowerment approach to social work practice which can be undertaken at various levels. Empowerment is defined as:

> A process whereby the social worker engages in a set of activities with client… that aim to reduce the powerlessness that has been created by negative valuations based on membership in a stigmatized group. It involves

identification of the power blocks that contribute to the problem as well as the development and implementation of specific strategies aimed at either the reduction of the effects from indirect power blocks or the reduction of the operations of direct power blocks.

Another lesson we learned from the engaged research is that the empowerment approach to social work practice could ensure that members of the leper community have equal access to the resources, services and opportunities. It could help expand choices and opportunities for this disadvantaged and oppressed group. Historically, people affected by leprosy have suffered from the various forms of stigma and discriminations, including segregation, unequal opportunities, and barriers to employment, social services, and education. Our project suggests that the empowerment approach provides a framework for understanding problems from different angles considering what the problem is and how it is defined, its history, why it's a problem, what values underlie it, the consequences of prevalence of the problem, and ways to address it.

Another unique lesson is related to the practice of health social work. The study provides a historical description of the setting and the complex misconceptions about the transmission of disease. It provides an opportunity to recognize the multifaceted forms of stigma and discrimination associated with leprosy. Health education could foster people's ability to make decisions about their own health-related problems and their relations with others. Participants raised several ways of reducing the negative implications of leprosy-related stigma and discrimination. Most participants have shown courage to openly discuss with members of the society outside the leper community about their strengths, potentials, and capabilities as well as their intention and readiness to fight against discrimination and prejudice and ensure their rights and entitlements to available opportunities.

Providing advocacy and awareness creation programs are essential in overcoming the stigma and discriminations experienced by the leper community. Members of the community are partly segregated and forced to feel that they are marginalized and even excluded from the benefits of the development schemes in that locality. Their vulnerabilities are mostly linked to lack of legal and policy frameworks that define the rights and entitlements of the members of the leper community. Understanding this marginalization is, therefore, important for social workers advocating for appropriate intervention programs intended to empower marginalized groups. In this engaged project, some members of the inquiry group argued that they need to speak up about the disease and their identity to improve public awareness. Some participants also noted that performing these tasks on individual basis is difficult, so collaborative work that engages the members of the leper community with other stakeholders is important to enhance people's awareness of the disease and bring about attitudinal change.

Influence on the Authors' Scholarly Direction

The project was conducted for the doctoral action research course. When the assignment of the course was given, we discussed how we could collaborate on an engaged research, selected a relevant topic, and jointly carried out this research. After completing the project, we conducted our respective dissertation research on topics different from that of this action research. Despite this, a fact that should not be overlooked is that our engagement enhanced our understanding of the current situation of leprosy in Ethiopia.

Thousands of new infection cases have been registered in the country. This shows that leprosy, a disease disappearing from many parts of the world, continues as a public health problem in Ethiopia. The leper community of Gebre Kirstos is one that survives in the sub-city of Addis Ababa, but social problems related to leprosy are not limited to Gebre Kirstos. As leprosy continues, the social dimension of the disease will affect negatively people with leprosy and their relatives struggling to survive in challenging circumstances. The study findings reveal that leper communities are among the most marginalized groups in the Ethiopian context. Hence, these communities deserve the attention of social work research, advocacy and intervention. Schools of social work and social science researchers should give attention to these unique circumstances of marginalization and join hands to empower these communities.

Our engagement in the research process also taught us about challenges and dilemmas that occur in the relationship between power and knowledge. In action research, the roles played by the researcher and study participants can be differentiated based on the power effects of knowledge and action taken in the course of interactions between the two parties. We learned that the power effects of knowledge are evident starting with defining the research question, all the way through the implementation processes, and acting on the research results.

As a result of the engaged research, we have obtained insights into the diverse ideas, views and perspectives propagated by prominent figures such as Habermas, Freire, Foucault, Marx, and Chambers who have a special place in critical social theory which underlies action research. The project also inspired us to think beyond the traditional roles of universities and work to strengthen relationships between communities and universities in our future careers. This could involve applying models of social change to empower marginalized social groups. Distinctive characteristics and core principles of action research are central to the intervention-oriented nature of social work. We practically experienced action research's cyclical, repetitive, and collaborative character as well as its democratic, participatory, and empowering nature.

Similarly, Reason & Bradbury (2006) noted that action research practices can be found in community development, organizational and business education, health care and medicine, social work, and in human social, psychological and transpersonal sciences. The purpose of action research is not to produce theories about action. Its primary purpose is to liberate the human body, mind and spirit in the search for a better, free world. The aim of participatory action research is to change practices, social structures, and social media, which maintain irrationality, injustice and unsatisfying forms of existence. Reason & Bradbury (2006) also indicated that action research is a participatory, democratic process concerned with developing practical knowledge in the pursuit of worthwhile human purposes, grounded in participatory worldview which, we also believe, is the real reason to conduct action research. It seeks to bring together action and reflection, theory and practice, in participation with others, in the pursuit of practical solutions to issues of pressing concern to people, and more generally, bring about the flourishing of individual persons in their communities.

Recommendations for Advancing Engaged Research

We would like to make some recommendations that would help promote engaged research endeavors by practitioners, researchers and the academia, especially in developing countries. Engaged research can be conducted on a wide range of issues and problems. It could be conducted when practitioners aspire to gain a better understanding of their previous or ongoing practice. It can be used when activists plan to foster social change, and when academics are invited to carry out action research in organizational settings to solve certain problems. In terms of advancing engaged research, one of the best strategies which we really appreciate is through what is written in the mission and goals of doctoral social work education in Ethiopia. It states:

> The PhD Program in Social Work and Social Development has been launched to prepare scholars who can undertake action research through community engagements that addresses the social development challenges Ethiopia faces, builds knowledge to strengthen community life and stewards of the profession of social work with in the nation (Addis Ababa University, 2007, p. 2).

We believe that the social work doctoral program is also intended to produce action researchers and engaged scholars who have the knowledge of core competencies and principles of social work and adopt methods and approaches appropriate to the Ethiopia context to address pressing problems that the country is experiencing.

In addition, we came to realize that engaged research projects can be enhanced through establishing university-community partnerships. The engaged project has inspired us to realize community-based action research in our respective universities that consider the practice models of social change as community-based research, civic engagement, collaborative and interdisciplinary research and practice. Community engagement describes the collaboration between universities and their local communities for mutual exchange of knowledge and resources in the context of partnership and reciprocity. In a more traditional paradigm, universities were viewed as ivory towers, distant and set apart from the community on the ground. Universities must be encouraged to denounce the professional-oriented experiences which let universities withdraw from larger society, turn inward and stay away from the most pressing civic, social, and economic problems. The process of community engagement can add new voices, ideas, insights, and perspectives to the intellectual process. The term university-community partnership incorporates concepts such as engagement, partnership, collaboration and participation, particularly involving people, groups, and communities who once were treated only as subjects.

Establishing Community-Based Research (CBR) is crucial to solve pressing problems of communities. In this engaged research, members of the leper community identified a problem, collected and analyzed information, and devised mechanisms to solve problems caused by stigma and discrimination. Minkler & Wallerstein (2006) note that different terms, sometimes used interchangeably, have been used to refer to community-based research including community-wide research, community-involved research and community-centered research. Conducting research rooted in community settings, serving community interests and frequently encouraging participation at all levels would create an enabling environment to solve pressing community problems. Scholars should work to champion this increasingly accepted function of community-based research that involves partnership among students, faculty and community members who collaboratively engage in the research process.

References

1995 Problems and Coping Strategies of Families Having Patients with or without

1995 Problems and Coping Strategies of Families Having Patients with or without

1995 Problems and Coping Strategies of Families Having Patients with or without

Addis Ababa University. (2007). Rationale and course description for a doctoral education in social work and social development. School of Social Work, Addis Ababa University, Addis Ababa, Ethiopia.

Barrett, R. (2005). The stigma of leprosy in Northern India. *Medical Anthropology Quarterly, 19*(2), 216-230.

Berhe, D., Haimanot, R.T., Tedla, T., & Taddesse, T. (1990). Epidemiological patterns of leprosy in Ethiopia: A review of the control programmes. *Leprosy Review, 61,* 258-266.

Freeman, D. (2002). *Initiating change in highland Ethiopia.* Cambridge: Cambridge University Press.

Freire, P. (2000). *Pedagogy of the oppressed.* NY: Herder & Herder

Friedman, V.J. (2006). Action science: Creating community of inquiry in communities of practice. In P. Reason & H. Bradbury (Eds.), *Handbook of action research* (pp. 131-143). Thousand Oaks, CA: Sage.

Goffman, E. (1963). *Stigma: Notes on the management of spoiled identity.* NY: Simon & Schuster, Inc.

Heron, J., & Reason, P. (2006). The practice of co-operative inquiry: Research with rather than on people, In P. Reason & H. Bradbury (Eds.), *Handbook of action research* (pp. 144-154). Thousand Oaks, CA: Sage.

Homan, M.S. (2008). *Promoting community change: Making it happen in the real world.* Belmont, CA: Thomson.

Idgens, L.M., & Bjerkedal, T. (1973). Epidemiology of leprosy in Norway: The history of the national leprosy registry of Norway from 1856 until today. *International Journal of Epidemiology, 2*(1), 81-89.

International Leprosy Congress. (1994). Editorial: Reflections on the International Leprosy Congress and other events in research, epidemiology, and elimination of leprosy. *The International Journal of Leprosy, 62*(3), 412-427.

International Leprosy Congress. (2002). Transactions of the sixteenth International Leprosy Congress: Reports on current issues and workshops. *The International Journal of Leprosy, 70*(4), 301-357.

Johnson, A.G. (Ed.) (2000). *The Blackwell dictionary of sociology* (2nd Edition). Malden, MA: Blackwell Publishing.

Lee, J.A.B. (1994). *The empowerment approach to social work practice.* NY: Colombia University Press.

Lee, J.A.B. (2001). *The empowerment approach to social work practice: Building the Beloved Community.* (2nd Edition). NY: Colombia University Press.

Melese, T. (2005). *Leprosy, leprosaria and society in Ethiopia.* Addis Ababa: Armauer Hansen Research Institute.

Mesfin, A. (1992). *Historical and social aspects of leprosy in Ethiopia.* Addis Ababa University, Addis Ababa, Ethiopia.

Midgley, J. (2010). *Social work and social development: Theories and skills for developmental social work.* Oxford: Oxford University Press.

Minkler, M., & Wallerstein, N. (2006). *Community-Based participatory research for health: From process to outcomes.* San Francisco: Jossey-Bass

Nicholls, P., Wiens, C., & Smith, W. (2003). Delay in presentation in the context of local knowledge and attitude towards leprosy: The results of qualitative fieldwork in Paraguay. *The International Journal of Leprosy, 71*(3), 198-209.

O'Brien, R. (2001). An overview of the methodological approach of action research. In R. Richardson (Ed.), *Theory and practice of action research.* João Pessoa, Brazil: Universidade Federal da Paraíba. English version Available at http://www.web.ca/~robrien/papers/arfinal.html

Pankhurst, R. (1984). The history of leprosy in Ethiopia to 1935. *Medical History, 28,* 57-72.

Rafferty, J. (2005). Curing the stigma of leprosy. *Leprosy Review, 76,* 119-126

Reason, P., & Bradbury, H. (2006). *Handbook of action research.* Thousand Oaks, CA: Sage Publications.

Shuttleworth, R., & Kasnitz, D. (2004). Stigma, community, ethnography: Joan Ablon's contribution to the anthropology of impairment-disability. *Medical Anthropology Quarterly, 18*(2), 139-161.

Sileshi, B. (2015). Leprosy in Ethiopia: Epidemiological trends from 2000 to 2011. *Advances in Life Sciences and Health, 2*(1), p. 31044.

Susman, G. (1983). Action research: A sociotechnical systems perspectives. In G. Morgan (Ed.), *Beyond method* (pp. 95-113), Beverly Hills, CA: Sage.

Tadele, T. (1988). *Leprosy.* In A.Z. Zien & H. Kloos, (Eds.), *The ecology of health and disease in Ethiopia* (pp. 252-265). Addis Ababa: Educational Materials Production and Distribution Agency.

Walsh, J. (2006). *Theories for direct social work practice.* Belmont, CA: Wadsworth Cengage Learning.

World Health Organization. (2006). Global leprosy situation, 200: *Weekly Epidemiological Record, 81*(32), 309-316. Available at http://www.who.int/wer/2006/wer8132.pdf?ua=1

Yohannes, H. (1973). *Some aspects of leprosy as a social problem.* Addis Ababa University, Addis Ababa, Ethiopia.

CHAPTER 6

THE IDDIR IN LOCALITY-BASED SOCIAL DEVELOPMENT

Tadesse Gobosho

This chapter presents qualitative action research results conducted in partnership with a local association in Ethiopia. The research focuses on the Debo Iddir association in Bishoftu town. The objective of the research was to explore how the association built common assets and engaged in ways of supporting its members who are living in poverty. I used focus group discussion as a data gathering tool. The primary objective of any iddir in Ethiopia particularly, the neighbourhood iddir, is to bury the dead and support members during the grieving process and during funeral. I report found that Debo Iddir worked beyond its primary objective. It built some common assets for the association and well as for its members living in poverty. Other iddirs could also use this model in building their assets and engaging in community development by supporting poor people. The research engaged members of the iddir in identifying the assets it has developed and identified the existing challenges the association faces in overcoming community problems.

Introduction

Ethiopia is one of the least developed countries in the world. Ethiopia faces multiple problems involving economic, social, and health issues, largely because many of its citizens live in poverty. Teller, Charles, Assefa, Tesfayi, and Ali (2009) point out that Ethiopia has suffered repeated droughts, famines, epidemics, wars, and instability over the past 35 years. Demographically, the population has been growing rapidly at an annual rate of up to 3% in the 1990s, to a total of 80 million in 2009, of which nearly 15 million people experience considerable food insecurity, requiring humanitarian assistance. Iddirs are one type of such voluntary local associations that operate across in almost all parts of Ethiopia. An iddir helps members when serious problems arise like the death of the member or death in the family of members or relatives.

Debo Iddir association serves as a relevant site for understanding how iddirs contribute to the well-being of their members. Two reasons motivated me to select this iddir. First, I could easily get access to information directly from iddir members since I had opportunity to work with that iddir as part of my other responsibilities. Second, I understood that local associations could contribute to community development in general. As Turner, McKnight and Kretzmann (1999) state, local associations contribute to community building through their ability to reach people and involve them in local action. Moreover, local associations have the capacity to involve people in meaningful roles, and to transmit information locally. Local associations can influence the attitudes and behavior of people and set norms and expectations for new forms of local action.

While most associations focus on one goal or interest, they take on additional functions that reach beyond their primary purpose. In many neighborhoods, a great deal of community improvement is the result of the primary and secondary activities of local associations. Asset Based Community Development identifies and taps the potential assets in a neighborhood. It involves the talents and skills of individuals, organizational capacities, political connections, buildings and facilities, and financial resources. Thus, associations represent a vital local vehicle for achieving community change and engaging in improvement.

For the research, I tried to include members of the iddir. I served as a facilitator to help participants identify the knowledge they sought and understand the assets that the iddir possesses. The iddir includes members who are poor, but also people who did not hold membership in the iddir but were living in the immediate neighborhood and experiencing poverty. Some people cannot afford the membership dues and cannot pay on a regular basis. My aim was to understand the iddir as a locality-based organization, the assets of which are critical to advancing neighborhood life. Based on these concepts of association and assets, I framed research questions focusing on understanding the association's assets and how the Debo Iddir association supports poor people at the neighbourhood level.

Framing the Engaged Research

In Ethiopia, several types of indigenous local associations offer mutual support to their members. Across rural as well as urban Ethiopia, these associations are commonly known as iddir, debo and equb. Iddirs are formed to assure financial and in-kind help at the time of a funeral for a group member or their deceased relative. For centuries, people have organized themselves in these local associations to help each other during critical periods such as weddings, death, accident or misfortune. By collecting fixed amounts of money and other in-kind materials from the members, iddirs act as a form of insurance, offering members ways of addressing the financial aspects of risk in their lives. Such insurance can be provided, for example, when one's house burns down, cattle get sick, accidents happen, or someone from the member's family or some close relative dies. In addition, members may volunteer their assistance during the days of mourning in the house of a member. Iddirs can make loans to members when they are in need for funds for marriage, or when imprisoned or fined by a court (Gezahegn, Bizuayehu, Fulle, & Tadesse, 2006). Membership insures people of some ability to survive after the devastating loss of crops or cattle (Pankhurst, 2004).

Most iddirs, especially those in urban areas, have written rules for membership, the contributions that members make, and the amount of money to be paid each month (Dejene, 2009). According to Bold and Dercon (2009),

> A striking feature of these associations is their degree of formality and sophistication. There are clear rules, an elected committee, and regular meetings. Iddir are primarily designed for providing insurance in the case of funerals and payouts are mainly made in cash but are also composed of in-kind gifts and labour services (p. 8).

Iddirs have a stable and clearly defined membership, usually based on written lists, and membership is built upon strong social networks that exist among relatives, friends, and neighbors. When a member dies, the iddir makes a payment to surviving family members in cash or provides in-kind resources (Dercon et al, 2007). Among the numerous types of iddirs, the most common one is the neighborhood iddir where people living in the same neighborhood voluntarily come together and form an association (Dercon, Hoddinott, Krishnan, & Woldehannna, 2007).

Iddirs in the Gondar area of the Amhara Region have formed a union and function together in response to problems. For instance, the union of iddirs provides access to money for emergencies, and for larger expenditures such as weddings and house construction when a member's house is destroyed by weather or fire. These activities are directly related to a problem-based or need-based approach (Muir, 2004).

Iddirs as Agents of Social Change and Development

In the past several decades, iddirs have incorporated a development perspective in their work. As voluntary organizations, they provide a leadership structure for addressing member needs through locality-based social development. The voluntarily, inclusive, and democratic or egalitarian qualities of their operations, administration, and institutional features are widely acknowledged. As non-market institutions, they operate through elected committees independent of local political forces. To access premium-based insurance, it is common for a person to be a member of several different iddirs to increase their coverage (Dercon, De Weerdt, Bold, & Pankhurst, 2006).

Tesfaye (2002) argues that iddirs have evolved to include social development functions. According to Dejene (2009),

> Many academics for example, claim that *iddirs* have transformed themselves from burial associations to multifunctional ones as *iddirs* have started undertaking a number of development work, business activities and credit activities. In accordance with the capacity of the *iddirs*, some work on sanitation development in the neighborhood, sharing responsibilities in building smaller infrastructures like feeder roads and sewerage systems, and secondarily good social (neighborly) relations, social control, day cares, schools and the likes (p. 538).

Most published research on iddirs share this common perspective on the increase in the scope of these local associations. Iddirs, in general, have changed from organizations that serve somewhat narrow well-focused functions, like burial and funerals, to broad multi-functional locality-based organizations that engage in an array of socio-economic, social service, educational, and infrastructure development activities. For example, it is now common for iddirs to provide support for orphans and vulnerable children in Ethiopia. Table 6A outlines Butcher's (2007) identifies the potential and constraints of iddirs working as agents of social change and social development.

Table 6A: Iddirs as Agents of Social Change and Development

Positive Aspects	Negative or Unknown Aspects
Voluntary and self-initiated	Decision making is not transparent to outsiders and this may be so for insiders, particularly if written rules are not in place.
Highly valued and respected	Size may be critical. Small associations may have less effect outside their neighborhood. Large associations may struggle with transparency and being responsive to the needs of all members.
A system of arbitration in disputes, of financial management and discipline	For historical reasons, iddirs may be suspicious of working with outside agencies or in coalitions with government.
Long term and stable	Despite having wide coverage, some marginalized social groups may be largely excluded.
Across socio-economic groups	In mixed gender iddirs, women may have less power, and little say in decision-making.
A variety of models adapted to the needs of different socio-economic groups	In mixed gender iddirs, divorced or separated women may be at a disadvantage.
Cope well with	There is difficulty in coping with problems such as crop failure or disasters that affect whole communities. This is particularly relevant with increased HIV/AIDS related deaths and the increase in orphans and vulnerable children.

Adapted from Butcher (2007, p. 23), based on information obtained from Dercon, Bold, De Weerdt, & Pankhurst (2004); Pankhurst & Mariam (2000); Pratt & Earle (2004).

Although the large literature on iddirs in Ethiopia recognizes these constraints, the literature far and above notes the positive aspects of iddirs and their important and evolving role and function in locality-based social development. From their comparative panel study of iddirs and other types of indigenous insurance associations in five villages in Ethiopia, Bold and Dercon (2009) summarize the promise of iddirs for local economic development:

> While some may argue that the prevalence of these institutions in developing countries signifies economic backwardness, and that they will rightfully become

obsolete if growth takes off, there is an alternative view which posits that these institutions are an integral part of a country's growth strategy especially in terms of achieving financial proliferation... This provides some hope that informal financial institutions can be steppingstones – rather than stumbling blocks – on the path to economic development (p. 53).

The Engagement Process

Debo Iddir is an informal local association in Bishoftu/ Debrezeit town kebele 01 at a village called Bole, about 47km east of Addis Ababa. The term *Debo* in Oromo society refers to a positive tradition in which a group of people come together to solve problems that an individual cannot accomplish alone. This helping tradition activity may be building a house, weeding, harvesting, tilling or ploughing land or other similar activities. However, the concept of *Debo* as the name given to the association in this research is quite different from the wider concept explained above. As I heard from the research participants and from reading their documents, the *Debo* name of their association is formed from two different words. "De" represents Debrezeit the Amharic name for the town of Bishoftu, and the letters "Bo" represent Bole, the specific villages where the members of the Debo Iddir association are living.

Debo Iddir was established by about 30 heads of households in January 1989, or in 1982 according to the Ethiopian calendar. The primary objectives in establishing the association were treating members equally in helping them with human and material resources and creating opportunities for using their existing assets. At the time of the research, there were 203 members, comprising approximately 1500 persons in all households where each person must pay a registration fee to become a member of the association. There are seven leaders elected by the members to lead the association. These leaders were trusted by members to improve their association. They were committed and played different roles, including that of chairperson, vice chairperson, secretary, vice-secretary, accountant, treasurer, and property store manager. The following four statements were developed as research questions. How does Debo Iddir define assets? How does Debo Iddir build common assets? How does Debo Iddir support people without assets in their membership? How does Debo Iddir develop plans for ways to build assets? These questions were answered through the process of engaged research.

Engagement in research is characterized by the principles that guide the research as well as the relationships between communities and those who seek to undertake research. Community-engaged research requires partnership, cooperation, and negotiation among researchers and participants, as well as a mutual commitment to addressing local needs in a way that participants find relevant or meaningful. I used participatory action research to engage with Debo Iddir and explore how the association supports its members who are considered poor and unable to fulfill what the association expects from them. According to Ahmed and Palermo (2010),

> Community engagement in research is a process of inclusive participation that supports mutual respect of values, strategies, and actions for authentic partnership of people affiliated with or self-identified by geographic proximity, special interest, or similar situations to address issues affecting the well-being of the community of focus (p. 1383).

I followed certain steps during the engagement processes. First, I contacted a previous chairperson of Debo Iddir since I knew him from my earlier work in the community. This person helped me establish a relationship with the present Chairperson of the association. During my meeting with him, I explained the research objective and clarified my motivation to better understand Debo Iddir. The Chairperson set up a time for me to meet with other leaders of Debo Iddir. When I met with Debo Iddir leaders for the first time, I tried to create an informal mutual relationship by greeting and introducing myself. Then, I told them why I was there and why I wanted to work with them. At first, I did not show them the official letter which I received from the School of Social Work at Addis Ababa University because I believed that creating an informal mutual relationship was more important than making it formal. However, when one of the leaders was unwilling to talk to me, I showed them the official letter which assured them that I was an appropriate person to work with them. This opened the opportunity to talk and discuss freely with the leaders, and as a result, their participation in this research began from the first day I met them.

From the beginning, I sought to communicate the ways the research could benefit the community, since I wanted to establish smooth mutual relationships and a sense of ownership among the participants. I was also forthright in telling them that I could not promise what we would accomplish together, neither could I promise any money for their work with me. After we formed a mutual understanding of these issues, all leaders were willing to participate in the action research. My co-researchers were the leaders of the association, and as such they were also participants in the research.

Doing action research means that one must communicate regularly since engaged research is based on cooperation among and between the co-researchers and research participants. Interest in engaged research should come from all co-researchers, not from the facilitator alone. Therefore, to achieve this objective, I negotiated to work with them, and was assured of their willingness and interest to work with me. I based our agreement on oral consent and promised not to disclose their personal or their association's private issues. I pledged not to dominate their discussions, and not lead conversations away from their interests. I also promised neither to interpret nor disseminate their ideas negatively. Similarly, they promised not to hide facts about their iddir and not to dominate others. They also gave their word to tolerate and accommodate differences in ideas.

I implemented the action research method in producing a mutually agreeable outcome for all participants, with the process being maintained by them afterwards. My involvement necessitated the adoption of many different roles at various stages of the process, including that of a planner, leader, facilitator, teacher, listener, observer, synthesizer, and reporter. I used focus group discussion for this research. As Dawson (2007) states, focus groups may be called discussion groups or group interviews, since several people are asked to come together in a group to discuss a certain issue. My main role, however, was facilitating dialogue and fostering reflective analyses among the participants, which I did up to the point where they could take responsibility for the process. In addition, I provided them with periodic reports, and wrote a final report when my involvement ended. These points were reached after they understood the methods and were able to carry on after I left.

Creating Awareness of Assets

After we created a mutual relationship, I talked with participants about the concept of assets. Since their awareness of various types of assets was weak, I prepared training materials on assets and translated the material into their own languages of Afan Oromo and Amharic. Concepts and definitions of assets, types of assets, and the benefits of assets and asset building were the major contents of the lessons, which I shared on three days for two hours per day. I encouraged all the research participants to talk on how, when and by whom their iddir association was formed. This was to know individuals who were champions of change in their community, their future vision about their iddir as well as their capacities to identify and organize interested individuals under one local association. Knowing these individuals and their vision and method helped me to easily facilitate the engaged processes. Additionally, they reflected on how they built their existing common assets. Based on their experience, they discussed the problems they faced. In relation to their common assets, I encouraged them to discuss whether they knew about the idea of assets, how assets could be built, and the effects of having assets. The participants generated different issues in terms of their strengths, weaknesses and constraints or problems they had been experiencing.

Through discussion and dialogue, I encouraged them to raise issues related to their iddir. The principal objective of creating awareness among research participant was to familiarize them with the concepts of assets. In order to create awareness, I also used discussion and dialogue methods. Then they actively participated in asking questions on issues that were not clear in order to understand things related to assets. For example, they asked me ways of identifying the assets of everyone in their iddir, and the way they would benefit from these assets as an association in general, and as individuals as well. I used techniques such as probing questions that could lead directly to key issues based on the assumption that iddir members were doing something and had some assets. For example, I asked, "What activities have you organized that built the iddir's assets in recent years?" "What happens when someone comes to you as a member who is unable to pay the monthly fee?" The participants reflected on and discussed the answers to these questions, and through group dialogue, common understandings emerged.

Data Analysis

Participatory action research acknowledges knowledge that is socially constructed. Thus, it has double objective. First, it aims to produce knowledge and action directly useful to people. Second, it is designed to empower people through the process of constructing and using their own knowledge (Miller & Brewer, 2003). These processes of knowledge and action which are directly useful to people should be done collaboratively. The construction of knowledge is grounded in the reflection of ideas and detailed dialogue and discussion. In order to be reflexive, scholars need to be aware of the many and varied ways in which they might create, or at least influence, the type of knowledge that is gained and used. There are at least four ways this might happen. First, knowledge is embodied and social in nature – it is mediated by physical and social lenses, which means that physical states and social positions will influence how scholars interpret and select information, and indeed how scholars are socially interpreted and interacted with. Similarly, knowledge is also mediated by subjectivity—that is the participants' experience and social position will influence what phenomena they see, and how they see them. Third, there is a reactivity element. This means that the knowledge obtained is at least partly determined by the kinds of tools and processes used to create it. So, participants own beliefs about what constitutes legitimate knowledge and its legitimate creation, and the types of methods scholars should and do use, will influence the findings. For example, information gathered from observation may be quite different from that gained through a conversation.

Analyzing action research data is an ongoing process. In this regard, participants went through the whole process of providing data and then analyzing it. Participants identified their problems and needs, prioritized their activities to act upon and set their future. Overall, the process consisted of building relationships, identifying problems and needs, discussing the issues, reflecting, dialoguing and discussing for analysis, generating ideas and further analysis. The ranking and prioritization of issues was another part of the analysis. Ranking identified needs and problems is important in action research because it is not possible to overcome all problems at once because of insufficient money, time, material, and human resources. After the participants listed their problems and constraints, they prioritized these issues according to the seriousness of the need, the manageability of the problem, and their potential use in planning and decision-making. As such, the process was an opportunity for mutual learning by doing.

Project Findings

Tangible and Intangible Assets

The concept of assets can be defined as the amount of wealth in a household. Assets include both tangible and intangible resources that human beings can use to improve their economic situation (Sherraden,

1991). During the focus group discussion, I observed that the concept of assets was seen only as tangible. They defined assets only as houses, farmland, factories, cars, shops, being employed and earning a salary, and similar things that can be seen and touched. In terms of tangible assets, Debo Iddir owns two houses made from wood and mud, one with four rooms and a three-room house with a meeting hall. They own one large tent made of plastic and another small canvas tent and forty benches. Assets for food service include two wide dishes made of metal for roasting and cooking meat and grain, 100 plastic pans used for eating *injera*, the Ethiopian cultural bread, or for eating grains on it, and 100 plastic glasses. Debo Iddir built these tangible assets through collecting money from members and through using their voluntary labor. Money was collected from members to buy the materials and members' labor was used to build the houses. Income was generated from house rent, bank interest, some charity organizations, and member's monthly payout. Money was also collected from all members of their association based on decisions of the General Assembly for special events or reasons.

After training on the concepts of assets, Debo Iddir leaders understood the concept of intangible assets. They identified their intangible assets as their existing social relationships, which are built and realized through coffee ceremonies, visiting each other during births and deaths, and helping each other psychologically when someone faces difficulty. Debo Iddir's social value of respecting each other was underscored as an intangible asset. Other intangible assets included skills, knowledge, professions, human labor, and the voluntary base of the association. Besides lending materials to members, Debo Iddir pays the monthly fee for its members who are unable to pay it. Five individuals were unable to pay the monthly fee. These individuals were treated as special cases, and the association covered their monthly expense, so they received services equal to that of other members. In this way, Debo Iddir is an intangible asset in supporting poor people among its members.

After discussing the nature and resources of their association, Debo Iddir leaders discussed their future plans. They thought of ways to build their common assets so members of the association would benefit, as well as poor people in the village areas. They raised points like building a clinic, youth recreation area and community shop, all of which would provide income for the association. They considered the absence of a clinic in their locality, a lack of recreation areas for youth, and the increasing price of commodities that made life difficult.

Their first proposed project is to build a community shop. According to Debo Iddir leaders, this is a timely issue because the community is affected by price inflation, and some of the traders are exploiting customers with the price hikes, which in turn, leads to poverty for the consumers. If they built a community shop, members could buy commodities for less cost than at individual trader's shops. The leaders expressed a sense of ownership for the community shop as it would minimize risk from inflation and be sustainable.

Their second proposal was to open a clinic. Although there is a governmental health center in their village that serves surrounding communities, the center is not open on weekends and does not have good service at night, so many people go to a private clinic in the town. The leaders agreed that such a clinic would have several advantages. Members could be served at a minimum cost, it could generate income for the association, and non-members who live nearby could benefit. Their last proposed project was optional because the Federal Sport Commission plans to build a medium stadium for the youth in Bishoftu, and its construction fence was already in place in their village. Since the project of the construction of the stadium is run by other bodies the Federal and the Regional Sport Commission, the beneficiaries of the stadium were not known. Once the construction was finished, the stadium may be open for certain age group of the youth who are expected to participate in the national sport teams, which do not involve all the surrounding youths. However, after identifying whether this stadium will provide recreational activities for certain ages levels of youth sports, the participants decide to create a youth recreational area by convincing the city administrators for permission.

Strengths, Challenges, and Lessons Learned

While the leaders discussed and agreed on the importance as well as the necessity of their planned projects, they did not forget the challenges. One predictable challenge was the lack of money to run the planned projects. Questions were raised by some of the reality of the projects, as well as sources of start-up income and funds to complete them. Even to start community shop, it was assumed to cost around 300,000 birr [$11,000 USD]. "How could these projects become true?" A second challenge was the issue of responsibility or determining who was going to run the project. "Are we going to hire an employee or going to serve with our own hands, and how?" They discussed among each other that at that moment, they had about 35,000 Ethiopian birr [$1275 USD] in their bank account. This money had accrued from members' monthly payments, and renting out their houses, glasses, pans, chairs, tents and so on. Then, drawing on the training they received on the concept of assets, one leader other suggested a solution by saying, "We should begin from where we are and with what we have."

To begin their plan, they discussed the need to identify the skills and gifts of each member of their association. One group member raised his hand and asked, "Is it not challenging. How can we identify the gifts and skills of all of the members or totally about 203 people?" The Secretary of the association answered that they can easily identify the skills or the jobs of current members just from their biography. The third person supported this idea and suggested that they call a meeting and tell all members the purpose of the meeting. After that, members could be asked to voice their gifts and the skills that they have, and what they will contribute to their association. The other participant supported the idea and added that the association should focus not only on those persons who were registered as family heads, but also on the skills and gifts of people in their family. Then, the leaders all agreed on the identification of the gifts and skills of members registered as family heads and the people in their family.

From the standpoint of the researcher, engaged research can be implemented and social development achieved when working with local voluntary associations such as iddirs. Such research can help the community move one step forward by organizing themselves to improve their lives. The iddir, especially, the neighborhood-based iddir includes many residents, all of which who have different gifts, skills, and talents, including those with financial and material assets. Engaged research with local associations is a means of mobilizing these assets in local communities. Nonetheless, unless research funds are available, the nature of engaged research is a challenge because of the necessary commitment of the researcher, his or her time, labor, regular living expenses, and pocket costs. Engaged research takes time to build partnerships, negotiate, plan and communicate with the target people. Moreover, the community-engaged research approach may not fit neatly within the academic status quo, thus making both funding and academic promotion challenging. Expectations for the dissemination of results are another challenge. Community members often expect to hear about results soon after the research is completed. They don't want to wait months or years before an article appears in an academic journal. Instead, the engaged researcher must complete and report the results of the research on an ongoing basis throughout the project, and in a timely fashion upon its end.

Finally, to bring about positive outcomes in engaged research, researchers should consider the following. Engaged research requires a strong partnership between the researcher and the community. Rapport-building and smooth relationships need to be created and sustained throughout research processes. Co-researchers in the community and researchers from outside the community should have shared and equal responsibility and control. In engaged research, the community should identify their own needs and problems, while outside researchers share knowledge and expertise with the community so that they can work to solve the identified problems. In a community-based participatory research, the real experts on community culture and community developmental issues should be the association, its leaders and its members. The academic researcher, practitioners, or other types of research should be in line with the interests of the community and facilitate their work by using his or her professional skills.

Influence on the Author's Scholarly Direction

In general, the Debo Iddir leaders' plan, their motivation to act on it, and their willingness to discuss issues energized me to use community based participatory research with a local association for my doctoral dissertation. This engaged research empowered me to look at poor people outside this association. I tried to observe the critical problem that rural communities around Bishoftu town were facing. Bishoftu town has been rapidly expanding to the farming communities in all directions. At the same time, because of the proximity of Bishoftu town to the capital city of the country, Addis Ababa or Finfine as well as because of the access to infrastructures, Bishoftu became the focus of investments. Hence, due to both the rapid expansion of the town and investment issues, the surrounding indigenous farming community became landless. The people lost their farmlands and they were changed from landowners to land losers and daily labourers, which resulted in a change from independent to dependent living. The problem negatively affected individuals, families as well as all the surrounding farming communities. Therefore, the existence of this problem on the ground initiated me to conduct an engaged research for my dissertation. I chose an engaged research because I observed that many academic researchers specially, in their doctoral dissertations do not want to conduct an engaged or an intervention research due to its consuming time, money and labor risks.

However, as a social work researcher, I decided to take this risk. I wanted to make a priceless contribution to poor people at risk just by working with a targeted community who were losing their farmland and experiencing unusual problems and risks. I set the title of my dissertation as *"Mobilizing and Utilizing the Assets of a Local Community in Ethiopia: Asset Based Community Development (ABCD) in the Abbo Iddir of Bishoftu Town"* (Tadesse, 2017). In short, the action research reported here with Debo iddir was the direct experience that led me to pursue and fully engage in participatory action research for my dissertation research.

The purpose of my dissertation was to understand the processes and outcomes of ABCD through action research with the Abbo

Iddir association, the components of which can offer a road map for planning, organizing, implementing, and evaluating an ABCD process with local associations in Ethiopia. The research process was evidence-based through photographs, videos and audios. Through my research, 25 individuals mobilized themselves and formed one local association called Kurkura Two Gudina Umata Consumers Cooperative Association in Bishoftu town. Currently, this association has grown to 750 members and 8000 customers. The engaged research shows that unconnected individuals can connect and mobilize through an association for common interests and build relationships among each other and the wider community.

This association created networks with nine different government and private institutions as well as local associations. It also provides practical and direct services to the community through providing different goods and services, especially basic commodities such as sugar, food oil and wheat powder with fair prices. By doing this, the association gives gains a small profit for itself. Economic opportunity was created and customers in the surrounding communities saved money. The members of the association bought shares, saved their money and gained profits. The association also created job opportunities for 13 jobless individuals in the community, especially for male and female heads of households who had no income. The association also built tangible and intangible assets.

Individuals are assets. The association has 750 members and 8000 customers where all of them registered and actively engaged and benefited. Associations and institutions are assets. This association created networks with nine associations and institutions in the town. Getting access to bank credit is another asset, namely the association has access to the Cooperative Bank of Oromia (CBO). Land for constructing a house in the town is another basic asset as farmland is a basic asset for rural people. The association has got 400m2 and 300m2 of land at two sites in Bishoftu town to construct houses for shopping, offices and stores. Constructing houses on one site is ongoing. Besides the permanent assets of the association, financial capital is another asset that the association has. The members started to contribute two birr at the beginning of the research process. Now the financial capital of the association increased to one million ETB (US $34,059) where the total capital is more than two million ETB ($68,118).

In general, community development involves a vision of how things might be changed so that sustainability and social justice can be achieved. This engaged research also implemented ABCD focusing on its sustainability. My dissertation prioritized identifying, mobilizing and utilizing the assets and skills of impoverished individuals instead of focusing on what they lacked. My experience in engaged research that is reported in this chapter showed me that implementing ABCD research with impoverished citizens through the Debo Iddir association was a viable topic for my dissertation, and one that could result in improving the lives of poor farmers in Bishoftu town.

Recommendations for Advancing Engaged Research

Two related areas should be addressed by engaged researchers. First, engaged research should be used by researchers, scholars, students, and practitioners to improve the work and build the capacity of iddirs in Ethiopia, and other such associations elsewhere. Concerning iddirs, they have existed in Ethiopia since the Italian occupation that occurred during WWII. Although the structure and function of these informal, local associations has been the subject of much anthropological and sociological research, little attention has been given to improving the work of iddirs through engaged research. My study is likely the beginning of such work with iddirs through participatory action research. Doing engaged research especially, by implementing asset-based community development is challenging since it is a complex process, consuming much time in addition to lack of enough research fund. However, regardless of its challenges and complexities, the research outcome is rewarding both for the researcher and the target community. Our environments, both social and physical, are surrounded by both problems and assets. At the same time little or no attention is given to mobilize the existing assets in order to solve the existing problems.

Mobilizations and utilization of these resources or assets can be done through engaged research. Although many things are expected from researchers and scholars, the importance of identifying the assets of impoverished communities, individuals, associations and institutions, and working through engaged research to address poverty through such processes is imperative.

Second, knowledge of tangible as well as intangible assets should be brought to the leaders of iddirs so they can develop plans to accumulate assets for the benefit of the organization, its members, and the local community. Perhaps iddir associations, in general, are like other locality-based associations in that they are not economically strong because they do not focus on building assets that generate their income. Although Debo Iddir has some houses which can be rented and used as a means of income, typically, iddir associations focus only on their members' insurance, except in special circumstances when they collect some amount of money and materials from their members. The long-term implication of this participatory action research is, therefore, aimed at making the Debo Iddir association economically and socially independent in a sustainable way. The vision is that poor people in this association will improve their life by getting accumulating assets, obtaining equitable social and economic services, and equally participating in society like non-poor people.

References

Ahmed, S.M., & Palermo, A.S. (2010). Community engagement in research: Frameworks for education and peer review. *American Journal of Public Health, 100*(8), 1380-1387.

Bold, T., & Dercon, S. (2009). Contract design in insurance groups. UK: University of Oxford. Retrieved from http://www.csae.ox.ac.uk/materials/papers/2009-04text.pdf

Butcher, C. (2007). Understanding the role of informal institutions in social accountability in Ethiopia. Available at https://pdfs.semanticscholar.org/ad10/481db7d5c74da1de62b2a4c499c91dae831a.pdf

Dawson, C. (2007). *A practical guide to research methods. A user-friendly manual for mastering research techniques and projects.* (Third edition). Oxford, UK: How to Books Ltd.

Dejene, S. (2009). Exploring iddir: Toward developing a contextual theology of Ethiopia. In E. Svein, H. Aspen, B. Teferra, & S. Bekele (Eds.), *Proceedings of the 16ᵗʰ International Conference of Ethiopian Studies* (pp. 535-547). Trondheim, Netherlands. Available at https://www.academia.edu/2161746/Exploring_iddir_Toward_Developing_a_Contextual_Theology_of_Ethiopia

Dercon, S., Bold, T., De Weerdt, J., & Pankhurst, A. (2004). Extending insurance? Funeral associations in Ethiopia and Tanzania, OECD Working Paper 240. Paris: OECD Development Centre. Available at https://www.oecd-ilibrary.org/docserver/103027727461.pdf?expires=1585157402&id=id&accname=guest&checksum=FCAC118BFBC18AC5FACC8534E06B5CFB

Dercon, S., De Weerdt, J., Bold, T., & Pankhurst, A. (2006). Group-based funeral insurance in Ethiopia and Tanzania. *World Development, 34*(4), 685-703.

Dercon, S., Hoddinott, J., Krishnan, P., &Woldehannna, T. (2007). Collective action and vulnerability: Burial societies in rural Ethiopia. "CAPRi working papers 83, International Food Policy Research Institute (IFPRI). Available at https://ideas.repec.org/p/fpr/worpps/83.html

Gezahegn, Y., Bizuayehu, A., Fulle, G., & Tadesse, M. (2006). *Ethiopian Village Studies ii: Turufe Kecheme: Shashemene Wereda, East Shewa Zone, Oromia Region.* Ethiopia Wellbeing in Developing Countries Research Programme, UK: University of Bath. Retrieved from http://www.bath.ac.uk/soc-pol/welldev/research/methods-toobox/cp-countries/ethiopia/Turufe%20community%20profile.pdf

Miller, R.L., & Brewer, D.B. (Eds.). (2003). The *A-Z of social research. Dictionary of key social science research concepts*. Thousand Oaks, CA: Sage.

Muir, A. (2004). *Building capacity in Ethiopia to strengthen the participation of citizens' associations in development: A study of the organizational associations of citizens*. Oxford, UK: International NGO Training and Research Centre.

Pankhurst, A. (2004). Conceptions of and responses to HIV/AIDS: Views from twenty Ethiopian rural villages. Department of Sociology and Anthropology, Addis Ababa University. Available at https://www.researchgate.net/publication/255588445_Conceptions_of_and_Responses_to_HIVAIDS_Views_from_Twenty_Ethiopian_Rural_Villages

Pankhurst, A., & Mariam, D.H. (2000). The iddir in Ethiopia: Development, social function and potential role in HIV/AIDS prevention and control. *Northeast African Studies, 7*(2), 35-58.

Pratt, B., & Earle, L. (2004). *Study on effective empowerment of citizens in Ethiopia*. Oxford, UK: International NGO Training and Research Centre.

Sherraden, M. (1991). *Assets and the poor: A new American welfare policy*. Armonk, NY: M.E. Sharpe.

Tadesse, G. (2017). *Mobilizing and utilizing the assets of a local community in Ethiopia: Asset Based Community Development (ABCD) in the Abbo Iddir of Bishoftu Town*. [Unpublished Doctoral Dissertation]. Addis Ababa University.

Teller, C., Assefa, H., Tesfayi, G. S. & Ali, H. (2009). Population dynamics, food/nutrition security and health in Ethiopia: Delicate balance of vulnerability & resilience. Paper presented at the International Union for the Scientific Study of Population, Marrakesh, Morocco. Available at https://www.researchgate.net/publication/275553242_Population_Dynamics_FoodNutrition_Security_and_Health_in_Ethiopia_Delicate_Balance_of_Vulnerability_Resilience

Tesfaye, S. (2002). *The Role of Civil Society Organizations in Poverty Alleviation: Sustainable Development and Change, the Cases of Iddirs in Akaki, Nazreth, and Addis Ababa*: (Unpublished Master's thesis) Addis Ababa University, Addis Ababa, Ethiopia.

Turner, N., McKnight, J.L., & Kretzmann, J.P. (1999). A guide to mapping and mobilizing the association in local neighborhoods. A community building workbook from the Asset Based Community Development Institute. Institute for Policy Research. Evanston, IL: Northwestern University. Available at https://resources.depaul.edu/abcd-institute/publications/Documents/Workbooks/MappingAssociations.pdf

CHAPTER 7

BUILDING CAPACITIES OF IDDIRS TO ASSIST POOR OLDER ADULTS

Samson Chane

Poor older adults seek the help of the family, relatives and neighbors, community-based organizations (CBOs), governmental organizations (GOs) and non-governmental organizations (NGOs). The purpose of this action research was to understand how community-based funeral associations called iddirs can help poor older adults in Dangila town, Ethiopia. The research was guided by this question: What are the strengths and limitations of iddirs to help poor older adults? A total of 18 members of the iddirs Executive Committee participated in the action research. This study applied action research, particularly Appreciative Inquiry (AI) to discover best practices, successes and strengths of the iddirs. The Nominal Group Technique (NGT) was employed to collect data. NGT allows study participants to explain, generate and crosscheck ideas focusing on the assets, strengths and constraints of iddirs. The research findings indicate the strengths of iddirs include human, material and financial assets, as well as the organizational structures of iddirs, their rules, regulations, and supportive cultural values. The existing assets and strengths of iddirs were not sufficient to meet the basic needs of older adults, change their life and make them productive and self-reliant. In spite of constraints such as inadequate finances and material, a lack of commitment among members, and the underutilization of existing resources and opportunities, iddirs continue to assist poor older adults. This action research helps the iddirs to identify their assets, strengths and limitations, and propose strategies to fill gaps. The research findings also have implications for social work research and practice in the areas of community-based elder care, support and asset building.

Introduction

In 2007, the total population of Ethiopia was 73, 918, 505. Of the total population of 3,565,161 (4.8%), older adults 60 years and older1,942,720 were men and 1,622,441 were women (Central Statistical Agency, 2008). Many older adults cannot meet their basic needs and do not have suitable caregivers and sources of support. Although the family is the major source of care and support for older adults, family members may not be able to fulfill the needs of older adults because of the rising cost of living (MoLSA, 2006). At the same time, older adults are productive and can make tremendous contributions to the welfare of their families and communities. Proponents of the productive aging movement argue that investing in older adults acknowledges their contributions to social development (Midgley & Conley, 2010). The Ethiopian Federal Ministry of Labor and Social Affairs (1996) called upon government organizations, non-governmental organizations, community-based organizations, and voluntary associations to support poor older adults. The policy emphasizes that the "Existing traditional and other grassroots' associations of the people shall be assisted and utilized for the initiation and implementation of developmental social welfare activities" (MoLSA, 1996, p. 80).

In Dangila town, people have established iddirs at the local level to voluntarily support one another in times of bereavement. Besides their traditional role, iddirs provide support to poor older adults. There are five iddirs in the town organized at the kebele level consisting of 2,367 members. Purposely, the iddirs of kebele 03, 04 and 05 were included in the study because of their efforts to help poor older adults. To diagnose and prioritize the issue, Appreciative Inquiry (AI) and the Nominal Group Technique (NGT) have been employed. Members of the Inquiry Group attended meetings and emphasized that the iddirs have limited capacity to help poor older adults and provide better services to the community. Ultimately, members of the Inquiry Group identified and prioritized the issue of building the capacity of iddirs to help poor older adults as the major area of focus for action research.

Framing the Engaged Research

Iddirs as Voluntary Indigenous Organizations

In Ethiopia, people voluntarily form indigenous organizations to address the socioeconomic challenges faced by their members and locales. Iddir is a funeral association that ensures a payout in cash and in kind at the time of a funeral for a deceased relative of a group member (Pankhurst & Haile-Mariam, 2000). The first iddir was founded in Addis Ababa during the Italian occupation from 1936 to 1941. The Italian invasion caused a loss of human lives and material destruction. This exposed many households to an acute shortage of money and created financial problems for covering expenses for burial and other purposes. Iddirs served as a collective strategy by helping members to manage financial crises, and the costs of funerals. Members come together and form an iddir based on sharing a common interest such as family membership, friendship, residence in the same district, affiliation by employment, and/or membership in the same ethnic group (Aredo, 1993). An iddir represents a way of achieving group solidarity and support, particularly during periods in which members experience considerable need and require resources they would be unable to access through other means.

Iddirs have written and well-defined rules and regulations related to membership procedures, duties, rights and obligations of members, and payout schedules. The rules and regulations hold a set of fines for nonpayment of contributions, stipulate frequency of meetings and offer guidance on the election of committee members. They collect regular monthly payments from their members and provide insurance in the case of funerals and payouts, mainly made in cash, in-kind resources, and in the form of labor services. The amount of payment is based on the relationship of the member to the deceased person (Bold & Dercon, 2009).

Apart from death, iddirs help in the event of crisis situations, such as fire and illness. They provide loans in cases when a member's oxen or other livestock have died, their houses burned, or they need money or materials to prepare feasts for wedding ceremonies (Hoddinott, Dercon & Pramila, 2005). They are a source of social capital, strengthen social solidarity among members, and extend their social networks (Pankhurst & Haile-Mariam, 2000). Iddirs have become involved in social development activities such as mitigating HIV/AIDS, supporting orphans and poor older adults, providing community services, and constructing roads and public utilities (Aredo, 1993; Kloos & Haile-Mariam, 2000; Chane, 2010).

In their more recent role of facilitating social development activities, iddirs work to build community capacity. Community capacity refers to the commitment of the community to create, deploy, and sustain assets, resources and skills so as to strengthen and find solutions to improve quality of life. Social capital and organizational resources are capacities that a community owns and can mobilize to meet its needs (Chaskin, Brown, Venkatech, & Vidal, 2001). To make a project sustainable, a community is expected initially to build its capacity from within (Mayer, 2002), and subsequently to get assistance from external sources. The community has the will and the resources to help itself, to identify and prioritize needs, and adopt appropriate strategies to build capacity (Delgado, 2000; Saleebey, 2002).

Related to the concept of capacity building, the strengths perspective is guided by principle that every individual, group, family and community have strengths (Saleebey, 2002). This principle allows for the recognizing community strengths and building upon the resources of the community to ensure sustainability for growth (Cassity-Caywood & Huber, 2004). The strengths perspective is change oriented that helps to identify and strengthen capacity to fulfill needs and foster social development. Its philosophy emphasizes the mobilization and utilization of the strengths or assets of families, groups and community-based organizations to achieve their goals and improve the quality of life (Healy, 2005).

Research Methods

Nominal Group Technique and Appreciative Inquiry

Participatory action research (PAR) is used to explore the assets and the roles of iddirs, and the ways of building their capacity to provide better services to the community and poor older adults. PAR is appropriate to address specific issues identified by local people, change practices and apply the results to solve problems. Members of a group or community identify a problem, collect and analyze data, and act to address the problems (Reason & Bradbury, 2006). Action research is participative in allowing people get directly involved in the research process. Action research also involves teamwork (Creswell, Hanson, Plano & Morales, 2007). It demands engagement from the researcher and participants at all levels of the research process (Heron & Reason, 2006; Martin, 2006). The engagement of the participants in the research process distinguishes the action research from basic and applied research (Park, 2006).

The Nominal group technique (NGT) was used to collect data because of its characteristics that fit this action research project. Several authors have described the uses of NGT from different dimensions. NGT increases participation of nominal group members (Young & Barrett, 2001), and their contribution and satisfaction with respect to participation in the data collection by motivating creative thinking (Ruyter, 1996). NGT is appropriate to identify and prioritize problems, needs and strategies, and facilitate group decision making, and it saves time to gather multiple ideas from several people on a particular issue (Witkin & Altschuld, 1995; List, 2001).

Appreciative Inquiry (AI) is a positive mode of action research that clarifies the creative and constructive potential of organizations and the community. In the AI approach, studying the best practices and accomplishments of the organizations and the community serves as input for building a better future (Ludema, Cooperrider, & Barrett, 2006). AI is the act of recognition, questioning, exploring, and discovering past and present strengths, successes, and the potential of a group of people, organizational members or community residents. It emphasizes the collective strengths and rich experiences of every organization and community, and offers a positive, strengths-based approach to organizational development and change management (Cooperrider & Whitney, 2005).

Engagement in the Field

I conducted field work in Dangila Town Administration in March and April 2011. Earlier contacts were established with experts working with older adults, community and iddir leaders. Preliminary data were collected on the number of older adults and iddirs, and iddir members. These people functioned as gatekeepers and created favorable conditions to build rapport with project participants. I introduced myself and established relationships with seven iddir leaders who formed the Inquiry Group. We discussed the purpose and process of the action research. This discussion was successful in clarifying the purpose and process of the action research and convinced them to participate.

NGT and AI were employed as methods to facilitate the identification of the issues inherent in supporting poor older adults, and the way in which iddirs could serve a role in offering support. During the Nominal Group, members of the Inquiry Group participated actively and raised relevant ideas related to elderly issues, the assets, strengths, the roles, and limitations of iddirs to assist poor older adults. The NGT and AI helped the Inquiry Group generate ideas about elderly issues in the context of the community serving as the place of engagement and identifying the strengths and limitations of iddirs to assist poor older adults. Members identified what they wanted to be studied, and the process to be used for the action research. In addition, the Inquiry Group nominated and convinced eleven members of the iddir Executive Committee to participate. The inclusion of these eleven individuals raised the total number of participants to eighteen, with the Inquiry Group continuing to play a facilitating role.

Together, we fixed the time and place to meet. To make the NGT manageable and efficient, the participants formed three small groups and nominated a facilitator and a recorder for each group. I communicated the purpose of the meeting and provided the questions in written form to the participants. Next, the group facilitators and I welcomed the participants and explained the purpose and procedure of the meeting. We shared information regarding what was expected of each nominal group member to do. I assisted the participants in understanding the guiding questions. The group facilitators explained the importance of each member's contribution and how to process the information gathered through NGT. Amharic was used as a media of communication since the participants were fluent speakers of this language.

During the process of new idea generation, the participants did not share their ideas with others. Individually and silently, each participant conceived ideas and jotted them down on a sheet of paper. Next, using key words, the recorder listed each participant's ideas on a sheet of paper. This was followed by a minimal level of discussion for clarification only. Then, I led the group discussion in which the participants that suggested ideas explained them more completely, and any new ideas were added to the list. To avoid repetition, similar ideas were combined, and the complete set of items was reviewed. Repetitions and non-relevant ideas were omitted. Major findings of the study were communicated to study participants before finalizing the research report, and participants forwarded reflections that were incorporated in the final report. I incorporated their comments and wrote up the final report.

Findings

Assets and Strengths, Limitations and Challenges

The participants identified the assets and strengths of iddirs as human, material, and financial assets, as well as cultural values. Human assets are crucial for the proper functioning of iddirs. At the time of this study, the iddirs had 2,538 members that came together mainly for the purpose of mutual help in time of bereavement. Members joined an iddir after fulfilling these criteria. The homes of the applicants were to be located in the area where the iddirs operated. Members were required to be a follower of the Orthodox faith and the head of a household. They had to have the capacity to pay entrance and monthly fees and be committed to obey the rules and regulations set by the iddirs. Iddir members were females and males, young and elderly people, some who attended only primary and secondary schools, and others who were college graduates. Members were civil servants, teachers, merchants running various business activities, handicrafts, daily laborers, and pensioners. Increasing number of the iddir members with diverse educational, economic and occupational backgrounds was a source of strength to the iddirs to enhance their capacities. This included assigning roles to members to assist poor older adults and address community affairs, including sharing knowledge and utilizing skills to manage the iddirs.

The iddirs had offices, meeting halls, tables and chairs, cooking materials, plates, cups, loudspeakers, tents, spade, bed, bells, bugles, digging tools, flags and ropes. The offices and meeting halls were constructed by iddirs members or given to them by the kebele, the lowest administrative of government. The iddirs collected money from members in the form of membership and monthly fees. The amount of monthly fee was birr 1.50 for a single person, and birr 3.00 for a couple. Totally, the iddirs had birr one-hundred thousand (or $5,882) in cash. They rented meeting halls to subsidize their income and used it to cover different expenses and to support poor older adults. Iddir members used the association's materials during funeral processions and funeral feasts. Whenever necessary, iddir members paid a small amount of money to rent chairs, tables, cups, plates and tents during wedding ceremonies and other feasts. Poor older adults and their families were exempt from payment when using chairs, tables, cups, plates and tents. The iddirs use a single room for their office and warehouse. To create an attractive working environment, they wanted to have relatively well-furnished rooms to use for different purposes. Financial assets were not adequate to fulfill needs of the iddirs, to give better service to their members, and to assist poor older adults. Iddir members shared common culture, religion and language, and adopted the tradition of mutual support, and tolerance. These attributions contributed to maintaining solidarity among members. Fundamentally, respecting older adults and acknowledge their roles is part of the social norm in the community. The local people have a supportive culture, and positive attitude towards elders, and they were interested to assist them.

The iddirs had functional structures with well-defined roles. The structure is comprised of a chairperson, vice-chairperson, secretary, auditor, treasurer, purchaser, fee collector, village representatives as each kebele is divided into village units, and members. The duties and responsibilities of each position, the number of people assigned in each structure, term of office, and penalties for breaching the rules were incorporated in a written document. The iddirs developed the tradition of auditing their properties annually. They held a general meeting to exchange views and make decisions on series of agendas, and to hear and comment on the annual reports of their performance. The structures, rules and regulations are not rigid. Whenever necessary, the iddirs call a General Assembly to amend the structures and rules and form an ad hoc committee responsible to identify poor older adults and orphans who deserved assistance.

Financial and material scarcity reduced the capacity of iddirs to assist poor older adults. Principally, their earned income from members' fees was insufficient to meet the demand of helping poor older adults in a satisfactory way. The support provided to poor older adults lacked continuity, and it was not enough to satisfy basic needs of older adults, and to change their life and make them productive and self-reliant. Sometimes, the local administrative units and development associations such as the Amhara Development Association and the Awi Development Association induced iddirs to contribute money to finance development projects like constructing roads, building schools and providing other infrastructure services. Of course, iddirs are expected to contribute for the cause of promoting development initiatives, but this kind of imposition tended to erode their autonomous status and shrink their financial capacity.

Most of members of the Executive Committee were government employees or had private businesses. They served the iddirs in their spare time even though their work required long hours and frequent engagement. Because of financial scarcity, the iddirs could not employ workers to reduce the workload of the Executive Committee. They were not able to maximize their human resources since some of members lacked the commitment to serve and share their knowledge and experiences. Limited financial and material resources constrained the capacity of iddirs to diversify its sources of income as a means to adequately support poor older adults.

The tradition of preparing a work plan is not firmly established among iddirs. Members Executive Committee had limited capacity in terms of leadership, planning, and project design, implementation, monitoring and evaluation. A list of activities and corresponding implementers, timelines, and budget breakdowns were not clearly stated as part of a written plan. The iddirs had close relationship with the kebele administration and Dangila Health Centre; but their relationships with Dangila Municipal Office, Office of Labour and Social Affairs, and HIV/AIDS Prevention and Control Office, and other government sectors were weak. Establishing strong linkages with other organizations was viewed as helpful to obtain financial, material, and technical support to poor older adults.

Assisting Poor Older Adults

Although the iddirs faced scarcity of material and financial assets and other constraints, they provided limited support to poor older adults. They supported older adults by decreasing or dismissing their membership fees. The iddirs embrace poor older adults as iddir members. Some poor older adults were members of iddirs for the last 20 or more years, even though some quit paying monthly fees due to financial problems. Nonetheless, the iddirs did not expel these persons, but rather allowed them to continue their membership. There were situations in which the iddirs admitted poor older adults as new members and exempted them from membership and monthly fees. Those who could do simple work were assigned to transport chairs, tents, plates, cups and cooking materials to the house of the family of the deceased person. Members attend funeral processions, and give condolences, financial and material support to the family and relatives of the deceased person. They dig the grave and carry the dead body to the cemetery. After the funeral ceremony, they accompany the family and relatives of the deceased person to their home and prepare food and drinks for guests for two days. Poor older adults were beneficiaries of all these services delivered by the iddirs.

Iddir members, together with voluntary groups, repair the houses of poor older adults. The iddirs work with the kebele administration to assist poor older adults to get rent houses owned by the kebele at low or no cost. Members contribute 0.25 to 0.50 birr monthly to help poor older adults and orphaned children. Only one iddir provided 90 to 100 Ethiopian birr [$3.27 to $3.60 USD] to poor older adults three times in a year, usually during the Ethiopian New Year, Christmas, and Easter. The other two iddirs provided grain, sugar, oil, flour bur rarely money due to scarcity of resources, and the need to give priority to support orphans. Iddirs gave stationery materials and seed money to orphaned children to run small business activities like renting bicycles, shoe shining, fattening sheep, selling articles and roasted groundnuts such as peas, beans, and chickpea. Under the sponsorship of the Global Fund, the iddirs purchased and distributed exercise books, pens, pencils, bags and school uniforms for 91 orphans.

In collaboration with the Dangila Health Institution, the iddirs facilitated the process to provide free medical support to poor older adults. The iddirs screened 120 poor people including older adults and offered them supporting letters to get free medical services at Dangila Heath Centre. The iddirs lent 100 to 300 birr to members including older adults to cover medical expenses. They organized joint programs with the health institutions, including teaching older adults and the community in general about harmful traditional practices such as female circumcision, the extraction of milk teeth, removing uvula, and early marriage. They conducted community conversation programs to raise community awareness on HIV/AIDS and the care and support of people living with HIV/AIDS, as well as conversations regarding orphans, older adults, family planning, primary health care, and prevention of malaria. Iddirs encouraged the community to adhere to vaccination programs and organize a campaign on environmental sanitation.

The iddirs support developmental activities in Dangila town, and at the zonal, regional and national levels. They made a financial contribution to upgrade water and power, renovate schools and the public hall, construct churches, offices, and repair roads. They gave financial support to the Amhara Development Association and the Awi Development Association. In doing so, the iddirs serve as a bridge between the government and the community to communicate information and implement government programs. In order to stabilize the market, the iddirs purchase teff, oil, sugar, and peas and sell them to members and other dwellers in the kebele. Sometimes, the iddirs subsidize expenses of poor older adults to buy these items.

Suggestions to Build the Capacity of Iddirs

The research participants forwarded suggestions to build the capacity of iddirs in order to provide better support to poor older adults, iddir members and the local community at large. Participants suggested engaging members in income generating activities like opening co-operative shops and introducing credit services to members who want to start small businesses. Strengthening the capacity of iddir members will build the capacity of the iddirs and increase the number of new members. This activity may change attitudes of the people towards iddirs and encourage them to join and contribute. It would develop a spirit of work and a feeling of ownership. Raising the amount of membership and monthly fees with the consent of iddir members, organizing fundraising programs, and looking for support from external sources would also strengthen the capacity of iddirs.

In collaboration with other organizations, iddirs could identify the interests and assets of older adults and assist them in engaging in income generating activities. This process could go hand-in-hand with identifying funders and credit services to provide the initial capital, advising elders how to manage their money, and marketing their products or services. The participants stressed the possibility of working together with elders' associations at the local level to represent the interests of older adults, make their voices heard, and defend their rights. The participants recommended offering two- or three-day seminars for members of the Executive Committee on leadership, planning and project design, implementation and evaluation. Establishing partnerships between iddirs and CBOs, GOs and NGOs would create opportunities for sharing experiences and working together to enhance the capacities of iddirs through technical, material, and financial support.

To conclude, the iddirs of Dangila town have the capacity to support poor older adults, but they are expected to exhaust their existing resources. Besides scarcity of resources, lack of attention and commitment to utilize opportunities limit the efforts of iddirs to support poor older adults. Iddirs are a culturally embedded institution with considerable capacities, sociocultural and economic values appropriate for culturally competent social work practice for social development. Iddirs are expected to do a lot of things, but what these iddirs in Dangila town are doing is exemplary, that is implementing a community-based elder support model.

Strengths, Challenges, and Lessons Learned

The research findings support previous studies in line with the roles of iddirs, the strengths perspective, and factors influencing capacity building. Pankhurst and Haile-Mariam (2000) and Bold and Dercon (2009) explain service delivery during bereavement, and financial and material support the iddirs provided to a deceased family or relative. Chane (2010) notes the participation of iddirs in supporting older adults and orphans, and Aredo (1993) illustrates their functions in the construction of roads and public utilities. The research reports of Kloos & Haile-Mariam (2000), and Hoddinott, Dercon and Pramila (2005) emphasizes the central role iddirs can play in the promotion of health development.

The strengths of iddirs can be explained by their capability to bind members from different backgrounds together. Members trust in iddirs, have a strong sense of ownership through them, and consider them as a source of security in time of bereavement and shock. Iddirs remain intact and continue to provide bereavement support to members and their families for the last 40 to 50 years. The role of iddirs is no longer restricted to supporting members and families of deceased people. Rather they have expanded their engagement to assist poor older adults and orphans and are involved in other developmental activities. From these experiences, other iddirs and community-based organizations may learn about the need to mobilize and bring members together and develop trust among members and clients. These are important qualities for social work practice with the groups, communities and organizations in promoting social development.

The iddirs create viable structures, rules and regulations that are fundamental for their existence. Readiness for change is the other experience of iddirs that can be shared with similar organizations working with the community. Iddirs are change-oriented and flexible in accepting new practices and approaches. The structures and rules of iddirs are not rigid. To a significant extent, they may be revised in the interest of members to make them more effective. Members participate in different activities, treat each other in line with the rules, and hold discussions to make decisions and exchange ideas. Iddirs have the experience of identifying their assets, strengths, achievements, and limitations, and developing ideas to deal with challenges they encounter. Iddir members have courage, aspire for change, and want to work collaboratively with organizations in the area of elder support and other issues.

The iddirs face challenges to support older adults and provide better services to members. These challenges may not be unique to the iddirs of Dangila town. The background to the occurrence of these challenges are mainly related to the internal situation of iddirs related to lack of and underutilization of resources, lack of commitment among members, limited interaction with stakeholders, and limitations to utilize existing opportunities. These challenges cannot stop the activities of iddirs. Still, the iddirs have the means to get out of these challenges and do better. In social work practice it is essential to get informed about the strengths and challenges of such organizations and strive to support them.

Influence on the Author's Scholarly Direction

This action research project raised my interest further to identify elder abuse and neglect as one of areas of scholarship in research and community service. The idea of doing my dissertation research on elder abuse and neglect was the outcome of the action research project. Alongside the main agenda of the action research project, participants discussed the socioeconomic and health problems of older adults in Dangila Town Administration and surrounding areas. The contents of discussions covered their lack of basic needs, poor health, lack of proper care and support, a decline in autonomy and respect, and the contexts, forms and perpetrators of elder abuse and neglect.

Thus, this engaged research project inspired me to focus on elder abuse and neglect. To me, it revealed specific issues that needed investigation, and thus it directed my reading. I tried to read some of previous studies on elder abuse and neglect in Ethiopia and other African countries, Asia, Europe, and America to have better understanding in the area, to think of the body of knowledge, and to some extent reflect on the research gaps. In Africa, information is scant about elder abuse; even the available research results are not widely disseminated. In Ethiopia, little is known about elder abuse and the lived experiences of abused elders that necessitates a need to understand elder abuse in-depth from social work perspective. I also learned the practice of organizing nominal group discussion and its importance in empowering people to explain their opinions and explore their needs, and to find out practical solutions to address problems. Doing action research has scholarly value in blending theoretical knowledge with practice. This helped me internalize the concept, methods and processes of action research.

Recommendations for Advancing Engaged Research

Action research is a continuous process that needs attention from planning to implementation stages. It blends theory, research and practice/action. In the action research, activities done in each process have contributions on the outcome of the research project. The researcher and the community are expected to identify, prioritize, and clearly understand the problems, interests and concerns of the community. Action research projects must be realistic in terms of time, material and human resources that are implemented to remedy problems and bring about change in the community. Stakeholders should be engaged actively, and their roles and responsibilities should be defined and communicated. Researchers and participants should find opportunities to proceed with research projects and utilize them effectively, anticipate potential challenges and introduce alternative solutions. The researcher and participants should develop sense of ownership of the project among stakeholders and encourage them exert maximum effort for the success of the project.

Following ethical procedures is part of process of the action research process, and community members, study participants and stakeholders should be briefed on the objectives of the project and expected outcomes. Ensuring trust and mutual respect between the researcher and participants develops a sense of ownership of the project in the community and maximizes engagement. Advancing engaged research means employing sound research methods but following eclectic and holistic approaches to align with the guidelines of action research. In action research it is important to apply culturally competent approaches, considering the knowledge inherent in indigenous systems, working towards the empowerment of participants, and giving attention to the views of study participants and insiders perspectives. Researchers should respond to comments so as to maintain effective communication, interaction and networking throughout the research. Researchers need to be open-minded and accept the idea that people can generate knowledge based on their experiences, negotiate ideas and engage in meaningful and critical reflection.

References

Aredo, D. (1993). The iddir: A study of an indigenous informal financial institution in Ethiopia. *Saving and Development, 1*(17)**,** 75-90.

Bold, T., & Dercon, S. (2009). Contract design in insurance groups. UK: University of Oxford. Retrieved from http://www.csae.ox.ac.uk/materials/papers/2009-04text.pdf

Cassity-Caywood, W., & Huber, R. (2004). Rural older adults at home. *Journal of Gerontological Social Work, 41*(3), 229-245.

Central Statistical Agency. (2008). *Summary and Statistical Report of the 2007 Population and Housing Census: Population Size by Age and Sex.* Federal Democratic Ethiopia Population Census Commission. Addis Ababa, Ethiopia.

Chane, S. (2010). *The roles and challenges of community participation in HIV/AIDS prevention care and support of PLWHAs in Dangila Town, Ethiopia.* Saarbruck: VDM Publishing House Ltd.

Chaskin, R.J., Brown, P., Venkatesh, S., & Vidal, A. (2001). *Building community capacity.* NY: Aldine de Gruyter.

Cooperrider, D.L., & Whitney, D. (2005). *Appreciative inquiry: A positive revolution in change.* San Francisco: Berrett-Koehler Publishers.

Creswell, J.W., Hanson, W.E., Plano, V.L.C., & Morales, A. (2007). Qualitative research descriptions: Selection and implementation. *The Counseling Psychologist, 35*(2), 236-264.

Delgado, M. (2000). *Community social work practice in an urban context: The potential of a capacity-enhancement perspective.* NY: Oxford University Press.

Healy, K. (2005). *Social work theories in context: Creating frameworks for practice.* London: Palgrave Macmillan.

Heron, J., & Reason, P. (2006). The practice of co-operative inquiry: Research 'with' rather than 'on' people, In P. Reason & H. Bradbury, (Eds.), *Handbook of action research* (pp. 144-154). Thousand Oaks, CA: Sage.

Hoddinott, J., Dercon, S., & Pramila, K. (2005). *Networks and informal mutual support in 15 Ethiopian villages.* Washington, DC: International Food Policy Research Institute.

Kloos, H., & Haile-Mariam, D. (2000). Community-based organizations and poverty alleviation programs in HIV/AIDS prevention and control in Ethiopia: A preliminary survey. *Northeast African Studies, 7*(2), 13-34.

List, D. (2001). The consensus group technique in social research. *Field Methods, 13*(3), 277–290.

Ludema, J.D., Cooperrider, D.L., & Barrett, F.J. (2006). Appreciative inquiry: The power of the unconditional positive question. In P. Reason and H. Bradbury (Eds.), *Handbook of action research* (pp. 155-165). Thousand Oaks, CA: Sage.

Martin, A.W. (2006). Large group processes as action research. In P. Reason & H. Bradbury (Eds.), *Handbook of Action Research* (pp. 166-175). Thousand Oaks, CA: Sage.

Mayer, S.E. (2002). *Building community capacity: How different groups contribute.* NY: The Foundation Center.

Midgley, J., & Conley, A. (2010). *Social work and social development: Theories and skills for developmental social work.* Oxford: Oxford University Press.

Ministry of Labour and Social Affairs (MoLSA). (1996). The Federal Democratic Republic of Ethiopia Developmental Social Welfare Policy. Addis Ababa: MoLSA.

Ministry of Labour and Social Affairs (MoLSA). (2006). *Collective Educational Materials Regarding Older Persons.* Addis Ababa: MoLSA.

Pankhurst, A., & Haile Mariam, D. (2000). The iddir in Ethiopia: Historical development, social function, and potential role in HIV/AIDS prevention and control. *Northeast African Studies, 7*(2), 37-53.

Park, P. (2006). Knowledge and participatory research. In P. Reason & H. Bradbury, (Eds.), *Handbook of action research* (pp. 83-93). Thousand Oaks, CA: Sage.

Reason, P., & Bradbury, H. (2006). Inquiry and participation in search of a world worthy of human aspiration. In P. Reason & H. Bradbury, (Eds.), *Handbook of action research* (pp. 1-15). Thousand Oaks, CA: Sage.

Ruyter, K.D. (1996). Focus versus nominal group interviews: A comparative analysis. *Marketing Intelligence & Planning, 14*(6), 44-50.

Saleebey, D. (2002). *Strengths perspective in social work practice.* Boston: Allyn & Bacon.

Witkin, B.R., & Altschuld, J.W. (1995). *Planning and conducting needs assessments: A practical guide.* London: Sage.

Young, L., & Barrett, H. (2001). Adapting visual methods: Action research with Kampala street children, *Area, 33*(2), 141–152.

CHAPTER 8

EXPLORING ASSETS OF YOUTH FOR THE PREVENTION AND CONTROL OF HIV

Andargachew Moges (PhD)

This study explored assets of youth for the prevention and control of HIV transmission. A participatory approach was employed to identify their assets and concerns. Thirty-five youth (25 males and 10 females) were involved as participants. Nominal Group Technique and Focus Group Discussion were used for data collection. Results indicated that young people have diverse internal (e.g. leadership, hospitality, self-efficacy, spirituality, positive self-concept, commitment and motivation for learning and work) and external (e.g. youth associations, positive cultural values and norms, adult and peer role models, and caring adult relationship) assets. As to their concerns, substance abuse, shortage of youth-focused recreational centers, unemployment, HIV epidemic, poverty, lack of access to information technology and harmful traditional practices were identified as major ones. The study encouraged the youth to participate in a similar and large scale engaged research and plan community-based and youth-focused comprehensive action to prevent and control the HIV epidemic.

Introduction

The National Youth Policy of Ethiopia marks a major step in recognizing and promoting the rights and strengths of young people. At the same time, youth in the nation still face a number of challenges, including inadequate access to sexual and reproductive health services, malnutrition, prevalence of HIV/AIDS, substance abuse, particularly khat, tobacco, alcohol and drug use, and persistent gender inequalities (Ethiopian Public Health Association, 2005). Young people in Ethiopia, ages 15-24 represent 22.8% of the population. The incidence of HIV infection among this age group, particularly among those who are unmarried, but sexually active, is very high. The 2016 DHS data shows that only 24.3 % of women and 39.1 % of men have comprehensive knowledge of HIV prevention, for example, knowing that consistent use of condoms during sexual intercourse and having just one uninfected faithful partner can reduce the chance of getting HIV. Urban youth have a higher risk of HIV infection than rural ones (Central Statistical Agency, 2017). Social and economic forces play a significant role in exacerbating the spread of HIV. Some of the factors which contribute to youth vulnerability are weakened social control, later age at marriage, multiple partners, changing sexual norms, economic pressures and the use of alcohol and other substances. In fighting against the epidemic, prevention and control efforts have resulted in increased awareness about HIV/AIDS and some positive trends in condom distribution and utilization, growing demand for voluntary testing and counseling (VTC) and a decline in national HIV incidence rate (Central Statistical Agency, 2017). Conventional HIV prevention and control programs designed for young people are not able to halt the epidemic effectively. Youth voices are lacking in the design and implementation of programs. Most programs are characterized as problems-based and focus on risk behaviors, and prevention interventions sometimes conflict with traditional sex education and practices. Youth are encouraged to use condoms to avoid unsafe sex, however cultural values and norms in Ethiopia discourage sex before marriage. As a result, HIV prevention campaigns lack synchronicity with cultural beliefs and values (DiClemente, Crosby, Salazar & Wingood, 2006). Creating opportunities for young people through engaging them in the design and implementation of HIV/AIDS intervention programs not only generates useful knowledge for individual young person but also provides opportunities for the development and empowerment of the youth (Vesely et al., 2004). Prevention efforts that concentrate on the assets or strengths of the youth are crucial to reversing the pandemic (Oman, Vesely, & Aspy, 2005).

This study poses the question: What assets do youth have that could be mobilized in preventing and controlling HIV transmission? To actively engage youth in the research process, the study used a participatory and strength-based approach with youth participants from 02/04 Kebele of Akaki/Kaliti sub- city, Addis Ababa.

Framing the Engaged Research

Youth is a period of rapid physical and emotional growth and development. It is a time of undergoing a process of self-discovery that accompanies the transition from adolescence to adulthood. This process often entails more risk taking compared to other life periods. In comparison with adults, some adolescents are high risk-takers, have high levels of impulsivity, or have a tendency for sensation seeking behavior. Such youth may place themselves at greater risk for HIV acquisition (DiClemente, Crosby, Salazar &Wingood, 2006; Odu & Akanle, 2008). Some young people become sexually active early. In some countries. boys and girls have sex before the age of 15 (UNAIDS, 2003). On average, men in Ethiopia initiate sexual intercourse at older ages than women. One in four (24%) women have their first sexual intercourse before age 15, and 62% before age 18. By age 20, 76% of women have had sexual intercourse. On the other hand, only 2% of men have first sex before age 15, 17% initiate sexual intercourse by age 18, and by age 20, 36% of men had sexual intercourse (Central Statistical Agency, 2017).

To reverse the impact of the pandemic, young people must be at the center of prevention actions (DiClemente, Crosby, Salazar & Wingood, 2006; UNAIDS, 2003). Engaging youth actively in prevention programs not only generates useful knowledge for young people about HIV/AIDS but also provides opportunities for the development and empowerment of participants, leading to benefits for young people. Youth participatory prevention programs are comprehensive and multifaceted, building on the assets or strengths of young people. Such programs are not focused on isolated problems-such as sexual risk behaviors but focus instead on holistic interventions creating diverse opportunities for young people (Pagliaro & Kiera, 2001; Powers & Tiffany, 2006).

Few intervention programs on HIV/AIDS involve youth actively in prevention activities. Most interventions are at individual level. Useful assets such as parental monitoring, parent-adolescent-communication, positive peer and community norms and values, social capital, enhanced youth-focused services are not exploited (Oman, Vesely, & Aspy, 2005). Most national and international prevention and control programs to combat HIV transmission among the youth have focused mainly on information and awareness campaigns aimed at increasing awareness of HIV transmission and prevention (Baptiste et al., 2006). In Ethiopia, the typical program is a top-down approach advocating condom promotion or monogamy or later age at first sex. Youth voices are lacking in HIV prevention and control programs and strategies, and there is lack of youth empowerment programs (Ethiopian Public Health Association, 2005).

Asset-based Approaches and HIV/AIDS Prevention and Control

Asset-based HIV/AIDS prevention relies on the strengths perspective. This perspective integrates concepts related to empowerment, hope and resilience. Rather than focusing on assessment and correction of youth problems or deficiencies, the strengths perspective is concerned with resources, skills, gifts and connections. An asset-based approach emphasizes self-mobilization and organizing for change and development by the youth themselves (Bergdall, 2003).

Asset-based approach to HIV/AIDS prevention and control is an approach based on the principles of appreciating and mobilizing individual and community assets such as resources, skills and capabilities. Rather than the effort being driven by external agencies, it is youth and community-driven (Cunningham & Mathie, 2002). The intervention is built on an appreciation of strengths, by identifying and analyzing the past successes of youth and the community. This strengthens young people's confidence in their own capacities and inspires them to take action. Asset-based HIV prevention and control recognizes the human, social, financial and environmental capital of youth and the community (Vesely et al., 2004).The asset-based approach assumes that there are many institutional or environmental obstacles to the protection of HIV transmission, and they cannot be overcome through individual action but instead must be addressed through the activities of youth and CBOs (Green & Haines, 2002). An asset-based approach focuses on the power of associations and informal linkages within the community, and the relationships built over time between community associations and external institutions. It is built on a participatory approach to empowerment and ownership of the prevention and control program. Such an approach mobilizes youth and community assets and resources focused on collaborative efforts and emphasizes engaging people as citizens rather than as clients in making communities and local governance more effective and responsive (Cunningham, 2008).

There are sets of methods that can be used in asset-based development. These include organizing a core group, mapping the assets of individuals, associations and local institutions, building a community vision, and planning and leveraging activities, investments, and resources from inside the community from its own associations and organizations before leveraging resources outside the community (Kebede, Getu &Negeri, 2011). In Ethiopia, asset-based approaches have been successful with poor communities and school children (Yeneabat & Butterfield, 2012; Butterfield, Yeneabat, & Moxley, 2016), but their use has not been applied to improving the health of people (Blickem, Dawson, Kirt, et al., 2018).

Research Methods

Engagement

This research explored the assets of youth that could be mobilized to prevent and control HIV transmission. It used a community-engaged approach that actively involved youth in the process. Community engaged research is a collaborative process between the researcher and participants to create and disseminate knowledge with the goal of strengthening well-being of the community. This approach is different from the traditional applied research paradigm in which the outside researcher determines many aspects of the study. In the traditional approach, youth have been engaged by researchers almost exclusively as subjects, respondents, and informants, but not as resources or partners in the discovery of new knowledge or the development of policies and programs (Powers & Tiffany, 2006). A community engaged approach to research involves equitably those who are affected by the problem and recognizes the unique strengths that each participant brings to the study. What is fundamental in a participatory engaged research is that the researcher acts as a partner with youth. The distinction between who does the studying and who gets studied is consciously muted. By doing so, young people's awareness of the assets they bring as researchers and agents of change in preventing and controlling HIV transmission is enhanced (Stoecker, 1999; Minkler & Wallerstein, 2008).

I identified the research issue and selected a community-based youth organization called Gelan Youth Oriented Development. I submitted a letter of cooperation from Addis Ababa HAPCO and Akaki/Kality Sub-city HIV/AIDS Prevention and Control unit to the head of the organization. Next, I discussed the research issue, purpose and process with the head of the CBO. A core research group to facilitate the investigation and serve as an advisory unit was formed. The core group included the head of the youth center, voluntary counseling and testing (VCT) experts, reproductive health (RH) service providers, the program and training coordinators of the CBO, and three youth representatives who had training on HIV/AIDS.

Gelan Youth Oriented Development was established to provide multi-dimensional services to young people. These include HIV counseling and testing, RH counseling, Internet, gymnasium, library and indoor and outdoor game services. Participants are young people in the age range 15-24. Ten young people who received training on HIV/AIDS prevention were invited to participate in the study. Orientation was given to the participants about the aim of the study and how the information would be used. Participants were told that their participation was voluntary, and they could stop participating at any time. Oral informed consent was obtained. A peer-to-peer recruitment technique was then used to nominate the other participants. Tiffany (2006) argues that participant-driven recruitment creates opportunities for engaging community youth in research to address their issues and utilize research findings within the community context. Each youth invited four or five peers to participate and most youth invited by their peers accepted the invitation and participated. A total of 35 youth, 25 males and 10 females participated. Most were high school students, while others were unemployed secondary school graduates. I used Nominal Group Technique (NGT) and Focus Group Discussion (FGD) as methods for data collection. Study participants were involved in NGT to generate data about their assets and concerns, particularly what they cared about. FGD was then held with representatives of the NGT participants to obtain answers to the following questions. How do the youth see conventional HIV prevention and control interventions in relation to their assets? How could the assets be used to prevent and control HIV transmission?

Nominal Group Technique

The Nominal Group Technique has the advantage of being more structured than the focus groups. Through NGT, everyone is given an opportunity to contribute while avoiding the likelihood of one person dominating the discussion. NGT can be used with small groups as well as with a larger number of participants, so it is possible to get a sense of priority concerns of group members (Witkin & Altschuld, 1995).

I used a 5-Step process to implement the NGT. *Step 1: Clarifying the activity.* After I explained the concept of assets, participants were assigned into 5 nominal groups, each with 7 members. Each group nominated a leader to serve as its moderator. The group leaders presented the topic for discussion and for the purpose of clarification, a brief moment of group interaction was allowed. *Step 2: Working independently.* In the nominal groups, each member was encouraged to think about the question and issue for a few minutes. Then, he/she worked silently and independently and generated his/her own assets in the form of words or short phrases. The group leaders encouraged members to list as many assets as possible.

Step 3: Gathering ideas. Using a flip chart, the facilitators of each group recorded answers. As each participant provided one list at a time, the facilitator directed them to respond or "pass" if the idea was already recorded. Participants were allowed to ask permission from the group to revise an earlier contribution or develop new ideas from their own list. Using the participants own words, the facilitators used only a word or phrase to describe each asset. No evaluation of ideas was allowed at this stage. This continued until no member had a new concept to add to the list. After each group exhausted writing their assets on the flip chart, a facilitator for the all nominated was identified and used the same process to compile the total. *Step 4: Clarifying assets.* The facilitator lead participants in discussion of each asset, one by one, to clarify, add to or meld it with another asset. Duplications were eliminated and the facilitator asked participants if all assets were clearly understood. Questions were not allowed about the merits, validity, or worth of any asset. Clear and concise lists of assets were then posted for all to see. *Step 5: Discussing the implications of the results.* Participants finally discussed about the implication of the asset exploration activity and the results. Participants took a break after they finished the asset exploration activity. After the break, they engaged in a similar NGT to list out their concerns. The asset exploration activity took two hours and identifying concerns took 40 minutes. All data collection and analysis were done in Amharic, the first language of the participants. Data generated from the NGT were refined by eliminating duplications and merging similar concepts together through the different stages of the technique

Focus Group Discussion

After the assets are identified by the NGT, Focus Group Discussion was followed for the two research questions: How do the youth see conventional HIV prevention and control interventions in relation to their assets? How could the assets be used to prevent and control HIV transmission? This is because the two questions are more of open-ended type and require an in-depth and interactive discussion. In focus groups, the interaction created in group dynamics results in the generation of relevant ideas. In addition, expressions other than those in verbal form such as gestures and stimulated activities can provide the researcher with useful insight (DiRuyter, 1996).

After participants finished the NGT sessions, they were asked to nominate seven youth to be involved in FGD. Ten candidates were suggested and seven were selected by voting. Their selection was based on their experience in HIV related prevention programs and their expressive language ability to communicate ideas. FGD was held the next day. A preview of the NGT results were displayed for the focus group participants before they began the discussion. I recapped the findings and used guiding questions to facilitate the group discussion. How important are the internal and external assets you identified by NGT in the effort to combat HIV/AIDS? What are the limitations of conventional prevention interventions in view of your identified assets? How can we mobilize the internal and external assets in the effort to fight against HIV/AIDS? Next, participants reflected on current prevention and control programs in relation to their assets and identified ways in which their assets could be mobilized in preventing and controlling of HIV transmission. Probing questions were raised based on the issues raised by the participants. The FGD took one hour. Data from FGD were transcribed verbatim. Themes were identified from the transcribed data. Interpretation was made with the research core group and sample participants. I translated the findings and produced the report in English.

Findings

Youth Assets and Concerns

Data obtained from NGT revealed that youth have several and diverse internal and external assets. Internal assets refer to the individual knowledge, skills, gifts or talents; and external assets are the ones that young people experience in their interaction with people and institutions in their community. Internal assets generated by the participants include empathy, leadership, hospitality, self-efficacy, goals and aspirations, spirituality, tolerance, positive self-concept, commitment and motivation for learning and work. Some of the external assets are youth associations, useful cultural values and norms, adult and peer models, community institutions, collaborative and team spirit, and caring adult relationship. The preliminary list of assets generated by the youth numbered more than 50, but these lists were reduced to 35 items by avoiding duplication and merging similar concepts. The final pool of internal assets of youth is shown in Table 8A, and the external assets of youth in Table 8B.

Table 8A: Internal Assets of Youth

	Internal Asset Name	Internal Asset Description
1	Talents	Youth have different talents like performing drama, composing, music, dancing, fashion show etc.
2	Leadership	Some youth have leadership gifts such as organizing, coordinating, planning, deciding
3	Hospitality	Youth welcome others (family, peers, elders, foreigners etc.)
4	Curiosity	Youth are curious for new things
5	Achievement motivation	Youth have high achievement motivation in school and life
6	Empathy	Youth are empathetic to family, peers and others
7	Self-efficacy	Youth believe that they have the ability to do something

8	Self-awareness	Youth are aware of themselves and their capacities, limitations
9	Goals and aspirations	Youth have their own goals and aspirations
10	Spirituality	Youth have their own religious beliefs
11	Tolerance	Youth have knowledge of and comfort with people of different cultural and ethnic backgrounds
12	Facing challenges	Youth are capable of facing different life challenge
13	Motivation	Youth have the motivation to learn and work
14	Creativity	Some youth have creative ideas and new ways of doing things
15	Positive self-concept	Youth have positive self-concept about themselves
16	Knowledge of HIV/AIDS	Youth have adequate knowledge about HIV/AIDS
17	Commitment	Youth are committed to their schoolwork
18	Courage	Youth have the courage to take risks, face challenge
19	Problem-solving	Youth solve problems they face in their life
20	Responsibility	Young people accept and take personal responsibility

Source: Author.

After participants completed the asset exploration activity, they held discussion on the implication of the results. The discussion created a sense of hope among the participants. They were surprised about NGT results because the pool of assets revealed the immense strength of young people. Participants discussed that assets could help them avoid potential harmful behaviors. They mentioned examples to substantiate their views. For example, youth who spend their time in sports and religious activities were less likely to use drugs and alcohol. Those who have positive peer role models often avoid potentially harmful behaviors like violence, risky sexual behavior, smoking and drug use. Students who are doing well in school and have great future aspiration rarely engage in risky sexual behavior. Participants said that before this research, they did not have the opportunity to discuss their issues and strengths in a systematic way. Academic researchers often ask them to complete questionnaires or reply to interview questions. They felt that the participatory way of dealing their issues and problems was more productive and educational. The youth became interested in a larger-scale study with young people in their community that would help them plan a youth-focused development program.

Table 8B: External Assets of Youth

	External Asset Name	External Asset Description
1	Youth associations	Young people have different formal and informal interest groups
2	Useful cultural norms, values and practices	Young people value useful cultural norms, values and practices
3	Community idols	Young people model peers and community people who are their idols
4	Community institutions	Young people value institutions--schools, clinics, churches
5	Society value youth	Society has high expectation of youth
6	Collaboration & team spirit	Young people have interest to work collaboratively with team spirit
7	Access to information	Young people have access to information (media, school, peers etc.)
8	Interpersonal relationships	Young people have positive relationships with family, peers, others
9	Youth-focused services	Young people have youth-focused services like VCT and RH
10	Participation in different activities	Young people participate in sport, religious activities, clubs etc.
11	Youth as resources	Young people have useful roles in the family, school and community
12	Huge in number	Young people represent a significant number of the population
13	Peer discussion	Young people have a culture of discussing with peers
14	Caring adult relationship	Young person experiences caring from parents' other adults
15	Linkages with different bodies	Young people link with Kebele administrators, community leaders, church leaders etc.

Source: Author.

Using the NGT, participants also identified and rank-ordered their concerns (see Table 8C). While prioritizing their concerns, the youth placed HIV/AIDS at the fourth rank. The rapid expansion of substance abuse in their Kebele is the primary threat for young people. One participant said- "Our Kebele seems to be the home for Khat and alcohol." Many youth spend their time chewing Khat and drinking alcohol. A shortage of youth-focused recreational services is their second concern. Other than school and home, youth have few places to spend their time. The participants said that HIV/AIDS is something that they can control easily if the drivers of the epidemic such as the expansion of alcohol and drug use, poverty and unemployment are alleviated. What the youth are really concerned about is the lack of a conducive environment for their growth and development to become useful citizens for the country.

Table 8C: Ranking of Youth Concerns

Youth Concerns	Ranking
Substance abuse	1
Shortage of youth-focused recreation centers	2
Unemployment	3
HIV epidemic	4
Poverty	5
Lack of access to information technology	6
Backward traditional attitudes	7

Source: Author.

Conventional HIV Prevention and Control Programs and the Role of Youth Assets

Participants in the FGD indicated that HIV intervention programs designed to reduce young people's risk of HIV infection in their community are fragmented, intermittent, short-term, and problem-focused. Most programs are accomplished through donor funds. The programs cease when the donor-based projects phase out. Prevention strategies are not youth-driven. Instead, they are based on the interests of NGOs or the government. Some prevention programs, for example, exclusively advocate for the use of condom which is contrary to the cultural values and religious beliefs of the society. As an example, they mentioned DKT International Ethiopia insistence for condom advocacy among young people so as to provide funds for HIV programs. Participants also denoted that HIV prevention and control programs have mainly focused on awareness creation. As one youth stated:

> I am bored of hearing the same information about HIV and AIDS now and then. I don't understand why the government is doing this. I believe almost all people know what is said on the media repeatedly about HIV and AIDS.

Participants credited their own community-based initiatives to prevent and control HIV/AIDS as more productive and sustainable than massive government or NGOs awareness creation campaigns. Another youth summarized this situation as follows:

> It is not the great deal money invested on prevention and control campaigns that is to be counted to appraise the success of preventions efforts. Rather, it is the motivation and initiative people develop to bring behavioral change for themselves, which indeed can be done without money.

Participants discussed that youth assets are strongly associated with a reduction in sexual risk behavior. They mentioned several examples. High school female students doing well in school and who have great future plans are less likely to engage in risky sexual practices. Youth who have different recreational places spend their time productively. Youngsters who are involved often in religious activities are faithful to their partners and rarely engage in premarital sex. Young people in families with high levels of cohesion or parental monitoring are less likely to engage in sexual risk behavior.

FGD participants also indicated that as youth they have tremendous capacity for combating the HIV epidemic. Some of their assets can help them be active agents in the prevention and control programs. A specific example is young people's collaboration and team spirit. On holidays, youth often engage in voluntary religious and community activities as a team. For Easter and similar holidays, they often raise fund from the community and support elderly and orphaned children. In general, what the youth need is the opportunity for participation and input into their own matters and ways to have a voice in decision making. Participants mentioned exemplary activities in preventing and controlling HIV transmission. One participant indicated that his peers have established an informal association which collects money from each member and support street youth by renting houses for them, paying the house rent, and giving some amount of money for basic necessities. Another participant indicated that his peer association is creating HIV/ AIDS awareness in the community and also provides food and other basic necessities in home-based care for people living with the virus. Through all their efforts, the participants reported that the Kebele administration did not support them with financial or material resources.

Concerning the strategies how the assets identified could be utilized in preventing and controlling HIV epidemic, participants suggested several approaches. These include adhering to cultural and religious norms and values, expanding youth-focused recreational centers, establishing youth associations that work on development activities, creating opportunities for educational access, and involving the youth in decision making regarding their own issues.

Strengths, Challenges and Lesson Learned

By applying engaged research, critical insights were added into the research and interpretation of the data. Conducting engaged research also helps to translate research findings more easily to real world settings and impact youth risky behaviors. Community-based engaged research design is more culturally appropriate and creates opportunity to own community interventions. In addition, the partnership established between the university researcher and community youth garnered the expertise and resources of both. The design of the research allowed community youth and the researcher to be clear about the extent of their collaboration, their respective roles and responsibilities, what they expected to gain from the research, and their anticipated contributions.

The results of the present study reveal that youth have diverse assets that could be mobilized for healthy and productive development. A strong and mutually beneficial partnership between the university researcher and community youth served as an essential bridge to the translation of research into meaningful interventions in the youth community. Studies on asset-based youth development programs provide support for this finding. These studies reveal that young people bring significant improvements in positive youth behaviors such as interpersonal skills, quality of adult and peer relationships, self-control, problem-solving, cognitive competencies, self-efficacy, commitment to schooling, and academic achievement (Vesely et al., 2004).

The above strengths are, however, accompanied by potential challenges that without adequate anticipation and planning, community-based engaged research can create problems for a research study. Some of the challenges or obstacles to engaged research concern the time required by the researcher to establish and maintain productive relationships. Many youth in the study site view research with suspicion because of well-documented breaches of research ethics, as well as that fact that participants were considered as simple passive participants in the research process. Other challenges include negotiating the differences between the expectations of the university researcher and community-based settings. The elements of these two cultures can affect a research study.

It is suggested that prevention programs targeting problem behaviors should not focus solely on reducing problems. Instead, youth-focused programs need to be comprehensive and multi-faceted, building on the assets and strengths of young people and assisting them to define goals, complete school, and plan their futures. Youth development seldom tackles isolated problems, such as sexual risk behaviors, but focus instead on providing holistic support and opportunities for young people. Youth development is a strategy that attempts to meet the needs young people. It allows them have life skills and enables them to be cared for and safe, and to be valued. This strategy also empowers young people to be useful and be spiritually grounded by building on their capabilities. Youth development approach assists young people to cultivate their own talents and increase their feelings of self-worth. This eases their transition into adulthood (Pagliaro & Klindera, 2001).

This engaged research developed greater appreciation and recognition of their assets among the youth. Youth also developed motivation and interest to engage in collaborative research. They valued the importance of university researcher and community collaboration to study youth problems and issues. This created a sense of ownership of interventions and a resulting sustainability of the effort. The youth involved in the research indicated their interest to participate in a more comprehensive study regarding their problems and concerns. The community-based youth organization coordinators also expressed interest to work in collaboration with the School of Social Work at Addis Ababa University in investigating youth problems and concerns.

Influence on the Author's Scholarly Direction

This engaged research impacted my scholarly direction and dissertation in many ways. I learned that my earlier conception of youth as a problem was erroneous. Young people have huge resources to bring to the classroom, community and different walks of life. In my classroom with graduate students, I learned that if we engage them in the learning experiences for each course, they can come up with creative insights. In my MSW class entitled Project Development and Evaluation in Social Work, for example, I was fascinated by a student's argument on the role of indigenous and untapped community resources and the importance of leveraging such resources for social work intervention. As a university professor, the significant value that I give to student engagement originated from the positive conception of my students as important resources.

My enthusiasm on youth assets and strengths directed my PhD dissertation. The dissertation theme, "Exploring assets of youth for positive development" (Andargachew, 2015) was out of a curiosity to probe more on this issue. From the research endeavor, I learned that young people in our context have diverse untapped internal and external assets that contribute to their positive development. These potential assets were not utilized in policy development or strategic interventions. Young people have the potential to play a significant role in the community's socio-economic and political development. Thus, recognizing their strengths and resources, it is important to create conducive context for youth to participate in an organized manner in the process of building a democratic system, good governance and development endeavors.

After completing my PhD study, I uphold the strengths perspective as one of my central theoretical assumption in my research and other professional career. In Ethiopia, individuals, families, groups, communities and organizations have inherent strengths. As a social worker we often diminish such resources of disadvantaged groups in the community. Our commitment, however, needs to be building on their inherent strengths. This will take us a long way to empower clients. Emphasizing and supporting even the smallest bits and pieces of client strengths helps them see chances and energizes them to reconstruct their lives and have hope for the future. The strengths-based approach is an empowering alternative to the traditional methods with disadvantaged groups.

The engaged research project has also enabled me to experience and appreciate participatory research. The university researcher's role here is muted. I learned that a community-based participatory research increases the relevance of the research both to the university researcher and those participating in the research process. This maximizes the translation of the knowledge gained through research into practice. Increased youth participation in the research augmented quality of this study. It led to some sustainability, at least of the concept of positive youth development and the transferability of results to the grassroots context. By being involved in participatory research, I developed interest to work collaboratively with the youth in dealing with community problems, challenges and issues. While working on my dissertation, I continued my partnership with the Youth Oriented Development, a CBO actively seeking new ways to deal with diverse youth problems.

References

Andargachew, M. (2015). *Exploring assets of youth for positive development.* [Unpublished Doctoral Dissertation]. Addis Ababa University, Addis Ababa.

Baptiste, D., Bhana, E., Petersen, I., McKay, M., Voisin, D., Bell, C., & Martinez, D. (2006). Community collaborative youth-focused HIV/AIDS prevention in South Africa and Trinidad. *Journal of Pediatric Psychology, 31(9),* 905-916.

Bergdall, T. (2003). *Reflections on the catalytic role of an outsider in asset-based community development (ABCD).* Chicago: Northwestern University. Available at https://resources.depaul.edu/abcd-institute/faculty/Documents/T.%20 Bergdall%20Catalytic%20Role%20of%20An%20Outsider%202.13.18.pdf

Blickem, C., Dawson, S., Kirk, S., Vassilev, I., Mathieson, A., Harrison, R., Bower, P., & Lamb, J. (2018). What is Asset-Based Community Development and how might it improve the health of people with long-term conditions? A realist synthesis. *Sage Open,* 1-3. Available at https://journals.sagepub.com/doi/pdf/10.1177/2158244018787223

Butterfield, A.K., Yeneabat, M., & Moxley, D. (2016). 'Now I know my ABCDs': Asset Based Community Development with Ethiopian primary school children. *Children & Schools, 38*(4), 199-207.

Central Statistical Agency (2017). *Ethiopia demographic and health survey 2011.* Addis Ababa: Central Statistical Agency and ICF International.

Cunningham, G. (2008). Stimulating asset-based development: Lessons from five communities in Ethiopia. In A. Mathie & G. Cunningham, (Eds.). *From clients to citizens: Communities changing the course of their own development* (pp. 263-289). Warwickshire, UK: Practical Action Publishers

Cunningham, G., & Mathie, A. (2002, February 21). *Asset-based community development: An overview.* Nova Scotia, Canada: Coady International Institute. Available at https://linkorgnz.files.wordpress.com/2017/01/abcd-overview-cunningham-mathie.pdf

De Ruyter, K. (1996). Focus versus nominal group interview: A comparative analysis. *Marketing Intelligence and Planning, 14*(6), 44-50.

DiClemente, R.J., Crosby, R.A., Salazar, L.F., & Wingood, G.M. (2006). Adolescents and HIV: Understanding risk factors for HIV infection and designing effective risk reduction strategies. In M. Paz Bermudez Sanchez & G. Buela-casal (Eds.), *Recent Advances in HIV Research* (pp. 1-48). Nova Science Publishers, Inc.

Ethiopian Public Health Association. (2005). *Identifying HIV/AIDS, sexually transmitted infections and tuberculosis research gaps and priority setting agenda in Ethiopia.* Addis Ababa: Ethiopian Public Health Association.

Green, G.P., & Haines, A. (2002). *Asset building and community development.* London: Sage Publications.

Kebede, W., Getu, M., & Negeri, D. (2011). *Insights from participatory development approaches in Ethiopia: Analysis of testimonies in Ethiopia.* Addis Ababa: Addis Ababa University/School of Social work & Oxfam Canada Ethiopia Program office

Minkler, M., & Wallerstein, N. (2008) *Community based participatory research for health: Process to outcomes* (2nd Edition). San Francisco: Jossey-Bass.

Minkler, M., & Wallerstein, N. (2008). Introduction to CBPR: New issues and emphasis. In M. Minkler & N. Wallerstein (Eds.), *Community- based participatory research for health: From process to outcomes* (pp.5-23). San Francisco: Jossey-Bass.

Odu, B., & Akanle, F. (2008). Knowledge of HIV/AIDS and sexual behavior among the youths in South West Nigeria. *Humanity and Social Sciences Journal, 3*(1), 81-88.

Oman, R.F., Vesely, S., Aspy, C.B., McLeroy, K.B., Rodine, S., & Marshall, L. (2004). The potential protective effects of youth assets on adolescent alcohol and drug use. *American Journal of Public Health, 94*(8), 1425-1430.

Oman, R.F., Vesely, S.K., & Aspy, C.B. (2005). Youth assets and sexual risk behavior: The importance of assets for youth residing in one-parent households. *Perspectives on Sexual and Reproductive Health, 37*(1), 25-31.

Pagliaro, S., & Klindera, K. (2001). *Youth development: Strengthening prevention strategies.* Washington, DC: Advocates for Youth.

Powers, J.L., & Tiffany, J.S. (2006). Engaging youth in participatory research and evaluation. *Journal of Public Health Management Practice,* Supp., 79-87. Available at http://www.health.state.ny.us/community/youth/development/docs/jphmp_s079-s087.pdf

Stoecker, R. (1999). Are academics irrelevant? Roles for scholars in participatory research. *American Behavioral Scientist, 42*(5), 840-854.

Tiffany, J.S. (2006). Respondent-driven sampling in participatory research contexts: Participant driven recruitment. *Journal of Urban Health, 83*(7), 113-124.

UNAIDS. (2003). *HIV/AIDS and young people: Hope for tomorrow.* Geneva: Switzerland. Available at http://data.unaids.org/publications/IRC-pub06/jc785-youngpeople_en.pdf

Vesely, S.K., Wyatt, V.H., Oman, R.F., Aspy, C.B., Kegler, M.C., Rodine, S., Marshall, L., & McLeroy, K.R. (2004). The potential protective effects of youth assets from adolescent sexual risk behaviors. *Journal of Adolescent Health, 34*(5), 356-365.

Witkin, B.R., & Altschuld, J.W. (1995). *Planning and conducting needs assessments: A practical guide.* California: Sage Publications, Inc.

Yeneabat, M., & Butterfield, A.K. (2012). "We can't eat a road:" Asset-Based Community Development and the Gedam Sefer Community Partnership in Ethiopia. *Journal of Community Practice, 20*(1-2) 134-153.

CHAPTER 9

YOUTH DEVELOPMENT IN STUDENT COUNCILS

Adugna Abebe

Engaging youth as partners in research projects offers many benefits for the youth and the research team. However, there is little systematic evidence for youth participatory research in youth-led organizations in Ethiopia. This research project was then designed to engage students so as to bring about improvement in the structure and role of undergraduate social work Student Council located at Akaki Campus, Addis Ababa University. A total of 17 participants were involved in this research project. Dialogue was holding the central position in collecting data, and the data were analyzed in thematic fashion. Essentially, this participatory research project resulted in the formation of two clubs (the Peace Club and the Anti-HIV/AIDS Awareness Club) under the Student Council. Findings indicated that the student engagement in this research provided them with positive development outcomes. Student engagement in research has implication for the development and empowerment of young students.

Introduction

The engagement of youth as partners in research and evaluation efforts is relatively new (Delgado, 2006). The practice of engaging young people as partners in the design and implementation of research has emerged out of a confluence of diverse practices, such as positive youth development (Lerner et.al, 2005), and the advancement of action research and community development practice (Sabo, 2003). The participation of young people in research not only generates useful knowledge for young people and communities (Kidd & Kral, 2005) but also provides opportunities for the development and empowerment of youth participants and communities (Powers & Tiffany, 2006; Zeldin, Camino, & Calvert, 2007). Having youth play influential decision-making roles in designing and conducting research is democratic and empowering (Fetterman, 2003, as cited in Delgado, 2006). While engaging youth in research occurs in multiple settings, this research project involves university students in opening the space for them to improve the function and structure of the Student Council.

Student Councils can be viewed as organizational settings that promote positive youth development. Youth councils are engaged in diverse activities and have the potential to benefit communities. They provide a realistic opportunity for enhancing social justice for young people at the community level (Collins, Augsberger, & Gecker 2016). Having students play important a decision-making role in designing and conducting research in Student Councils is democratic and empowering. Student Councils have long been in colleges and universities in Ethiopia. Student Councils are student self-governing organizations in universities in which members are elected by students. They not only offer avenues for the protection of students' rights and representation of students' interests in their institutions but also serve as student liaisons to the university administration. Such councils promote the organization of extracurricular activities and address social and administrative issues that students can face in higher education.

Though student councils have long history in the context of Ethiopia, the mechanisms of the activities of student councils are not yet well established in the way of providing students with meaningful opportunities for participation and positive development (Gebremariam, 2009). First, a large number of students usually assume that the student council is established only for facilitating service delivery such as meeting daily living needs within a university. Second, still many members of professional and administrative staff do not value student participation. For that reason, university officials use student councils for administrative functions without genuinely transferring authority to students. Third, there is a lag in understanding the role student councils can play in shaping youth development.

Research done in the West demonstrates that student participation in Student Councils increases the effectiveness of student involvement on campus and promotes positive youth development (Lizzio & Wilson, 2009; Martin, Pittman, Ferber & McMahon,2007). However, there is little systematic evidence for these effects in Student Councils established in Universities in Ethiopia. Further, there have been little participatory research projects done in Student Councils in the country to better understand students and their development in the context of their Council.

This research project was designed to engage students so as to bring about improvement in the structure and role of undergraduate social work Student Council located at Akaki Campus, Addis Ababa University. This Council was selected because I used to live in the same campus and was familiar with the practice of the Council. I worked with seventeen students (hereafter, called the research team) who were members of the Student Council. The research team framed the research question: How can we improve the Student Council for student development? This framework enabled the research team members to get engaged as fully as possible in every stage of the research project and helping them to take ownership over the whole process. This helped the team democratize the research process and build the capacity of students to analyze and transform their own lives and the Student Council.

Framing the Engaged Research

Positive Youth Development

Positive youth development encompasses a strength-based conception of youth. This approach has arisen in competition with deficit view of human behavior and development, which views youth as problems or the potential for problems (Lerner et.al. 2005). Within the deficit paradigm, the best interests of youth are under the influence of adults so that youth are vulnerable to exploitation in all spheres of their lives (Delgado, 2006). Alternatively, positive youth development views youth both as partners and central figures in their development process. Positive youth development is then a strength-based approach that focuses on youth strengths and directs the programs and services available in institutions and communities to all young people (Hansen, Larson, & Dworkin, 2003).

Positive youth development addresses both protective factors and risk factors. It shifts the dialogue from one that just focuses on youth with recipient to one that asks how communities and institutions can help youth develop the confidence, competence, compassion, connections and character to contribute in meaningful ways so that they grow up into healthy adults (Lerner et. al., 2005). Richmond (2000), cited in Delgado (2006), notes that giving youth responsibility and expecting accountability is at the core of most successful youth development organizations. Young people are learning by doing and youth organizations and their youth experience ripple effects. This paradigm shift places youth in positions of power, as researchers instead of research subjects. In practice, this participatory action research involved collaboration between the researcher and university students in the design and implementation of the research project. At the center of this research project was the involvement of students in every stage of the research process, from identifying the research question to formulating action proposals derived from the research results.

Theories on Youth Development

Humans, especially children and adolescents, are motivated to develop. They have natural dispositions to learn and to grow. Despite this continuous development, researchers suggest various ways of understanding about the process of human development. Various models for youth development include constructivist theory, collaborative learning theory, and sociological theories. According to constructivist theory, young people are viewed as producers of their own development. As stated by Lerner (2002), cited in Larson & Walker (2005), social constructivist theorists observed that organisms creatively adapt to their environment, and humans are particularly good at this. Young people are highly motivated to learn. The most influential of these scholars, Jean Piaget, stated that children and youth mentally construct concepts and realities through the process of active experimentation and reasoning (Larson & Walker, 2005). The implication is that young people learn best on their own. This model then helps us to think about the powerful natural tendencies of youth to develop and to organize their experiences into understanding. However, the risk of this model is that it undervalues the role of experienced adults in guiding youth development.

According to Larson and Walker (2005), collaborative learning theory states that development comes from the interactions between young and experienced adults. In other words, learning starts with the interaction and development is a collaborative process (Vygotsky, 1962, 1978; cited in Larson & Walker, 2005). Vygotsky stressed that youth are still active producers of their development, but they are active in cooperation with others. He underscored that youth-adult partnership is a vehicle of learning and development. In the partnership, an experienced adult provides guidance or scaffolding for youth's learning in multiple ways. The frame of this model is essential to youth development programs in which young people and adults need to develop partnership for promoting positive youth development.

Sociologists view development as a process of learning the norms of a group and acquiring social capital through social interaction.

Recent sociological theories stress that people are active in the socialization process. In other words, when youth enter society, many rules, norms and ways of thinking are in place. Youth may accept norms, create new meanings for old ones or they may create new norms. These sociological processes occur within youth programs. Adults may try to set norms for programs, but youth may modify them, adhere to them selectively or create some of their own norms. Studies demonstrate that usually the norms youth learn in a program are positive which helps them function effectively within a community and develop group norms for mutuality and responsibility (Larson & Walker, 2005). Homan (2008) pinpointed that development approach builds on strengths, identifying opportunities and/or resources within the individual, the organization, the group or the community that can be more fully cultivated and utilized. These developmental actions emphasize potential and help to improve a condition by augmenting the strengths to promote the well-being of people. Equality in power relationships, mutual ownership of possibilities, partnership, focusing on strengths and assets, ongoing change, linking people with shared interests, and contributions are underpinnings of development actions (Homan, 2008; Larson & Walker, 2005).

Organized Youth Activities

Youth participation is important because young people have a social right to participate in any decision-making processes that influence their lives (Checkoway, 2011). The involvement of youth in research has positive benefits for youth, community-based organizations that serve youth and the broader community (Ford, Rasmus & Allen, 2012). Such promising benefits of youth participation highlight participatory action research as one of the effective strategies to address social problems and social injustice that many youth face. Participatory action research seeks to develop practical knowledge for social change through collaborative partnerships (Powers & Tiffany, 2006).

Higher education settings provide a range of formal and informal mechanisms for student engagement in governance (Lizzio & Wilson, 2009). Gomez and Ang (2007) underscore that schools have the capacity to provide positive people, positive places and positive opportunities that promote positive youth development. In the study investigating what adolescents learn in organized youth activities, Hansen, Larson and Dworkin (2003) found that adolescents in organized youth activities, such as extracurricular and community-based activities, reported more experiences related to personal development(identity work or personal exploration; initiative; emotional, cognitive & physical skills) and interpersonal development (social competence; interpersonal relationships; connection to adults and social capital). Larson (2000) analyzed that structured voluntary youth activities provide the young people with fertile environments for positive development, particularly the development of initiative.

Building on available youth development research and theory, Pittman (1999) offered the model of 5 Cs as a framework for understanding positive youth development outcomes: Confidence-a sense of self-worth and mastery, having a sense of self-efficacy (belief in one's capacity to succeed); Character - taking responsibility, a sense of independence, individuality, connection to principles and values; Connection - a sense of safety, structure, and belonging, positive bonds with people and social institutions; Competence - the ability to act effectively in school, in social situations, and at work; Contribution - active participation and leadership in a variety of settings, making a difference. As the key goal of participatory action research is positive youth development (Vaughn, Wagner, & Jacquez, 2013), engaging youth in research and evaluation provides opportunities for the development and empowerment of youth participant, leading to benefits for young people, organizations and the research process (Powers & Tiffany, 2006). This participatory research demonstrated that involving young people in research as partners created opportunities for fostering positive youth development.

Research Methods

The Process of Engagement

Including young people as partners in research reveals an understanding of young people as not only assets, but also as agents of change (Ginwright & James, 2002). My focus in this research project was on student participation as an approach which took seriously their agency and capacity. MacDonald (2012) articulated that participatory action involves an action researcher and community or organization members who are seeking to improve their situation. This research project thus used participatory action research approach that I developed with seventeen undergraduate social work students who were members of the Students Council located at Akaki Campus, Addis Ababa University.

Initial contact was made with leaders of the Student Council. Because action research project is carried out to improve programs and community life, and involves open communication among people involved, frequent discussions were held with the student leaders for the purpose of participatory action research. Following these discussions, the Research Team which consisted of the researcher and 17 participants from the Student Council was formed. Participatory action research emphasizes a mutual interaction between researchers and participants in creating knowledge (Kim, 2016). Based on this epistemology, the Research Team used dialogue as the main methodological strategy in this project. Written materials (articles) on participatory action research and positive youth development were distributed among the research team members in order to create space for dialogue. Feedback from these discussions created student engagement framework grounded in the experiences of students at Student Council. The essential result of this engagement was that the Research Team framed the research question: How can we improve Student Council for university student development?

Because the goal of participatory action research is to democratize research and achieve useful, practical and just outcomes which improve real-life situations (Kemmis & McTaggart, 1988), the researcher and participants worked together in relationships of equal ownership and influence throughout the inquiry process. This ensured that the researcher and participants felt comfortable and welcomed to express themselves. In practice, the Research Team took shared responsibility for exploring opportunities for the Council and setting priorities to improve the role and structure of the Student Council. Participatory action research emphasizes empowerment and active and democratic participation by people. Action research is both recursive and iterative (Kekäle & Pirttilä, 2006; Stevenson, 2003).

In this project, the researcher followed four principles of participatory action research throughout the inquiry process. The first principle is the interaction cycle between research and action which involves the transformation of reality from a world as it is to a world as it could be (Kekäle & Pirttilä, 2006; Kemmis & McTaggart, 1988). Through this inquiry, theory informs practice, and practice refines theory in a continuous transformation. The two are intertwined in effecting positive changes. The second principle entails the appreciation and valuation of the knowledge and experience of participants in the study. The research team members actively involved in enacting this principle. The implication is that people under study act as co-researchers and have a significant role in contributing to new knowledge (Kekäle & Pirttilä, 2006).

The third principle involves open and dialogical communication between the researcher and study participants. Some scholars state that through dialogue people can move from analyzing their experiences to innovative discussions (Buchy & Ahmed, 2007). Throughout this inquiry, dialogical communication strategically places the researcher and study participants, including their values, at the center of the research and therefore under research scrutiny. The fourth principle is the ideal of democracy, enabling the participation of all (Kekäle & Pirttilä, 2006). As action research has an important place in the empowerment of people, this research project ensured that students have the right and ability to contribute to decisions that affect them and to knowledge that is about them.

Study participants exchanged their experiences and ideas about the situation of the Student Council through the principles of active participation and equality. I organized and interpreted information obtained from each dialogue and reported these to participants for verification. Data generated from a series of dialogues and interviews were refined through the different stages of dialogue sessions. Through this classification process, relationships among categories of data were identified, and subsequently, I organized the data into themes. Interpretation of these themes was made by the research team members of each club. Finally, I organized findings and produced the report.

Implementation

This action research consisted of three stages: exploration, intervention, and reflection. After permission was obtained during the engagement phase, the research team took an exploration role in the process to take joint action in the student council through democratic dialogue and reflection among involved participants. The team followed ground rules which emphasized the participatory, practice-oriented, dialogical and reflexive aspects of the change process. They scheduled hour long meetings for 9 weeks in the Student Council office. The opening sessions were idea-storming meetings concerned with examining the organizational situation of the Council. Dialogue created a social space in which participants shared experiences and information and created common meanings. Barge (2002) defines dialogue as a collective and collaborative communication process whereby people explore together their individual and collective assumptions and predispositions. In this study, dialogue was a continuous mutual exchange of views, ideas and opinions.

The participants articulated the ill-structured conditions in their Council and identified opportunities or strengths which are helpful to construct a desirable future. Some literatures on positive youth development and structured youth activities for the participants were shared among the research team members to deepen their knowledge regarding positive youth development. Subsequently, participants voluntarily formed two groups and took the reading materials with them to their dormitory for further discussion. During the next session, each group presented its discussion. Each presentation concluded with a discussion of what participants learned from the reading materials and the presentations. Members critically discussed the possible linkage between the knowledge acquired from the literature and opportunities in the Council. As a facilitator, I played the role of a devil's advocate by raising questions. Team members grew more confident of their ownership of the inquiry process by attending every session. Participants began suggesting a variety of feasible extracurricular activities during the ensuing dialogues.

The intervention phase involved a series of planning meetings which were informed by reflection on the key findings from the exploration phase and a proposal of the way forward. The need to organize extracurricular activities under the Student Council became a major point of consideration. It was agreed that participants needed a deeper understanding of the role of extracurricular activities in fostering positive youth development. I offered additional materials which highlighted the role of structured youth activities. Gradually, the research team suggested and prioritized interventions after a detailed dialogue that generated ideas and conclusions.

Developing Action Plans

The process of identifying intervention activities and developing action plans involved five meetings. These meetings allowed participants to think through all identified options before the final selection of activities. In the fourth and fifth sessions, participants decided what they needed to do. Having discussed a number of issues and coming to agreement, the research team selected two extracurricular clubs, a Peace Club and an Anti-HIV/AIDS Awareness Club. Following this, participants joined a club of their preference, with eight members selecting the Peace Club, and nine the Anti-HIV/AIDS Club. The members of each club took responsibility for development activities but took different paths to realize their mission.

The Peace Club grew out of two points from the series of dialogues. The first was the need to exercise cultural sensitivity practices in the everyday working of the Student Council. Cultural sensitivity provides students with context in which they familiarize themselves with the history, values, belief systems and behaviors of the members of another ethnic group through dialogue. This corresponds to the work of Cross et al. (1989) in that using conversations, students create context where they learn from each other irrespective of their cultural backgrounds. It promotes social justice and equality in cultural diversity and brings about a more peaceful environment. Secondly, when participants get the opportunity to exercise cross-cultural work in campus life, they can acquire the knowledge and skills which help them effectively work in cross-cultural off-campus contexts. Club members organized an hour-long meeting each week to dialogue on cultural issues. They organized several meetings around culture and cultural diversity in which each member shared the values, beliefs and behavior patterns of his or her culture. Following these discussions, the Peace Club held cultural sensitivity workshops promote cultural knowledge and cultural awareness among all campus students. Participation was open to any student interested in cultural diversity. Professionals were invited to engage in dialogue.

Participants joined the Anti-HIV/AIDS Club to improve communication and decision-making skills of themselves and their peers through interactive discussion. Other purposes were to educate regarding proper condom use, promote abstinence as an option, and increase awareness of the AIDS. I challenged members to reach agreement on the practices that were most effective in preventing the spread of HIV among on-campus students. They reached at consensus that peer education and fostering communication skills promote safe sexual behaviors. Peer education typically involves members of a peer group trying to educate others to change their attitudes, beliefs or behaviors. Through peer education, they learned about other risk reduction behaviors, the dissemination of HIV-related information, and techniques to reduce peer pressure. Like members of Peace Club, members arranged an hour-long meeting each week to discuss HIV prevention measures. The Club staged role plays, drama, and debates on HIV/AIDS. To attract other on-campus students and involve them in the process, members publicized debatable issues, meetings and other activities well in advance of their scheduled meeting. Members invited some individuals living with HIV/AIDS to share experiences.

There was evidence of reflection in every dialogical session as participants critically analyzed and evaluated questions of morality and values. Active participation in dialogue, planning and implementing activities developed collective autonomy and a sense of ownership. In what Park (1999) calls reflective knowledge, this marked engagement in change producing activities required conscious reflection on the part of the actors involved. Such collaborative reflection ensured that involvement in the action research process captured the mental and physical potential of participants to perform extracurricular activities through the Student Council.

Findings

This participatory action research was aimed at exploring opportunities and strengths of Student Council members and organizing them into some structure. The pursuit of this aim led to the foundation of two clubs that promote positive youth development: Peace Club and Anti-HIV/AIDS Awareness Club. The results support the notion that participation in extracurricular activities is related to the demonstration of positive developmental outcomes. Five themes emerged from the engaged research project. These include sense of ownership, initiative, social support and communication skills, cultural competence, and safe sex behavior.

Sense of Ownership

As facilitator of the research process, I consciously tried not to control the action research. From the very beginning, participants were involved actively in dialogue, planning and implementing activities. In doing so, a gradual sense of shared activity emerged among participants. As a result, participants' confidence in the ownership and responsibility for the action plans increased. One participant from the Peace Club remarked, "At the beginning, we were suspicious of taking active roles in the inquiry process because of our previous experience, but as we started group discussion and planning, we gradually developed confidence and felt responsibility for what we discussed and planned." Constructivist theorists suggest that people are active producers of their development and have the ability to shape their own lives (Larson & Walker, 2005).

Feedback from participants notes that democratic dialogue helped them take ownership of the process. The learning opportunities and their participation boosted their confidence. Members of each club commented that they felt a sense of ownership, which translated into genuine commitment and motivation to sustain their participation and recruit other students to participate. In support of this, Hansen, Larson and Dworkin (2003) argue that structured youth activities are contexts for the development of personal exploration, leadership skills, initiative and long-term goals. Larson (2000) points out that adolescents who participate in extracurricular activities report high levels of intrinsic motivation, devotion of thought and effort directed toward a goal.

Taking Initiative

Initiative developed through long term planning and engagement. Participants both in the Peace and Anti-HIV/AIDS clubs were motivated to do synergistic activities directed toward goals. As one member stated, "Taking part in this inquiry process has enabled us to mobilize our attention, mental and physical power on deliberate courses of action." This supports Larson's (2000) definition of initiative as the capacity for devoting effort overtime toward achieving a goal. In the same way, Hansen, Larson and Dworkin (2003) note that adolescents involved in structured youth activities develop skills for developing plans, organizing their time, using contingency thinking and problem solving. During reflective discussions, I encouraged participants to direct and regulate their actions in pursuit of goals. A general view expressed by one member was that "they felt more self-efficacious, more confident in their ability to make difference." Bandura, a famous social learning theorist, proposed that the development of self-efficacy within the psychological domain of a person leads to empowerment (Robbins, Chatterjee & Canda, 2006).

The participatory action process provided a platform for discussing and critically analyzing the opportunities and activities of the Student Council. Their involvement gave them a different perspective on the development of young people. Through dialogue on positive youth development and structured youth activities, they discussed the existing opportunities and strengths in their Council and engaged in meaningful activities instead of focusing on problems and how to fix them. Richmond (2000), cited in Delgado (2006), argues that giving youth responsibility and expecting accountability is at the heart of most successful youth development initiative since they are learning by doing and the community and its youth are experiencing ripple effects. Lerner et. al. (2005) believes that concentrating on strength-based approaches in youth programs helps young people develop confidence, competence, compassion, connections and character.

Social Support and Communication Skills

This inquiry process is related to a dramatic increase in the use of language skills, altruistic behaviors, and social connections and learning skills. Participants learned to work with others and developed leadership skills. This observation matches with the work of many scholars (Barber & Stone, 2003; Larson, 2000; Rubin, Bommer & Baldwin, 2002). In the reflective discussions, participants reported that involvement brought them together and created team spirit through transparent communication. They became actively involved in running activities. Assertive behavior was welcomed as a norm which fostered teamwork and mutual support. Gomez and Ang (2007) suggest that adolescent participation in extracurricular activities provides the opportunity to develop social connections, personal confidence and character. Sociological theorists consider development as a process of learning the norms of a group and acquiring social capital through social interaction (Larson & Walker, 2005).

Volunteer participation in extracurricular activities provides adolescents with the opportunity to be personally expressive and to communicate openly (Barber & Stone, 2003). Activities in each club helped the members develop better communication skills so they can pass on information to their friends in assertive manner. According to one participant in the Anti-HIV/AIDS Awareness Club, "When we are surrounded by our peers, we often feel more comfortable and accepted. This is why we felt very effective in communicating information about HIV/AIDS and educating our peers to make informed choices. "In Anti-HIV/AIDS Club, members showed great commitment and enthusiasm for the fight against HIV/AIDS on campus and off-campus as well. "It is through our dedication and hard work that the next generation of youth will be protected from HIV infection. We are all pleased by the contributions we make to fight against HIV/AIDS." Youniss, Yates, and Su (1997), cited in Larson (2000), suggest that participation in youth activities creates personal confidence and responsibility that increase the participants' likelihood of engaging in public service in other contexts. In supporting each other, participants of this research validated their own concerns and their commitment to achieve the aims of the clubs. One participant remarked that "working with club members has reinforced our perception of the empowering nature of a group and the joy of working with motivated group members to jointly reach a common goal." This is consonant with the basic principle of collaborative theory in that young people's learning and development result from interactive processes (Vygotsky, 1962, 1978; cited in Larson & Walker, 2005). In a similar vein, constructivist theorists argue that development is the result of an active, cooperative enterprise of persons in relationships (Larson & Walker, 2005).

Cultural Competence

Participants familiarized themselves and others with the cultural values, beliefs and behavior patterns of their various cultures through dialogue. Their involvement opened up the possibility for learning to appreciate cultural variations. As one participant from Peace Club summarized:

> Initially, we were afraid of openly discussing ethnic issues for fear of reinforcing stereotypes. In fact, we used to view the culture of others through our own cultural lens. But participation in this inquiry has provided us with the opportunity to have cultural contact and recognize cultural differences. It helps us have direct cross-cultural communication so that we feel cultural awareness. We found this participation vitally important because, as social work students, we need to accommodate cultural differences. We believe that the knowledge and skills we have acquired from participation in this inquiry will help us effectively communicate with culturally diverse communities outside of university life.

In the Peace Club, participants gained an experiential understanding and acceptance of the beliefs, values, and ethics of others as well as the demonstrated skills necessary to work with peers of diverse cultural backgrounds. One participant noted, "By participating in the club, I have become more aware of and respectful of the beliefs, values, and ethics of other cultures. I understand the cross-cultural skills necessary for delivering services and working with diverse individuals and groups." Extracurricular activities are productive contexts for promoting better understanding of peers from diverse ethnic groups (Hansen, Larson & Dworkin, 2003) and for developing social competence (Gomez & Ang, 2007). Participation in structured extracurricular activities provides important opportunities for development and growth (Mahoney, Larson, Eccles, 2005).

Safe Sex Behavior

Youth activities serve as context for cross-ethnic friendships and understanding (Hansen, Larson & Dworkin, 2003). Stevenson (2003) argues that open dialogue in participatory action research results in the empowerment, collaboration, the acquisition of knowledge, and social change. One participant from Anti-HIV/AIDS Club summed the group's view that AIDS talks and peer education resulted in positive changes in understanding and attitudes:

> ...in relation to understanding of HIV prevention, it seems to us that we indeed gained knowledge of cultural, religious and scientific perspectives of HIV/AIDS. We tried to debate about HIV to explore various viewpoints on it and to discuss variety of safe sex behaviors. This seems to have had a long-lasting impact.

Holland and Andre (1987) point out that participation in extracurricular activities prevents students from being involved with problem behaviors. The exercise of open dialogue in participatory action research results in the empowerment of participants, collaboration, acquisition of knowledge, and social change (Stevenson, 2003). In the Anti-HIV/AIDS Club, participants made their own choices about their safe sex behavior from discussion and peer education. Members are very concerned in their sexual health. Some felt that involvement in Anti-HIV/AIDS Awareness Club increased their awareness of safe sex behaviors. One member recapped a small group's conversation:

> We felt that the Club is very effective in HIV prevention because the content of peer education, debates and discussions were focused on being anti-AIDS, but not being anti-sex. We feel that young people are very interested in their sexual life, so it is better to say love safely, live longer... Because we talked openly in our deliberation about sex, negotiating for safe sex,

resisting negative peer pressure, and knowing the facts about sexual health, we have started changing our risk behaviors. Activities in the Club have enabled us to reduce our risk of infection by improving our decision making, communication and condom negotiation skills. Because of this we are so committed to the Club and keen for it.

Another outcome is the realization of safe sex behavior. Participants felt that their involvement in this research created an awareness of safe sex behaviors, such as condom use, open partner communication, and sexual decision-making. One participant reported on a discussion with her group partner:

> ...because of involvement in dialoging and organizing various participatory activities in our Club, we experienced psychological readiness and felt responsibility to reduce risk behaviors. This research provided us a great opportunity to play active roles in discussing and planning HIV/AIDS prevention, instead of being a passive recipient of information on HIV prevention delivered by professionals. We are dedicated to sustaining our involvement in HIV dialogue and other activities in our Club.

Participants gain increased awareness and skills and appear to ready to use this awareness to modify their sexual relationships. This supports Pittman's (1999) position that youth engagement in structured activities increases positive outcomes for young people.

Strengths, Challenges, and Lessons Learned

This project was successful in creating positive developmental opportunities and meaningful roles for students. Through engagement study participants have become realized the nature of positive youth development and the roles organized youth activities play in facilitating positive youth development. Reflection from the participants ensured that this research provided them with meaningful opportunities and helped them gain decisions-making and leadership skills. The realization of positive youth development inspired participants to engage in the inquiry process.

I was keen on observing and learning about the nature and process of participation within the dialogues, the motivation of participants, and their expectations and challenges of working in teams. The dialogical approach allowed participants to take charge of their situation and act. In both clubs, students learned about the process of doing research and developed various skills including how to work with each other, leadership, planning actions, confidence in ownership and responsibility as well as knowledge of culturally specific practices.

The participatory process presented an opportunity for students to transform themselves. It is this process that I attempted to understand through the application of reflective learning, to reflect or look retrospectively on the processes involved. I found that through involvement and deliberation, participants developed capacity for ongoing learning and engagement in organized activities. I learned that action research focused on participation, the plurality of knowing, and practical outcomes, can lead to new and enduring structures. The concepts of validity, reliability and methodological objectivity as traditionally used in empirical analytical approach are not helpful because they are dissonant with the fundamental nature of participatory action research.

Influence on the Author's Scholarly Direction

As a doctoral student in social work education at Addis Ababa University, I was given the opportunity to conduct action research project as a fulfilment of the course *Action Research and Models of Social Change*. The purpose of the project was to facilitate social change through engaging with Student Council of undergraduate social work students at Addis Ababa University. I felt appreciated that engaging students in research as partners provides a structured approach to create meaningful and developmentally rich opportunities for students. Student engagement in this research helps participants experience a wide array of developmental outcomes. Participants acquired knowledge of engagement and understanding of democratic dialogue directed by the Student Council. The knowledge of engagement and democratic dialogue has implications for sustaining participants' commitment in the improvement of Student Council as well as in their development.

At the outset of this action research project, I was concerned with engaging students as full as possible in every stage of the research project and helping the students to take ownership over throughout the process. In order to build the research team for this action research project, I wanted the team members to feel at home and made it clear that I considered them equal partners with me in the research process, as competent agents and experts in understanding the Student Council. It was also crucial to address power within the research process in which I honestly specified my role as a facilitator and collaborator within the collective research process.

A primary role as a facilitator was to create a safe space for truthful dialogue where everyone involved would feel comfortable to express themselves and contribute. At times this involved energetically facilitating everyone's participation or disrupting dominant voices by creating regular opportunities for group reflection (e.g. Do we all have the same opinion? The reason why/why not?). Part of my role in this project involved being an active listener, working confirm members' contributions, and checking in my understanding of what was being said. Such practice became particularly relevant when we were trying to articulate and understand theoretical interpretations offered by individual research team members, which, in turn, enabled richer analysis of our data. In practice, this meant that participatory learning within the research team play a key role in their development of research skills.

I learned that authentic participatory research is collaborative in its nature. As co-researcher I was also involved in the research process and had opinions about our dialogues, whilst I kept balancing my contribution in order not to dominate or derail discussions throughout the process. I was very careful about the grounds on which I make contribution to the research process. In practice, I was speaking from my own experiences and standpoints without making any claim to authority. Furthermore, I frequently shared my interpretations with my research team confirming and clarifying my understanding with the team so as to gain further understanding and challenge my assumptions.

I found the collaborative aspect of the research team worked well. Research in Student Council was not only a very useful learning experience, but also enjoyable and rewarding. In the research process, I observed that students work with one another and actively involved in planning and facilitating meetings and activities. Such engagement helped students to develop skills of decision-making and leadership to run various activities. I observed that engaging youth in participatory research provides positive development opportunities for students as well as helps them to improve the functions of the Student Council.

My experience with the research team shows that students had different strengths and characteristics that help them carry out the research project with greater success. Students with good social skills took on more organizing and leading activities while others having art skills took on performing activities in the research process. The experience of having participants with diverse skills has enriched the quality of the research. I learned the importance of considering participants' diverse skills and using these skills as strength within the development of the project.

Student engagement in the participatory research generated useful research data that enabled the research team to design a realistic plan of action for the organizational improvement of the Student Council and energize student mobilization around relevant social issues on-and off campus. Because of their involvement in this research, students learned that they are active agents in their development process. In practice, they developed skills for time management and working toward goals. This has implication for youth in governance involves youth as decision makers on a variety of efforts. They also showed promising signs that participation in their clubs and their interest in research would continue in the future.

The most critical problem confronting me in the process was keeping students engaged, connected and involved in the research. I and the research team members addressed this challenge through reflective practice which allows us to critically re-examine our daily experiences in the project. As times went on, I learned that experience coupled with reflection is much more powerful impetus for keeping young people engaged in the research project. As a research facilitator, I have found great value in incorporating cyclical process of action and reflection for deepening the research. More importantly, I felt that involving students in participatory research project empowers them and leads to sustained change and growth in programs that support them. Furthermore, from this research project, I experienced a transforming change in my professional practice, in my attitude toward the use of participatory research. I perceived the practice of engaged research as a vehicle of positive development and empowerment involved in it. Ultimately, this research project has influenced me to ground my scholarly direction in youth development research.

References

Barge, J.K. (2002). Enlarging the meaning of group deliberation: From discussion to dialogue. In L.R. Frey (Ed.), *New directions in group communication* (pp. 159–177). Thousand Oaks, CA: Sage.

Buchy, M., & Ahmed, S. (2007). Social learning, academics and NGOs: Can the collaborative formula work? *Action Research, 5*, 358–377.

Checkoway, B. (2011). What is youth participation? *Children and Youth Services Review, 33*(2), 340-345.

Collins, M.E., Augsberger, A., & Gecker, W. (2016). Youth councils in municipal government: Examination of activities, impact and barriers. *Children and Youth Services Review, 65,140*-147.

Delgado, M. (2006). *Designs and methods for youth-led research.* Thousand Oaks: Sage.

Eccles, J., & Templeton, J. (2002). Extracurricular and other after-school activities for youth. *Review of Education, 26*, 113-180.

Gebremariam, E.B. (2009). *Youth and Politics in Post-1974 Ethiopia: Inter-generational analysis.* Unpublished MA Thesis, The University of Manchester.

Ford, T., Rasmus, S., & Allen, J. (2012). Being useful: Achieving indigenous youth involvement in a community-based participatory research project in Alaska. *International Journal of Circumpolar Health, 71*, 1-7.

Ginwright, S., & James, T. (2002). From assets to agents of change: Social justice, organizing, and youth development. *New Direction for Youth Development, 96*, 27-46.

Gomez, B.J., & Ang, P.M. (2007). Promoting positive youth development in schools. *Theory into Practice, 46(2)*, 97–104.

Hansen, D.M., Larson, R.W., & Dworkin, J.B. (2003). What adolescents learn in organized youth activities: A survey of self-reported developmental experiences. *Journal of Research Adolescence, 13(1)*, 25-55.

Holland, A., & Andre, T. (1987). Participation in extracurricular activities in secondary school: What is known, what needs to be known? *Review of Educational Research, 57*,447-466.

Homan, M.S. (2008). *Promoting community change: Making it happen in the real world* (4ᵗʰ Edition). Belmont, CA: Brooks/Cole.

Kekäle, J., & Pirttilä, I. (2006). Participatory action research as a method for developing leadership and quality. *International Journal of Leadership in Education, 9(3)*, 251-268.

Kemmis, S., & McTaggart, R. (1988). *The action research reader* (3rd edition). Victoria, Australia: Deakin University Press.

Kidd, S.A., & Kral, J.M. (2005). Practicing participatory action research. *Journal of Counseling Psychology, 52(2)*, 187-195.

Kim, J. (2016). Youth involvement in participatory action research: Challenges and barriers. *Critical Social Work, 17(1)*, 38-53.

Larson, R.W. (2000). Toward a psychology of positive youth development. *American Psychologist, 55(1)*, 170-183.

Larson, R.W., & Walker, K. (2005). Process of positive development: Classic theories. In P.A. Witt & L.L. Caldwell (Eds.), *Recreation and youth development* (pp. 131-147). Urbana, IL: Venture Publishing.

Lerner, R.M., Lerner, J.V., Almerigi, J.B., Theokas, C., Phelps, E., Gestsdottir, S. …von Eye, A. (2005). Positive youth development, participation in community youth development programs, and community contributions of fifth –grade adolescents: Findings from the first wave of the 4-H study of positive youth development. *Journal of Early Adolescence, 25(1)*, 17-71.

Lizzio, A., & Wilson, K. (2009). Student participation in university governance: the role conceptions and sense of efficacy of student representativeness on departmental committees. *Studies in Higher Education,* 34(1), 69-84.

MacDonald, C. (2012). Understanding participatory action research: A qualitative research methodology option. *Canadian Journal of Action Research, 13(2),* 34-50.

Mahoney, J., Larson, R., & Eccles, J. (2005). *Organized activities as contexts of development*. Hillsdale, NJ: Erlbaum.

Martin, S.; Pittman, K., Ferber, T., & McMahon, A. (2007). *Building Effective Youth Councils: A Practical Guide to Engaging Youth in Policy Making*. Washington, DC: The Forum for Youth Investment.

Park, P. (1999). People, knowledge and change in participatory research. *Management Learning, 30(2)*:141-57.

Pittman, K. (1999). *Youth today: The power of engagement*. Washington, DC: Forum for Youth Investment.

Powers, J.L. & Tiffany, J.S. (2006). Engaging youth in participatory research and evaluation. *Journal of Public Health Management and Practice,* (Suppl), S79–S87. Available at http://citeseerx.ist.psu.edu/viewdoc/download?doi=10.1.1.540.1179&rep=rep1&type=pdf

Robbins, S.P., Chatterjee, P., & Canda, E.R. (2006). *Contemporary human behavior theory: A critical perspective for social work*. Boston: Pearson Education.

Rubin, R.S., Bommer, W.H., & Baldwin, T.T. (2002). Using extracurricular activity as an indicator of interpersonal skill: Prudent evaluation or recruiting malpractice. *Human Resource Management, 41*(4), 441-454.

Sabo, K. (2003). Youth participatory evaluation: A field in the making. *New Directions for Evaluation, 98,* Special Issue, pp. 1-92.

Vaughn, L.M., Wagner, E., & Jacquez, F. (2013). A review of community-based participatory research in child health. *MCN The American Journal of Maternal/ Child Nursing, 38*(1), 48-53.

Zeldin, S., Camino, L., & Calvert, M. (2007). Toward an understanding of youth in community governance: Policy priorities and research directions. *Analise Psicologica,* 1(xxv), 77-95.

CHAPTER 10

RECLAIMING HEALTH EDUCATION AT BESEKA HIGH SCHOOL

Kerebih Asrese

Health education in schools is expected to teach healthy behaviors to youth and mitigate the consequences of high-risk health behaviors like casual sexual practices, or challenges like unwanted pregnancy and child bearing at early age, unsafe abortion, and sexually transmitted diseases including HIV/AIDS. The health education activities of the Anti-AIDS and Reproductive Health Club at Beseka High School in Akaki-kality Sub-city of Addis Ababa are minimal. This study explores the question: Why is school health education neglected in Beseka High School? Teachers and students representing members in the Club participated. Findings reveal that poor coordination and lack of commitment among members in the Club, weak networks with stakeholders working on health issues, a lack of support, and poor facilities are factors that hamper health education activities. The participants devised actions to improve the activities of the Anti-AIDS and Reproductive Health (RH) Club and advance the health education program.

Introduction

In Ethiopia, young people constitute about one-third of the total population (Central Statistical Authority, 2010). This group is exposed to high risk reproductive health problems such as casual sexual practices, unwanted pregnancy and childbearing at an early age, high risk abortion, HIV/AIDS, and other sexually transmitted diseases (Ministry of Health [MoH], 2003). The situation is aggravated by the overall poor socioeconomic environment and harmful traditional practices (Govindasamy, Aklilu, & Hailom, 2002). As part of the national health development program, the government has introduced the adolescent reproductive health extension packages, and schools are noted as important settings to communicate health information. It is believed that health education at schools develops attitudes of self-responsibility for health, raises awareness of health promoting behaviors, increases community participation in health development, and discourages harmful traditional practices (MoH, 1993). Schools provide opportunities to deliver organized and continuous health education to students, teachers, and administrative staff. Health education at schools develops health promoting behavior. The importance of health education in a high-risk situation underscores the necessity to offer education to youth, teachers and staff so they can assume control over their own health, and produce positive health outcomes. Early sexual debut, unsafe sexual practices, substance use, violence, and other problematic health challenges justify the advancement of health promotion strategy at schools (Federal Democratic Republic of Ethiopia, 2006).

This project focuses on how to improve a club devoted to health promotion in Beseka High School. The Anti-AIDS and Reproductive Health coordinator in Beseka High School explained that the Club was established at the beginning of the year with a view to communicate information about reproductive health, HIV/AIDS prevention and control, and harmful traditional practices for the school community, particularly for students. With the support of local non-governmental organizations, six teachers and five students took life skills training to become health educators. The Club planned different activities such as life skills training, entertainment dramas on harmful traditional practices and HIV/AIDS prevention, and a series of mini-media presentations on the impact of substance use, early sexual debut, and safe reproductive health behavior. The Club, however, does not function well. Of its planned activities, only a session on the impact of substance use was presented to the school community.

The purpose of this action research was to explore the factors that hinder health education activities at Beseka High School. The research was guided by the following research question: Why is school health education neglected in Beseka High School in Akaki-kality Sub-city of Addis Ababa? The study employed a participatory action research approach to explore the factors that hinder health education in Beseka High School, and to develop a plan to advance activities. The Anti-AIDS and RH Club is responsible for health education. The Club has 164 members of which 67 are male students 60 are female students, and 37 are teachers and 127 are students. Seven teachers who are committee members and Coordinators of the Club, 10 students who represent members, and two school officials participated in the study.

Framing the Engaged Research

Schools as Settings for Health Promotion

A recognition of the importance of the total environment in determining health has shifted the emphasis from curative medicine to health promotion (Denman, Moon, Parsons, & Stears, 2002). This shift brings the settings approach to health (Dooris, 2009), which emerged following the statement in the Ottawa Charter for Health Promotion that "health is created and lived by people within the settings of their everyday life; where they learn, work, play, and love" (WHO, 1986, p. 4). Settings are places or social contexts where people engage in daily activities and their interaction may affect their health and well-being (WHO, 1998). Schools are one of the settings where children and youth learn basic knowledge, skills, and develop attitudes for their future lives. Schools are potential settings for promoting children's health (Denman, Moon, Parsons, & Stears, 2002). They provide opportunities to reach many children and youth effectively and through a relatively continuous intervention at critical times in their lives (Hoffman & Jackson cited in Jackson, Perkins, Khandor, Cordwell, Hamann, & Buasi, 2007). Adolescence is a special age in an individual's life. It is an age of transition, experimentation and risk taking. Adolescents will experiment with their sexuality before settling with stable partners; some will experiment with smoking, drugs, and alcohol. Therefore, they should get information to enable them to participate in their own health care, engage in their own health promotion, and maintain their well-being. "Adolescents are a key target for health promotion, since adolescence is the time for consolidating health related values, attitudes, lifestyles and also making decisions a variety of behaviors which have important consequences for future health" (Ochieng, 2001, p.79). Although worries related to infectious diseases have declined, new threats which are social and behavioral in origin to children's health have emerged. Trends in teenage pregnancy, smoking, patterns of alcohol use and experimentation with illicit substances threaten the health of adolescents. "Of all the possible settings that provide opportunities for promoting the health of children, schools hold the greatest potential" (Denman et al., 2002, p.2). Education and health are inextricably linked; improvements in one dimension will bring improvements in the other.

McCall and McKay (2004) suggest that schools should provide sexual health information for adolescents. Schools, in cooperation with parents, the community, and health-care professionals can play a major role in sexual health education and promotion. It is necessary for all youth to receive educational and health services that prepare them for the realities and responsibilities of sexual behavior. The lack of effectively designed and implemented programs limits the rights of young people to make informed choices about their health, places them at increased risk for negative health outcomes, and fails to prepare them for healthy adult lifestyles.

The importance of schools as sources of reproductive health information is also recognized in the literature (Hindin & Fatusi, 2009; Lee, Cheng, & Leger, 2005; Teric, 2008). A study of opportunities for teenage health promotion found that school speakers, drama, peer groups and teachers were important sources of reproductive health information (Walker, Townsend, Bell, & Marshall, 1999). In a comprehensive review of school-based sexual health education interventions in Sub-Saharan Africa, programs have the potential to promote condom use among young people (Sani, Abraham, Denford, & Ball, 2016).

An investigation of school children as change agents in Tanzania found that school-based health education programs helped pupils develop basic knowledge on how diseases are caused, transmitted and prevented (Mwanga, Jensen, Magnussen, & Hanson, 2007). Participation as peer educators in school-based health education increased student commitment to communicate health messages to their families and the wider community. Similarly, an evaluation in rural Nigeria found that a school-based program had a positive impact on students' knowledge of reproductive health issues. Students in the intervention schools reported a decreased number of sexual partners, and increased condom and contraceptive use. They exercised abstinence, improved their academic results, and developed positive attitudes towards their school. The program made teachers and students responsible for the reproductive health education, and that created a social environment that favored open discussions on reproductive health. Reproductive health knowledge was higher in a school with a peer education and trained teacher intervention program than in a school with only peer education or a trained teacher program (Ajuwon & Brieger, 2007).

School-based Anti-AIDS Clubs as Sources of Health Promotion in Ethiopia

In response to the increasing AIDS epidemic, anti-AIDS clubs were established in schools in Ethiopia by the Ministry of Education in collaboration with the Ministry of Health (Haile Gabriel, 2008; Kloos,

& Haile, 2000), and this was believed to curb the epidemic. In 2002/03, there were 8360 anti-AIDS Clubs, 7600 in primary and junior high school, 360 in high schools and 400 out-of-school clubs. These clubs engaged in school-based AIDS education and peer education, which aimed to bring about changes in knowledge and behavior to reduce the risk of HIV exposure and infection. The clubs use drama, literature and songs, information, peer education and communication materials such as newspapers, magazines and brochures to communicate HIV/AIDS and RH issues to the school community. The clubs also invite people living with HIV/AIDS as guest speakers to educate the school community about the realities of infection (HIV/AIDS Prevention and Control Office, 2006). Youth HIV/AIDS and RH clubs create opportunities for promoting reproductive health and the prevention of HIV/AIDS. The clubs also promote VCT services by being role models (Admassu, cited in Degaga, 2006).

Acquisition of health information through these various means increases knowledge about HIV/AIDS and other RH issues thereby influencing behavior change among audiences. For example, Zimmerman, Kebede, Smith, Matuza, and Hovde (n.d.) in their study of school-based anti-AIDS clubs in Addis Ababa reported that students who had higher levels of exposure to sex education were more knowledgeable about HIV and AIDS. Despite these promising efforts, the clubs had challenges in pursuing and achieving their goals. A study in Addis Ababa at three high schools indicated that such programs are not popular among students (Kloos, cited in Kloos and Haile, 2000). The lack of support from concerned authorities, lack of office space, insufficient funding, and lack of project development and management skills were challenges (Degaga, 2006). The lack of appropriate follow up and supervision also contributed to what is too often the low performance of the clubs (Haile Gabriel, 2008; Kloos & Haile, 2000). In sum, schools are important settings where the new generation can be molded for future life. Importantly, schools are ideal places to address and prevent health issues. Although the school setting is influential in addressing many issues that impair the lives of students directly and the community indirectly, it is underutilized (Ajuwon & Brieger, 2007).

This is true at Beseka High School and thus, efforts to reclaim health promotion and education should be the ongoing business of the school community.

Theoretical Basis for the Settings Approach for Health Promotion

The social ecological model serves as a strong theoretical basis of the settings approach to health promotion. This model assumes that health is influenced by complex interactions of multiple aspects of the physical and social environments where people live (Burke, Joseph, Pasick, & Barker, 2009). The model emphasizes the importance of interactions between environmental, organizational, and personal factors for health and well-being (Dooris, 2009). The social ecological model for health promotion addresses multiple levels of social and physical environments. Intervention focuses on different targets at these different levels—from the individual behavior at the intrapersonal and interpersonal levels, to organizational change at the community and institutional level, and on to policy change at the systems level (Emmons, cited in Burke et al., 2009). Health and well-being are the results of a series of complex processes in which an individual interacts with other people and the environment (Naaldenberg et al., 2009).

The settings approach to health promotion addresses the context within which people live, work, and play (Poland, Krupa, & McCall, 2009). The approach has been widely advocated as it offers opportunities to situate practice in its social context, optimize interventions in specific contextual contingencies, and target crucial factors in the organizational context influencing behavior (Rootman, cited in Poland et al., 2009). Under the umbrella of the social ecological model of health, the settings approach to health promotion recognizes that individuals exist and interact within complex subsystems including families, peer groups, organizations, communities, culture, and physical and social environments. These various systems can enhance or damage health and are the focal point of the settings approach to health promotion.

Therefore, a settings approach utilizes interventions geared towards modifying the context within which individuals live, work and play.

The Engagement Process

In *Harmful Traditional Practices and Violence against Women* (Asrese & Abebe, 2007), I learned that a majority of the people were reluctant to use modern health services. Rather, they prioritize visiting traditional health consultants such as fortune tellers and witchdoctors. This traditional practice of managing health disproportionately affects women, youth, and children, who are relatively powerless to decide on their own health care and health decisions (The Transitional Government of Ethiopia, 1993). About 60% – 80% of the disease burden in Ethiopia is attributed to preventable communicable diseases such as tuberculosis, malaria, diarrhea, and sexually transmitted diseases including HIV/AIDS), as well as the negative consequences of harmful traditional practices including female genital cutting, tattooing, milk teeth extraction, early marriage, and food prohibition for pregnant women and children (Ministry of Health, 2005; National Committee on Traditional Practices of Ethiopia, 2003). Reproductive health problems such as teenage pregnancy, unwanted pregnancy, unsafe abortion, obstructed labor, still birth, infant mortality, maternal mortality, and underweight children are pervasive. These problems disproportionately affect youth (Central Statistical Agency and ORC Macro, 2006).

Schools are one of the settings for health promotion. This action research was conducted at the Beseka High School in Akaki-Kality Sub-city located at the fringe of Addis Ababa. I took a support letter from Addis Ababa University, School of Social Work and introduced myself. I explained to the school officials that I planned to work with the School's Anti-AIDS and RH club for a couple of months. I received permission and the officials introduced me to the school Anti-AIDS and RH Club coordinator.

I met with the Club Coordinator and two other teachers. I explained my stay with the Club, and we initiated a dialogue on the general overview of health education activities. The Club Coordinator and his colleagues stated that they were not satisfied with the Club's activities. The Club planned many activities to be implemented, but unfortunately, many plans failed to come to fruition. The Coordinator and his colleagues believed that actions to improve the Club's activities will be welcomed. To that end, we agreed to have meetings with the Club's committee and members of the club. In a follow-up session, three fourths of the committee members attended the meeting, and we reiterated the earlier memo. After a brief discussion, participants discussed issues such as the performance of the Club in the current academic year, success stories, the contributions of members, and major areas of activities. We also discussed the relationship of the Club with other stakeholders such as governmental organizations (GOs), non-governmental organizations (NGOs), and individuals and interested groups, as well as the school's support, the Club's networks, and the challenges faced in implementing its plans. The participants held a brainstorming session during which every participant wrote her or his own priority areas of concern. We tallied the responses of the participants and identified three basic areas of concern, the Club's performance, networks, and challenges. We developed the discussion guides for each area of concern. Two focus groups were arranged to be held for the coming sessions, in-depth interviews with school officials.

A focus group discussion was held among teachers who were committee members of the club. Similar discussions were held among students who represented the club members. A total of 17 individuals (7 teachers and 10 students) participated in the focus groups. In-depth interviews were held with the school principal and administrative and finance officers. The discussions were tape recorded and transcribed verbatim. In the follow-up meeting, the data were analyzed with the active participation of the respective discussants. Field notes and memos were used throughout all of my visits to the school. I did this to collect information which was not recorded on tape. In addition, documents in the school related to anti-AIDS and RH plans and activities were consulted. I analyzed the data and the findings were presented for the discussants at a joint meeting. They worked together to interpret the findings. In this meeting, the Club's plan for the academic year was presented by the Coordinator and the participants evaluated the performance of the Club. In this session, the participants discussed ways of improving activities in the school and developed an action plan for its implementation. During this meeting, the school officials, namely the principal and the administrative and finance officers, also participated.

Findings

The Anti-AIDs and RH Club Plan and Performance

An inspection of the Club's plan for the academic year indicated that with the support of local NGOs, 20 students will be trained life skills training to be peer educators. The trainees were expected to provide life skills training for all the needy academic and administrative staff and all students, numbering 3,080 people in the school. The club also planned health education programs on distinct reproductive health topics (safe sex, sexually transmitted diseases including HIV and AIDS, unwanted pregnancy, emergency contraception, and gender-based violence) and harmful traditional practice (early marriage, female genital mutilation, and rape).

The education messages were planned to be communicated using mini media early in the morning before students go to class, during class break time, and in each classroom using the peer educators. Moreover, the Club planned music and drama shows twice a year when it would solicit funds for its activities and communicate health education for the school and neighboring community. With the support of the nearby health center, the Club also planned to provide HIV and AIDS voluntary and testing services for 600 school community members, both academic staff and students. Both groups of discussants reported that the club did not fully implement its plan. Only 10 students took life skills training. Though they planned to provide life skills training and voluntary counseling and testing (VCT) services and undertake income generating programs, it did not implement these activities according to the proposed schedule. The third quarter implementation report indicated that the Club provided life skill training for 20 administrative staff, 82 teachers, and only 70 students. The club did not organize and provide VCT services, and it did not undertake music and drama shows for income generating purpose.

The club planned to offer peer health education services for all students. Five students from each section were nominated to give peer health education in the classroom. This plan was not implemented, and a student explained that most students did not have the skill to teach such issues. The discussants also mentioned that the poor coordination between teachers and students contributed a lot to the Club's poor performance. In particular, the school did not allocate extra periods for such programs in the daily timetable. In a joint meeting with the research participants, school officials also shared their discontent. Although they did not thoroughly evaluate activities, they felt that the Club was not working as intended. They compared its performance to that of previous years and commented on its dwindling activities. As one official stated, "The club is known for its diverse programs in the school. There were series of entertaining and educative programs in the previous years presented to the school community. Such a passion is weak this year."

The discussants pointed out that the club has relationships with some GOs and NGOs working on anti-AIDs and RH issues. It has relationships with the Women's Affair Bureau and other local NGOs such as Family Guidance Association of Ethiopia (FGAE), Talent Youth, and Safe Life. The third quarter plan implementation report indicated that Women's Affair Bureau provided training on gender issues for some students and teachers. The FGAE provided training of trainers on life skills for three female students. The Coordinator and two students received life skills training by Talent Youth. Talent Youth also provided training materials and financial support for refreshments. Similarly, Safe Life provided training of trainers on life skills for five teachers.

Most discussants believed that these networks were opportunities that supported activities in the school. Notwithstanding, these networks were initiated by the organizations, and the Club was passive in assessing and exploiting such opportunities to build its capacity. They evaluated that the Club as weak in its capacity to establish such networks and maintain existing ones. It does not have capability to influence and negotiate with the school officials to meet its purpose in the school. The Coordinators, on the other hand, argued that the school official's support to initiate and facilitate the link to different stakeholders was insufficient, and they maintained that stakeholders need official invitations and recognition by the school. The school officials, however, did not place a lot of emphasis on these networks, and considered these issues as the responsibility of the Coordinators.

Challenges and the Development of an Action Plan

The teacher focus groups, as well as the student focus groups, shared the challenges faced by the Club. Poor support by the school's officials was reiterated by both groups. For example, the discussants in the teacher focus groups reported that poor attention of the school officials towards the club, financial problems, lack of facilities (office, equipment, mini-media), and poor documentation of previous activities of the Club are current challenges. The discussants emphasized that the lack of mini-media facilities in the school thwarted efforts to provide life skills education on a continuous basis. Lack of commitment by members to implement activities and lack of experience also contributed for the low performance of the Club.

Student focus groups shared similar opinions. In addition, the students identified poor coordination between the teacher and student activities, lack of supervision and follow-up by the Coordinators, lack of skills and commitment among teachers coordinating the Club, and lack of recognition and incentives for the Club's work discouraged the student initiatives. Student focus groups emphasized that the school and the teachers coordinating the Club are not supportive of activities. The discussants shared that their plan to present entertainment drama on HIV/AIDS prevention for the school community failed because of lack of support from the school and the Coordinators.

The students reported that activities are not participatory, and that they did not participate in developing the annual plan. The plan did not include activities that might be easily implemented by members. Rather, it consisted of activities such as provision of VCT services that were beyond the member capacity. Because of this, there was lack of congruence between Coordinator and student interest. Students pointed out that their initiatives to present poems, songs, and drama at different times were not valued by the teachers.

Once the data were analyzed, the findings were presented for the discussants in a joint meeting. The participants worked together and interpreted the findings. The Club did not accomplish its intended purposes. They figured out the main obstacles and drafted an action plan to improve activities in the school. The action plan calls for concerted efforts of all stakeholders and members to advance the activities of the Anti-Aids and RH Club in the school, and implementation was set for the next academic year, with activities to be done before the new academic year as a precondition for effective future activities.

Strengths, Challenges, and Lessons Learned

This research enabled me to read lots of material on health promotion in general and school health education in other parts of the world. I learned much about anti-AIDS and Reproductive health clubs at schools at different levels of education. The Anti-AIDS and Reproductive health Club coordinators, both students and teachers, actively participated throughout the research process by identifying the problem, figuring out the discussion points, participating during discussion, interpreting the findings, and developing action plans to improve activities. This was a unique way to do research, a way which is not the same as with what I was familiar. One interesting thing is the way we dialogued in the groups during various sessions. We always discussed things in great detail and sometimes the discussion was heated, but we reached a consensus by the end. The research project has given me the opportunity to learn how people critically examine their concerns in defining problems and finding solutions. In the research process, there was a dialogue among the participants on their role in the Club with its current status and their role in the next steps. The active participation in the dialogue enhanced the participants' communication among themselves and they became active in identifying and defining the action agendas for future activities of the Anti-AIDS and Reproductive Health Club.

Despite the aforementioned strengths, doing such type of research has challenges. Knowing the history that all the Club's plans were not implemented due to financial constraints, bureaucracies, and an unsupportive environment, some members were reluctant to put their time and effort into something that might not make a difference. It was difficult to convince them to participate in the research process. One member for more than five years argued, "What can we do to push the group members implement the Club's plan without an adequate budget, an unsupportive school bureaucracy, and limited commitment?" Moreover, the involvement of the participants in the research process was not continuous or predictable. Some teachers and students who agreed to participate also had other tasks to be accomplished so that there was fluctuation within groups during sessions.

During the research process, every participant has the chance to forward her or his feelings and thoughts. Such a process sometimes brought the sessions to be a talk shop and it was difficult to differentiate the relevant and less relevant suggestions. I found some participants consistently had divergent views on the Club's performance and its challenges. Sometimes, we had trouble coming to consensus. Even so, the research brought individuals and groups together around a common agenda, that of improving the activities of the Anti-Aids and Reproductive Health Club. Having the groups involved in the research process to make change in the Club's activities enhanced communication, which may bring cohesion and collaboration among group members and with other stakeholders. The participants evaluated the performance of the Club clearly and identified major challenges and barriers for its activities. The findings of the research motivated the club to develop action plans for better performance. By the end of the action research project, the participants owned the findings and developed action plans to improve health education provision. The active involvement of the stakeholders in identifying the problems and designing alternative courses of actions for the solutions is a learning process that improves the capacities and skills of participants. These competencies and skills can be used to solve problems in other comparable problematic situations in the future, even in broader contexts. Thus, engaged research is important for social work practice, and social workers may use such engaged research processes in their practice settings.

Influence on the Author's Scholarly Direction

When I was taking the course Knowledge Building in Social Work and Social Development, I completed a literature review on health promotion and its development, the theories that guide health promotion practices, health promotion evaluation and measurement of outcomes, and research on health promotion. I learned that health promotion is a contemporary approach to health and health care provision. It is a unifying concept that represents a mediating strategy between people and their physical environments synthesizing personal choices and social responsibility in health to create healthier future (WHO, 1984).

Health promotion embraces actions directed at strengthening the skills and capabilities of individuals and actions directed towards changing social, environmental and economic conditions to alleviate their impact on public and individual health. It enables people to increase control over the social determinants of health and thereby improve their health (Nutbeam, 2006). Therefore, this action research project was initiated to assess health promotion activities. Health education is one of the components of health promotion. The health promotion literature depicts health education at school as an ideal approach to communicate healthy lifestyle messages for youth and the community at large (Denman, Moon, Parsons, & Stears, 2002). This same intention is clearly articulated in the Health and Policy of the Ethiopia (Ministry of Health, 1993). Despite all this, the findings of my engaged research reveal that the health education activities in the school I visited were minimal. The findings informed me to revisit the literature and read on health promotion and then try to relate to Ethiopia's reality. I learned the premise that preventing a disease, or a trauma is better than to cure it after it happens.

In conclusion, the engaged research immersed me into a body of knowledge that has direct relevance to human wellbeing in health. I learned that the increasing demand for health care services has shifted the paradigm from clinical medicine towards health promotion—that is, health improvement and prevention to manage health care more effectively. There are health status disparities attributed to differences in individual, societal, and environmental factors. My engagement with young people during the research process and readings informed me that there are different sectors of the population, including children, youth, women, and older people, that are disproportionately affected by ill health problems. Such conceptualizations enlightened me to read more on women's health. In my reading on women's health, I found a catchy phrase: "Women are dying while giving life." It tells that many women are dying not from disease, but during normal process of procreation. Women are dying by preventable causes attributed to individual, socio-cultural, and environmental factors (Nanda, Switlick, & Lule, 2005).

As a beginner scholar, I worked my dissertation on roles that social context and social networks have on women's decision of the place of giving birth. The findings reveal that the decision on place of delivery for a woman is a social process and many stakeholders around the woman have considerable roles. Social networks have greater roles in deciding place of delivery than individual attributes (Asrese, 2014). Findings were consistent with the literature on the roles of social networks in developing healthy behavior in general and health service utilization in particular. Currently, I am working on importance of social and environmental determinants of health in general reproductive health in Ethiopia.

References

Ajuwon, A., & Brieger, W. (2007). Evaluation of school-based reproductive health education program in rural south west Nigeria. *African Journal of Reproductive Health, 11(2)*, 47-59.

Andersen, R. (1995). Revisiting the behavioral model and access to medical care: Does it matter? *Journal of Health and Social Behavior, 36*(1), 1-10.

Andersen, R., & Newman, J. (2005). Societal and individual determinants of medical care utilization in the United States. *The Milbank Quarterly, 83*(4), 1-28.

Asrese, K., & Abebe, M. (2007). *Major harmful traditional practices and violence against women in Amhara Region,* Bahir Dar, Ethiopia. (unpublished document).

Asrese, K. (2014). *Women's social networks, use of skilled birth attendants, and experience of quality in delivery services in Jabi Tehinan Woreda of Amhara Region, North West Ethiopia.* [Unpublished Doctoral Dissertation]. Addis Ababa University.

Burke, N., Joseph, G., Pasick, R., & Barker, J. (2009). Theorizing social context: Rethinking behavioral theory. *Health Education and Behavior, 36*(1), 55-70.

Central Statistical Authority. (2010). *2007 Population and Housing Census of Ethiopia.* Addis Ababa, Ethiopia.

Crosby, R., Kegler, M., & DiClemente, R. (2002). Understanding and applying theory in health promotion practice and research. In R. DiClemente, R. Crosby & M. Kegler (Eds.). *Emerging theories in health promotion practice and research* (pp. 1 – 15). San Francisco: Jossey-Bass.

Degaga, A. (2006). *Empowerment of Youth Club: Experience, Opportunities and Challenges: The Case of 'sele tselote egi' Youth RH /HIV/AIDS club in Oromia and 'kal' RH/HIV/AIDS Club in Addis Ababa Region Ethiopia.* (Master's thesis), Addis Ababa University.

Denman, S., Moon, A., Parsons, C., & Stears, D. (2002). *The health promoting school: Policy, research and practice.* London: Routledge.

Dooris, M. (2009). Holistic and sustainable health improvement: The contribution of the settings-based approach to health promotion. *Perspectives in Public Health, 129*(1), 29-36.

Federal Democratic Republic of Ethiopia (2006). *National adolescent and youth reproductive health strategy 2007 – 2015.* Addis Ababa: Ministry of Health.

Govindasamy, P., Aklilu K., & Hailom B. (2002). *Youth reproductive health in Ethiopia.* Calverton, Maryland: ORC Macro.

Haile Gabriel, A. (2008). The challenges and opportunities of mainstreaming HIV and AIDS intervention in Ethiopia's higher education: What roles for tertiary education? In *The HIV/AIDS Challenge in Africa an Impact and Response Assessment: The Case of Ethiopia* (pp. 1-70). Addis Ababa, Ethiopia: OSSREA.

Hindin, M.J., & Fatusi, A.O. (2009). Adolescent sexual and reproductive health in developing countries: An overview of trends and interventions. *International Perspectives on Sexual and Reproductive Health, 35*(2), 58-62.

HIV/AIDS Prevention and Control Office. (2006). *Report on Progress towards Implementation of the Declaration of Commitment on HIV/AIDS*. Addis Ababa, Ethiopia.

Jackson, S., Perkins, F., Khandor, E., Cordwell, L., Hamann, S., & Buasi, S. (2007). Integrated health promotion strategies: A contribution to tackling current and future health challenges. *Health Promotion International, 21*(51), 75-83.

Kloos, H., & Haile Mariam, D. (2000). Community-based organizations and poverty alleviation programs in HIV/AIDS prevention and control in Ethiopia: A preliminary survey. *Northeast African Studies, 7*(2), 13-34.

Lee, A., Cheng, F., & Leger, L. (2005). Evaluating health-promoting schools in Hong Kong: Development of a framework. *Health Promotion International, 20*(2), 177-186.

McCall, D., & McKay, A. (2004). School-based and school-linked sexual health education and promotion in Canada. *J Obstetric Gynecology Canada, 26*(6), 596–600.

Ministry of Health. (1993). *Health Policy of the Transitional Government of Ethiopia*. Addis Ababa, Ethiopia.

Ministry of Health. (2003). *Adolescent Reproductive Health Extension Package*. Addis Ababa, Ethiopia.

Mwanga, J., Jensen, B., Magnussen, P., & Hanson, J. (2007). School children as health change agents in Magu, Tanzania: A feasibility study. *Health Promotion International, 23*(1), 16-23.

Naaldenberg, J., Vaandrager, L., Koelen, M., Wagemakers, A., Saan, H., & Hoog, K. (2009). Elaborating on system thinking in health promotion programs. *Global Health Promotion, 16*(1), 39-47.

Nanda, G., Switlick, K., & Lule, E. (2005). *Accelerating progress towards achieving the MDG to improve maternal health: A collection of promising approaches.* Washington, DC: The World Bank.

Nutbeam, D. (2006). Using theory to guide changing individual behavior. In M. Davies & W. Macdowall (Eds.). *Health promotion theory* (pp. 24 -36). London: McGraw-Hill.

Ochieng, B. (2001). Health promotion strategy for adolescent's sexual behavior. *Journal of Child Health Care, 5*(2), 77-81.

Poland, B., Krupa, G., & McCall, D. (2009). Settings for health promotion: An analytical framework to guide intervention design and implementation. *Health Promotion Practice, 10*(4), 505-516.

Sani, A., Abraham, C., Denford, S., & Ball, S. (2016). School-based sexual health education interventions to prevent STI/HIV in Sub-Saharan Africa: a systematic review and meta-analysis. *BMC Public Health, 16*, 1069.

Teric, L. (2008). Back-to-school health promotion. *American Journal of Lifestyle Medicine, 2*(6), 402-405.

Walker, Z., Townsend, J., Bell, J., & Marshall, S. (1999). An opportunity for teenage health promotion in general practice: An assessment of current provision and needs. *Health Education Journal, 58,* 218-227.

World Health Organization. (1984, July). *Health promotion: A discussion document on the concept and principle. Summary report of the Working Group on Concept and Principles of Health Promotion.* Copenhagen: WHO Regional Office for Europe.

World Health Organization (1986). *Ottawa Charter for Health Promotion.* Geneva: World Health Organization.

World Health Organization (1998). *Health Promotion Glossary.* Geneva: World Health Organization.

Zimmerman, R., Kebede, W., Smith, G., Matuza, M., & Hovde, A. (n.d.). School-based Anti-AIDS clubs in Addis Ababa, Ethiopia: What impact do they have on HIV-related knowledge, attitudes, and behaviors? School of Social Work, Addis Ababa, Ethiopia. (Unpublished manuscript).

CHAPTER 11

STUDENT ENGAGEMENT IN CAMPUS-BASED COMMUNITY POLICING

Demelash Kassaye

This action research explored students understanding on the consequences of crime and develop the plan of action to deter the trend of crime through campus-based community policing. Ten males and four females were selected haphazardly. Focus group discussion was a tool used to generate qualitative data. The data gathered has been analysed thematically. Freire's method of dialogical process that makes participants active in identifying and solving their problems was used. To this end, a series of steps have been in place to first make participants familiar with basic principles and philosophies of community policing. The findings of this study indicate that Akaki being a place to traffic drugs, *khat*, and contraband goods, intruded from East and South parts of Ethiopia exposed many students to addiction of using substances and commit crime. The types of crimes committed are picking monies, stealing properties, bullying, and violence against female students. The consequences of these crimes devolved confidence, peer relation, compassion, and trust among students. The effect it posed on the teaching learning process is explained in terms of class absenteeism, gloomy in group thinking, polarization, ill relation with campus management, fear of crime and predicaments to friendly interaction. After delineating the consequences and types of crimes, they were able to develop action plan uplifting the crime fighting spirit of students through campus-based community policing.

Introduction

Community policing can achieve success in reducing crime rate, fear, social problems and disorder, if both the police and the community mobilize resources into shared values and strategies. The mobilization process needs to entertain the expectations of the people and the country. Community policing is built on the foundation of socio-geographic neighborhood in which citizens have a personal stake in their immediate surroundings and therefore are more willing to support neighborhood improvement (Bass, 2000; Thurman & Reisig, 1996). Practitioners acknowledge the increasing influence of a community-oriented approach in policing (Cordner, 2001; Greene, 2000), and its popularity is rising among urban police departments (Fridel, 2004). In forging police-community relationships, building trust, and fostering citizen involvement is necessary. This is complex and difficult to do, but police officers can play a positive and critical role in this regard (Lewis & Ramakrishnan, 2007; MacDonald & Stokes, 2006). To this end, community policing requires the active participation of local government, civic and business leaders, public and private agencies, residents, churches, schools, and hospitals (Bureau of Justice Assistance, 1994).

One feature of democratic policing is the promotion of partnerships between police and the community. Ethiopia adopted democratic principles in its police service soon after the 1990 downfall of the Derg Regime. Compared to traditional policing, the philosophy of community policing involves broadening the nature and number of police functions. Community policing is based on the idea that public safety is best achieved when police and community members work together to solve problems. Through the direct contact with citizens, police officers have the potential to create an environment that not only improves public safety but also enhances citizen engagement and involvement and builds a sense of community. Another way to explain community policing is that it engages citizens as "co- producers" of public safety (Skolnick & Bayley, 1988, p.18). Coproduction is the involvement of citizens in producing and delivering public services (Ostrom & Ostrom, 1971). Although coproduction is typically viewed as a means of reducing costs (Alford, 2000; Osborne & Gaebler, 1992), it can also be a vehicle for community building.

Schools and higher educational institutes have been disregarded in community policing programs. Excluding youth and members of the school communities has an enormous effect on these social institutions so much so that this may impact the entire program of participatory policing. The community of inquiry in this action research refers to my role as the engaged researcher, and to third-year Bachelor's in Social Work students at the Akaki Campus, Addis Ababa University. The rationale of this action research was not to produce student police officers, but to seek student engagement in identifying crime problems and putting forth solutions to curb the tendency of crime in the area. The study enhances student knowledge about community policing and identifies ways to solve problems by partnership with police, as well as increasing student comprehension about policing, their interest in partnering with the community to identify and solve problems and examining student awareness of the power of community policing. In doing so, it hoped to lessen crime on campus by helping students identify crime problems and developing a plan of action pursuant of community policing. How do students experience crime and its consequences on campus? What activities do they plan to engage in to promote a crime-free school through campus-based community policing?

Framing the Engaged Research

Definitions of Community Policing

Scholars in criminology define the concept of community policing in various ways. While some give emphasis to partnership, others consider the importance of improving the quality life in community settings. "Community policing is a new philosophy of policing, which emphasizes the working partnership between police officers and citizens in creative ways to solve community problems relating to crime, and neighborhood disorders" (Trojanowicz & Bucqueroux, 1990, p.5), Similarly, Newman (2006) describes community policing as "A policing philosophy that promotes and supports organizational strategies to address the causes and reduce the fear of crime and social disorder through problem solving tactics and police-community partnerships" (p.46). Although there are many definitions, community policing can be described, in the broadest sense as a "style of policing in which the police are close to the public, know their concerns from regular everyday contacts, and act on them in accord with the community's wishes" (Fielding, 2005, p. 460). Through direct contact with citizens, police officers have the potential to create an environment that not only improves public safety but also enhances citizen engagement and involvement and builds a sense of community. In this sense, community policing provides an immense opportunity for community residents to proactive policing, especially in identifying police priorities and intervention strategies. Community policing involves a belief that partnerships will reduce the fear of crime, and ultimately lead to a reduction in crime rates. Viewed from this standpoint, police and communities are co-producers of crime control and safety services, indicating a shared responsibility for maintaining law and order in a community.

Fear of Crime and Crime Reduction

In a brief recounting of the history of policing, Scheider, Rowell, and Bezdikian (2003) report "three primary and interrelated functions: crime control, order maintenance, and service provision" (c.f., Trojanowicz & Bucqueroux, 1990). Kelling and Moore's (1988) history of policing explains how professional policing moved away from order maintenance and service provision to a focus on crime control and criminal apprehension. According to Scheider et al. (2003), the community policing "model moves away from police-dominated crime control through reactive responses to calls for service and moves toward proactive problem solving centered on the causes of crime and disorder and on fostering partnership between the police and the community" (p. 365) (c.f., Scott, 2001; Wilson & Kelling, 1998).

According to the Bureau of Justice Assistance (1994), "Community policing is democracy in action. It requires active participation of social institutes operating at local level to community welfare such as agencies, residents, churches, schools, and hospitals" (p. 4). This means that the function of police must include bettering the lives of people. A typical strategy of community policing is building partnerships based on trust and confidence with the community. According to Dietz (1997), reduction in the fear of crime is also a pillar of successful community policing. "Reducing the fear of crime has become an essential element and an often explicitly articulated goal of the community policing philosophy" (Scheider et al., 2003, p. 365) (c.f., Thurman, Zhao, & Giacomazzi, 2001).

From the inception of professional policing, the relationship between the police and the community has been an important consideration. As a result, the police and communities would be considered "co-producers" of crime control and safety services, indicating a shared responsibility for maintaining order in a community (Skolnick & Bayley, 1986). The movement toward community policing was based on the notion that this style of policing could help reduce both fear of crime and disorder and ultimately lead to a reduction of crime rates. Bayley (1994) has argued that "the police do not prevent crime. This is one of the best kept secrets of modern life. Experts know it, the police know it, but the public does not know it" (p. 3). This is certainly a strong sentiment but is true that the field's assessment of the efficacy of community policing is less than clear. Although there is evidence, that this strategy reduces disorder and increase positive community-police relations (c.f., Kelling, 1981; Lurigo & Rosenbaum, 1994), its effect on crime rate is mixed (MacDonald, 2002). Indeed, Cordner (2001) found that only a slight majority of the 60 studies he reviewed revealed a decline in crime rates after a community policing model was implemented.

However, the results acquired in fighting crime are not as such encouraging due perhaps to the failure of spreading the philosophy of community policing to students in public and private schools and higher educational institutes. The prevailing reason articulated in police community forums is the belief that police need to control schools by increasing the number of beat officers thereby heightening the perceived risk of apprehension. It seems, however, that police have failed to incorporate schools, where half of the Ethiopian young population are found, in community policing efforts.

The Engagement Process

Reason for Selecting the Topic

I am a policeman by profession. In that role, I taught and assessed community policing programs implemented in some units of the Federal Police Bureaus and National Regional Police Institutes. The aim was to bring about a paradigm shift that favors community policing rather than the philosophy and management style of traditional policing. The initial step was to improve public awareness of community policing to gain community engagement and set forth a new way to sustaining peace and social order. Citizens came together to deal with on issues of community policing, to exchange information, identify and prioritize local problems, develop strategies to address them, and begin to raise resources that could be used to implement problem-oriented policing. As a similar department training bulletin notes, "Beat meetings ensure community input in the problem-solving process" (Chicago Police Department, 1993, p.1). Police chiefs are directed to form advisory committees that would broadly represent interests in the community.

They were to advise the commanders about matters concerning the community and ask them to help evaluate the effectiveness of projects within their jurisdiction. This gave me to get the opportunity to assess the implementation of community policing philosophies and principles as practiced in various levels of police services.

At the time of this action research, I was a doctoral student enrolled in the Social Work and Social Development program at Addis Ababa University. The program was headquartered on the Akaki Campus located in Akaki Sub city populated with about 85,000 people. The City Council of Addis Ababa demarcated the area as a zone for the expansion of industry and factories. This became an external factor to pull many people into the area for employment as daily laborers. The situation brought crime in various ways. The crime profile of the sub city (Addis Ababa Police Annual Report, 2002) indicated that murder, burglary and trafficking stimulants and psychotropic substances were the dominant crimes reported to police. Most crimes were committed by adolescents addicted to khat and other stimulants and psychotropic substances.

The campus is safeguarded by security officers responsible to maintain a safe and secured environment. However, the data obtained from the logbook reported that many students have been victims of local gangs. For example, in front of the main gate of the campus, the cell phone of one female student was taken and her arm was wounded. Such crime decreased the confidence of the campus community to move, especially at night, without fear of crime. It is easy to imagine how fear of crime can have negative consequences for the students that may outstrip the psychological harm resulting from any criminal act.

Before making the study, I explored whether the problem was increasing. Assuming that they are aware of or have experienced more traumatic experiences than first- or second-year students, and to try to understand those who had the most experience over time, I chose 14 (10 male and 4 female) 3rd year BSW students, Ideally, the activities of engaged participants, both individually and collectively, should be explicit. Consequently, I chaired the group to ensure that the issue was focused clearly and summarized in an organized way. I also enhanced the issues being discussed. My goal was to assess students' perceptions on community policing and engage them as the main implementers of an intervention plan to create a safe and secure environment for productive learning. Noting the importance of seeing participants as co-researchers and contributors, I pursued some of the procedures advocated by O'Brien (2001). In carrying out the research, I treated participants equally and fairly as they expressed their opinions. To make the research participatory, I encouraged participants to express their views, thoughts, feelings, and experiences.

The Process and Steps of Engaged Research

In action research there are the steps researchers can take to ensure the findings are scientific. These include paying attention to planning the project and designing the research strategy, methods of data collection, and data analysis by taking the objectives of the study into account (Heron, & Reason, 2006). Friedman (2006) uses the term community of inquiry to refer to a group of researchers and practitioners who redefine their roles and formulate common values, norms, terminologies and procedures throughout the engaged research process.

Action research involves a cyclical process, which means monitoring what has been done, reviewing and evaluating the outcomes, modifying the next action steps, and so on. Kemmis' model (cited in Hopkins, 1983) sketches action research as a cyclical process consisting four phases: planning, acting, observation and reflection. The process commences from planning and then is followed by action, observation and reflection. The process continues until the problem is solved. Susman's (1983) model begins with identifying the problem, developing an action plan, taking action, and evaluating the outcomes of the action taken. This project follows Friedman's (2006) first step of establishing a community inquiry is meeting with participants, which in this case are selected undergraduate social work students. I used a three-stage process in this engaged research.

In Stage 1, the process of engagement, students were selected to participate in the research, and two action meetings were held. I held a session to inform students on the intent of community policing, the goals of the research, and what was expected of them. The students selected the Chair and Committee members of the Student Council as gatekeepers or entry points for the research. The prime objective of this stage was to inform students of the intended objectives, obtain their consent and willingness to participate. After explaining the potential risks and benefits of participation, I obtained informed their consent. A second action meeting informed students of the philosophical underpinnings, management approaches and the concept of partnerships in community policing. Participants cautiously discussed these concepts, and brainstorming was employed to foster critical and creative thinking.

After ensuring participants were acquainted with the concepts and philosophies of community policing, I approached my co-researchers with a blank sheet of paper and some predetermined items for discussion. Some exploratory questions were included to make the discussion lively and productive. I employed Paulo Freire's (1976) constructs of dialogue, conscientization, praxis, transformation, and critical consciousness dialogical process to identify the problems, produce the codes, see the situation as experienced by the participants, and engage the student co-researchers in analyzing the situation, and acting to change it. According to Sharma (2002),

> Paulo Freire (1976) in his book, *Education: The Practice of Freedom*, explicates the framework of his methodology that in essence is a simple three-phased process. The first phase is the *naming* phase where one asks the question, 'What is the problem?' or 'What is the question under discussion?' The second phase is the *reflection* phase where one poses the question, 'Why is this the case?' or 'How do we explain this situation?' The third phase is the *Action* phase characterized by the question, 'What can be done to change this situation?' or 'What options do we have?' The unique feature of this pedagogical

approach is *'process centered'* as opposed to *'outcome-centered'* or *'product centered'*. It does not prescribe any acceptable end product in the beginning but only specifies the approach to be adhered.

This Freirean approach was used to produce a wide variety of ideas, or solutions, to a novel situation or problem. Participants enumerated the major causes of crime and social disorder on campus and in the nearby communities where they resided. This dialogue increased their understanding of community policing, provided ideas, and enhanced commitment among participants. Brainstorming and group discussion were used with groups of five to six members in the classroom and other venues on campus. Points dealt and agreed with at the end were recorded and compiled to use as potential references for further discussion.

With the aim that the co-researchers were directed to increase student participation in the implementation of campus-based community policing, Stage 2 consisted of a workshop and three dialogue sessions. The Workshop focused on reflection and discussion of the theories, philosophical thoughts, principles and practices of community policing. Presentations consisted of summaries and short synopsis that were read, with copies distributed to members in advance In Dialogue 1, five or six participants were grouped together. Questions for measuring participants' understanding about community policing were presented. Group recorders presented a summary of their group's discussion. This has confirmed participants' acquaintance towards the epistemological foundations, various theories of policing, management approaches and principles and values of community policing. Dialogue 2 focused on assessing the extent to what they are familiar with the underlying theories, principles and philosophies of community policing. Exercises were constructed to measure participants understanding on the general ideas of community policing. The aim was to lay down the premise that helps to avoid such ambiguities of concepts that may appear in the next two succeeding sessions easily. Dialogue 3 refined and reconstructed the facts covered in the previous two dialogues to check the reliability of the group dialogue sessions. This backward and forward discussion allowed participants to express their own views freely and gave the group a process through which to refine their views through collective reflection. In Stage 3, the students and I, as co-researchers, prepared an action plan together. The data gathered during focus group discussions and brainstorming sessions were analyzed using verbatim analysis to synthesize the data generated in the form of reflections, views and opinions. The findings of the sessions were reported to members before moving into the next session. In doing so, the groups deleted the statements that they viewed as inconsistent with what had been raised in various discussion sessions. They approved points they accepted as relevant. Participants commented on the first draft report of the study and edited it. The draft analysis was given back to participants again to gain their consent regarding the authenticity and originality of the analysis.

Findings

Student Experiences of Crime

Students examined the consequences of crime and its adverse effect on students' interrelations. Of the crimes reported to police and security personnel, the principal crimes are against students and their properties. Students are victims of crimes in buildings and housing, both classrooms and dormitories. One participant explained,

> I lost my personal items from my dormitory and reported it to campus police to get help. Members of the campus police still watch the student as suspect in the campus. However, when my roommates hear the rumor that I reported this to campus police, they hated me and started seeing me as their enemy rather as their roommate. You can guess how it is bad to be looked at as an enemy by students living with you in one dorm.

The most frequent types of crimes perpetrated day and night are stealing items and money from dormitories, substance abuse (chewing khat, smoking marijuana), fighting one another, bullying, and violence against female students. Speaking for the group, one student summarized the issue:

> We recall a phenomenon that appeared a year back on a female student who was stabbed by gangs. They grabbed her cell phone in front of the main gate. This was a recent traumatic experience when we learned about it. The situation has quickened the entire campus community to fight against youths living in the surrounding. It was dread to many of us while hearing the incident. Recalling what has happened helps to sensitize us to the adverse effect it posed on our peaceful learning. Therefore, all we should think responsibly about the problem and set alternatives to reduce the possibility of the prevalence of violence.

The consequence of these crimes has undermined student confidence, peer relations, empathy, and trust among each other. It has exposed them to class absenteeism, physical loss, negative group thinking and polarization. Such consequences also include increased their fear of crime and ill relations with campus management and the School of Social Work. In support of this, one student commented,

We all are victims of its consequence, especially in damaging group interactions in promoting cooperative learning. I can also say that we lost our opportunity to develop inter-communication skills, which are essential to our professional development in the future. Therefore, I may be wrong in pointing out this idea, but the School is producing educated thefts, those who will be criminals and drug users in the community. You can imagine how these students are looked at as gangsters and troublemaking youths in society instead of being seen as wanting to serve the people who need help from them as social work professionals.

Problems are aligned with substance abuse (chewing khat, smoking marijuana and cannabis), drinking alcohol, and breaking campus rules were identified as factors playing a great role in these crimes. This area is a place of destination for contraband goods and substances flowing from the Eastern and Southern parts of the country. The group pointed out that the area contributes student access to drugs. A great number of students started smoking and chewing khat after joining the campus. Students addicted to substances need money to buy stimulants to satisfy their need. Therefore, the new habit they acquired drives them to steal monies and items of their roommates to buy khat and other substances for chewing and smoking.

Student Responses to Campus-based Community Policing

The consequences students sensed made them think and identify ways to reduce the fear of crime and create a safe and secure environment for learning. With this regard, one student asked the group to "retrieve points raised in the sessions prepared to discuss views and perspectives that community policing advances." One student commented,

> the definition of community policing is fully democratic and well professionalized so long it involves public participation in identifying and solving social problems together with police. I have firm belief that campus-based community policing outweighs other alternatives to invent a crime free area and reduce fear of crime. I diligently ask you all to put forth your maximum effort for the realization of community policing in our immediate surroundings to avoid disorder and maintain good relationships amongst us.

In continuing, students consented to strengthening a body in charge of coordinating students to plan and implement campus-based community policing. They realized the need to develop a guiding manual, to accommodate diversity, and provide awareness-raising training on harmful substances. There should be psycho-social support for students addicted to khat, substances and alcohol, and social clubs working against crime and substance abuse. Their plan included empowering females, cooperating with local police and community policing offices, and staging forums on character education. In support of each other, speaking with the consent of others, one student summarized the group's response: "Educating students about harmful substances, empowering females to defend their rights, providing psychosocial support to students affected by the consequences of crime can be realized only if we employ the perspectives of community policing."

Strengths, Challenges and Lessons Learned

This action research encountered various strengths and challenges. The challenges experienced are partly related to retain students' free time and willingness to repeatedly participate in group discussions. Nonetheless, the results of this engaged research provided vivid information to the campus community at Addis Ababa University to develop an implementable plan of action. The project revealed the trend and status of crime in a higher educational institution and developed the strategy in place of letting crime and the use of substances to prevail. I was able to identify the challenges and factors affecting the idea of community policing in a real context and learn more about the feasibility of community policing on campus. The project report charged the School of Social Work to enhance student understanding of community policing in courses dealing with community development and criminal justice.

The action research entitled 'Student Engagement in Campus-based Community Policing' was made to fulfill the course 'Action Research and Models of Social Change. This action research has been carried out to solely satisfy the partial requirement of the course Action Research and Models of Social Change, given to doctoral students in School of Social Work. Community policing is useful as an area of future engagement in research, teaching and serving the community. This project helped me comprehend the status of community policing in schools, a gap which led me to further study this area through my dissertation research. In that research, I widened my work the capacity of community policing in deterring crime and reducing the fear of crime in a given neighborhood. Reviewing literatures, theories and practices of the philosophy helped me determine my conceptual framework and research paradigm to see community policing from the viewpoint of the community, as ingredient to raise awareness and improve police community relations.

References

Addis Ababa Police Annual Report. (2002). *Annual Crime Report*. Addis Ababa Police Commission, Ethiopia.

Alford, J. (2000). A public management road less travelled. *Australian Journal of Public Administration, 57,* 128-137.

Bass, S. (2000). Negotiating change: Community organizations and the politics of policing. *Urban Affairs Review,36,* 148-177.

Bayley, D.H. (1994). International Differences in community policing. In D.P. Rosenbaum (Ed.), *The challenges of community policing* (pp. 278-281). Thousand Oaks, CA: Sage.

Bureau of Justice Assistance. (1994). *Understanding Community Policing: A Framework for Action*. Office of Justice Programs. Washington, DC: US Department of Justice. Available at www.ncjrs.gov/pdffiles/commp.pdf

Chicago Police Department. (1993). *Together We Can: A Strategic Plan for Reinventing the Chicago Police Department*. Chicago: Chicago Police Department. Available at http://www.chicagocop.com/wp-content/uploads/A-Strategic-Plan-for-Reinventing-the-Chicago-Police-Department-1993-October.pdf

Cordner, G.W. (2001). Community policing: Elements and effects. In R.G. Dunham & G.P. Alpert (Eds.), *Critical Issues in Policing: Contemporary Readings* (4th Edition) (pp. 493-510). Prospect Heights, IL: Waveland.

Dietz, A.S. (1997). Evaluating community policing: Quality police service and fear of crime. *Policing: An International Journal of Police Strategy and Management, 20,* 83-100.

Fielding, N.G. (2005). Concepts and theory in community policing." *The Howard Journal of Criminal Justice, 44*(5), 460-472.

Freire, P. (1970). *Pedagogy of the Oppressed*. NY: Seabury Press.

Fridel, L. (2004). The results of three national surveys on community policing. In L. Fridel & M.A. Wycof (Eds.), *Community Policing: The Past, Present, and Future* (pp. 39-58). Washington, DC: Police Executive Forum.

Friedman, W. (2006). The community role in community policing. In D.P. Rosenbaum (Ed.), *The Challenge of Community Policing: Testing the Promises* (pp. 263-269). Thousand Oaks, CA: Sage.

Greene, J.R. (2000). Community policing in America: Changing the nature, structure, and function of the police. In J. Horney (Ed.), *Criminal Justice: Policies, Processes, and Decisions of the Criminal Justice System, Volume 3* (pp.

299-370). Washington. DC: U.S. Department of Justice, National Institute of Justice.

Heron, J., & Reason, P. (2006). The practice of co-operative inquiry: Research 'with' rather than 'on' people. In P. Reason & H. Bradbury (Eds.). *Handbook of Action Research* (pp. 144-154). London: Sage Publications.

Hopkins, D. (1983). *A Teacher's Guide to Classroom Research*, (3rd Edition). NY: Open University Press.

Kelling, G.L. (1981). *The Newark Foot Patrol Experiment.* Washington, DC: The Police Foundation. Available at https://blueravenintelligence.com/wp-content/uploads/2016/10/Newark-Foot-Patrol-Experiment1.pdf

Kelling, G.L., & Moore, M.H. (1988). The evolving strategy of policing. *Perspectives on Policing, 4,* 1-15. Washington, DC: National Institute of Justice. Available at https://www.ncjrs.gov/pdffiles1/nij/114213.pdf

Lewis, P., & Ramakrishnan, S.K. (2007). Police practices in immigrant-destination cities. *Urban Affairs Review, 42,* 874-900.

Lurigo, A., & Rosenbaum, D. (1994). The impact of community policing on police personnel. In D.P. Rosenbaum (Ed.), *The Challenge of Community Policing: Testing the Promises* (pp. 147-166). Thousand Oaks, CA: Sage.

MacDonald, J.M. (2002). The effective of community policing in reducing urban violence. *Crime and Delinquency, 48,* 592-618.

MacDonald, J., & Stokes, R.J. (2006). Race, social capital, and trust in the police. *Urban Affairs Review, 41,* 358-375.

Newman, O. (2006). *Defensible Space: Crime Prevention through Urban Design.* NY: Macmillan.

O'Brien, R. (2001). An overview of the methodological approach of action research. In R. Richardson (Ed.), *Theory and Practice of Action Research.* João Pessoa, Brazil: Universidade Federal da Paraíba. Available at http://www.web.ca/~robrien/papers/arfinal.html

Osborne, D., & Gaebler, T. (1992). *Reinventing Government.* Reading, MA: Addison Wesley.

Ostrom, V., & Ostrom, E. (1971). Public choice: A different approach to the study of public administration. *Public Administration Review, 31,* 203-216.

Scheider, M.C., Rowell, T., & Bezdikian, V. (2003). The impact of citizen perceptions of community policing on fear of crime: Findings from twelve cities. *Police Quarterly, 6*(4), 363-386.

Scott, J. (2001). Assessing the relationship between police-community coproduction and neighbourhood-level social capital. *Journal of Contemporary Criminal Justice, 18,* 147-166.

Sharma, M. (2001). Freire's adult education model: An underutilized model in alcohol and drug education? *Journal of Alcohol & Drug Education, 47*(1), 1-3.

Skolnick, J.H, & Bayley, D.H. (1998). Theme and variation in community policing. *Crime and Justice, 10,* 1-37.

Susman, G. (1983). Action research: A sociotechnical systems perspective. In: G. Morgan (Ed.), *Beyond Method: Strategies for Social Research* (pp. 95-113). Newbury Park, CA: Sage.

Thurman, Q., Zhao, J., & Giacomazzi, A.J. (2001). *Community Policing in a Community Era.* Los Angeles: Roxbury.

Thurman, Q.C., & Reisig, M.D. (1996). Community oriented research in an area of community-oriented policing. *American Behavioural Scientist, 39,* 570-586.

Trojanowicz, R., & Bucqueroux, B. (1990). *Community Policing: A Contemporary Perspective.* Cincinnati, OH: Anderson.

Wilson, J.Q., & Kelling, G.L. (1998). Making neighbourhoods safe. *The Atlantic Monthly, 263*(2), 46 52.

CHAPTER 12

INVOLVING FACULTY AND STUDENTS IN ENGAGED RESEARCH

Wassie Kebede, Alice K. Butterfield

Introduction

This chapter presents the principles and characteristics of engaged research and cross-cutting themes in engaged research as identified by doctoral students who contributed chapters in this book. We discuss the way in which policy contexts can be addressed through engaged research and the contribution of such engagement to future scholarship and models of social change. The chapter briefly presents the implementation of engaged research in social work profession and other disciplines, and concludes by presenting ways to use the book to teach engaged research

Principles and Characteristics of Engaged Research

Before discussing the themes identified in the engaged research studies that make up majority of the chapters in this book, it is useful to briefly reiterate the fundamental principles and characteristics of community-engaged research. Engaged research is defined as research that involves the active participation of both the scholar/researcher and community participants. According to James (n.d, para.7), engaged research has seven principles, including developing reciprocal relationships, being long-term and future-oriented, understating the nature of spatiality, conducting efforts in relation to lived places, and working with differences not to dissolve differences. Knowledge and inquiry are bound with power and practice and methodological decisions are sensitive to ethical and practical consequences. Avila-Linn, Rice, and Akin (2012) developed a comprehensive diagram that demonstrates the interlinked principles of academic engaged research. Principles of academic engaged research include (1) faculty-community partnership are robust; (2) faculty-community partners collaborate as co-educators.co-researchers; (3) students are well prepared for community engagement; (4) dialogue about culture, identity and power among partners is welcome and prevalent; (5) strategies to balance inequitable power are generated; (6) reflection is integrated before, during and after community engagement; (7) faculty and community partners agree on how students will be supervised and coached; (8) partners document and share their work; (9) partners celebrate their work and thoughtfully bring closure; and (10) academic learning and community experience are interwoven and seamless.

As defined above, engaged research which involves the scholar and community participants is comprised of several important characteristics in the framework for conducting the research. These include the use of both qualitative and quantitative methods, building on community strengths, characterized by principles that guide the research and requiring partnership development. Cooperation, negotiation, and collaboration among the scholars and community participants is essential (McDonald, n.d). Involving community and collaborating with members are integral components of engaged research process. Scripps Translational Science Institute and Scripps Whittier Diabetes Institute, (n.d, p. 8) note that in engaged research, community participants:

> Play primarily in defining relevant research questions, conducting the research, and disseminating the results. Participants and researchers contribute equally, shared decision making is an integral part of the process, findings and knowledge benefit all partners, researchers and community participants recognize each other's expertise, partners commit for long term research relationships and priority is local capacity building and empowerment.

Engaged research "responds to community-identified research interest, assets and needs; utilize the skills, passion and knowledge that academic and community co-researchers have and developed" (p. 4).

Cross-Cutting Themes in the Engaged Research by Doctoral Students

There is no standard listing of cross-cutting themes either in the development or research literature. However, in the development literature, a cross-cutting theme is defined as "topics that are gaining such importance with respect to the objectives of development cooperation that they should be considered and integrated into all development interventions and policies" (Institute for Evaluations and Social Analyses, n.d, p.3). Cross-cutting themes in research generally involve the issues (areas of focus) and the targets (specific groups) being investigated. What is defined as a cross-cutting theme can vary by time and place, but major cross-cutting themes in contemporary research include gender equality, diversity and inclusion, environmental sustainability, livelihood development, poverty reduction, including employment and income generation, general well-being and technology.

The concept of cross-cutting themes is more common in development and policy agendas compared to research in general, and particularly in academic research. Most universities have shifted their research agenda from "pure" research to applied and development-oriented research where issues of cross-cutting themes are more pronounced. Research units are established by universities in thematic areas to focus the attention of academics and students. Also, in line with this, universities recognize the importance of involving community groups in research, which ultimately contributes to the emergence and development of engaged or participatory research. In the process of developing thematic research, university leaders are likely to consider cross-cutting themes a mandatory requirement. For example, Debre Markos University in Ethiopia identified 17 cross-cutting themes for research by academics and students. "Thematic areas are designed as a result of a thorough analysis of the problems that the nearby communities are facing, needs of society, personal experiences of researchers and the national development agenda" (Debre Markos University, n.d, para, 1). Similarly, cross-cutting themes are identified based on consultation and participation of beneficiary communities. Such thematic research is multidisciplinary, which emanates from social problems and the most important and researchable problems (Bahir Dar University, 2014). Themes in crosscutting in research are "instrumental in reducing fragmentation of activities and duplication of efforts, enhancing efficient utilization of resources, easing coordination, and management of different research activities" (Haromaya University, 2014, p. 6).

Outside of Ethiopia, the same is true. For example, research collaboration between Chinese universities and those in other nations focuses on the areas of "sustainable urbanization, environment-friendly energy, sustainable agriculture, sustainable aquaculture, cooperation on infrastructure, health innovations, etc." (The Research

Council of Norway, n.d, p.2). Monash University (2020) in Australia established its thematic research under four areas including artificial intelligence and data science, better governance and policy, health science and sustainable development. Research by this university is believed to contribute to changing the nature of work and human interaction, improving innovation, enterprise and social inclusion, and the quality of life in health care, and contributing toward the United Nations Sustainable Development Goals. The British Council (2018) explains that the thematic research areas of Kenyan universities are aligned with a "knowledge-based policy and development trajectory which clearly connected knowledge, higher education and sustainable development" (p.16).

We reviewed the engaged research conducted by the authors in consideration of their cross-cutting themes. Table 12A shows these cross-cutting themes, including the issues addressed and the target groups considered. The table also summarizes the policy context addressed by the engaged research.

Table 12A: Cross-Cutting Themes & the Policy Context of Engaged Research

Research Title	Cross-Cutting Themes	Addressing the Policy Context	Research Participants
Ch. 3 The Khairat Muslim Women's Empowerment Organization by Yania Seid-Mekiye	Female Empowerment Gender Equality	Women empowerment and gender equality	Muslim Women University Students
Ch. 4 - Women and Economic Development by Abiot Simeon	Microenterprise	Women economic emancipation, decision making and economic empowerment	Women Microenterprise
Ch. 5 - Leprosy: Stigma and Discrimination in an Ethiopian sub-city by Getaneh Mehari & Getu Ambaye	Discrimination	Health services, social protection, and addressing discrimination	Persons with Leprosy
Ch. 6 - Supporting People in Poverty Through a Local Association by Tadesse Gobo.	Poverty Community Development	Local capacity building and community empowerment	Local Associations (Iddir) Impoverished Farmers
Ch. 7 - Building Capacities of Iddirs to Assist Poor Older Adults by Samson Chane	Elder Abuse & Neglect	Social protection, welfare and social security, social insurance	Local Associations (Iddir) The Elderly
Ch. 8 - Exploring Assets of Youth for the Prevention and Control of HIV by Andargachew Moges	HIV/AIDS Youth Empowerment	Youth development, health services and local asset building	Youth - High School Students
Ch. 9 - Youth Development in Student Councils by Adugna Abebe	Youth Development	Youth empowerment, participatory decision making and youth representations	University Students
Ch. 10 - Reclaiming Health Education at Beseka High School by Kerebih Asres	Health Education HIV/AIDS	Health services, community education, youth representation, information dissemination	Youth - High School Students
Ch. 11 - Student Engagement in Campus-based Community Policing by Demelash Kassaye	Victimization Female Empowerment	Police services, human right issues, gender equality, girls empowerment	University Students

The authors addressed various cross-cutting themes as the focus of their action/engaged research. Women/female empowerment, poverty reduction, HIV/AIDS, youth development/empowerment, vulnerability/discrimination, health education, and livelihood improvement are some of the themes. Local associations, youth, disabled persons and women are the groups targeted. These cross-cutting themes and targets are relevant and focused on understanding contemporary issues in Ethiopia. Illustrations of some of these cross-cutting themes follow.

Local associations, also named community-based organizations (CBOs) are relevant entities in Ethiopia in addressing critical social and economic problems such as poverty, HIV/AIDS, elder support and adolescent/youth misbehavior including involvement in drug use and alcohol consumption. Kloos, Wuhib, Haile-Mariam and Lindtjjorn (2003) note that CBOs provide immense support to government in the prevention of HIV and other communicable diseases by serving as traditional birth attendants, health extension workers, community health agents, reproductive health agents, and so on. Youth unemployment is a challenge not only for economic prosperity but also causes various social instabilities such as crime, drug abuse and related health and social illnesses. As noted by Nayak (2014, p.34), youth unemployment in Ethiopia "...continue to be serious social problems...." In traditional research approaches, issues related to youth unemployment are much covered, but the voices of youth are unheard. In Chapter 8, Andargachew Moges documents the assets of youth, to address their HIV/AIDS and unemployment problems, which are suggested by youth. This is a relevant piece of engaged research that draw lessons from the participants in engineering strategies to address problems and further the lives of the youth for the better.

Other critical areas are female empowerment, and the vulnerabilities and discrimination of elders and persons with disabilities. Women in Ethiopia are still devoid of many rights including the right to own property, equal access to quality education and participation in political and social affairs that affect their life. According to Jones, Tafere and Woldehana (2010), not only are women are denied of voices in national and community arenas but also in their households.

Considering women's issues and their economic opportunities relate to two cross-cutting themes. Women's voices are heard in the engaged research conducted in Chapter 3 by Yania Seid-Mekiye and Chapter 4 by Abiot Simeon. Such engaged research towers above traditional approaches, both qualitative and quantitative, that consider women only as sources of data in conducting research. Focusing on vulnerable groups and engaging them in research to hear and document their voices is critical. Such a focus is found in in Chapter 5 by Getaneh Mehari and Getu Ambaye who document the voices of persons with leprosy. Samson Chane's engaged research in Chapter 7 is conducted with local associations that provide economic and social support to elders who are unable to support themselves, lacking the necessary social protection from government or other responsible bodies. Although this engaged research did not directly target elders, the voices of leaders of the local association directly reflect the voices of elders as both share a similar social and economic environment. Other studies conducted on the roles of local associations in providing services to vulnerable groups have supported the idea that these associations represent the voices of the voiceless such as children, elders, persons with disabilities, and so on (e.g., Stuer, Okello, Wube & Steinitz, 2012; Fenta & Getachew, 2015; Miriti, 2009).

All the action-engaged research projects identified in this book are good examples leading to social work theses or dissertations in social development. In developing countries, social development is linked with "community-based projects … such as microenterprises, women's groups, cooperatives, maternal and child welfare programs, the provision of safe drinking water, and the construction of schools and clinics" (Midgely, 2014, p.3). Social development is multi-disciplinary, touching upon all aspects of human life including "health, education, economic development, safety, social protection and welfare services" (Patel, 202015, p. 87). In line with these foci of social development, Chapter 10 by Kerebih Asres generates data on youth assets to address HIV/AIDS as a health problem. Chapter 6 by Tadesse Gobosho and Chapter 7 by Samson Chane present the roles of local associations in mitigating poverty and ensuring the economic wellbeing of community members, for example, among poor farmers and the elderly. Abiot Simeon's engaged research in Chapter 4 provides insights about the role that women can play by participating in microenterprise activities for their own economic development. Finally, safety is a concern for social development. Chapter 9 by Adugna Abebe uses engaged research to promote the development of knowledge and skills to protect them from substance abuse, and cultural incompetence. Chapter 11 by Demelash Kassaye emphasizes the safety needs of university students and the strengths and challenges of community policing through active student participation in the research.

Addressing the Policy Context through Engaged Research

Policies influence the context of research and particularly engaged research. Engaged research as an emancipatory process, influences policy formulation and implementation by empowering people through their engagement and decision making. When the policy environment provides freedom for researchers, engaged researchers are free to unearth social realities and contributing policy solutions is critical. In contrast, when policies are unable to provide a favorable environment for research, the methodologies and actions of researchers remain peripheral, and engaged research is unlikely to occur. In the absence of a supportive policy environment, researchers follow traditional approaches in which participant engagement in research is minimal or not present at all. Scholars argue that the "...research-policy link is now moving towards a more dynamic and complex view that emphasizes a two-way process between research and policy..." (Young & Shaxson, 2006, p. 3). Accordingly, action research or engaged research can contribute to evidence-based policy if (i) the engaged research fits within the political and institutional limits and pressures of policy makers, (ii) the evidence is credible and convincing, provide practical solutions to current policy problems and (iii) researchers and policy makers share common networks, trust each other and communicate effectively.

Engaged research is a good approach to address existing gaps between policy and community interests. Engaged research provides the opportunity for forming policy by soliciting priorities that communities want and need to address. As indicated in Table 12.1, the engaged research generated impressive issues that community participants voiced during their participation. For example, in Chapter 3, Muslim research participants aired their views about the place of Muslim women in Islam religion and Muslim families. They stated that what is written in Qur'an about the place of women in society and the actual practices by society often are incongruent. Engaging more Muslim women to voice their understandings of Islam and their position in society holds promise to influence policy contexts such as the Sharia law and its related practice in society to improve the life of Muslim women.

A further articulation of engaged research and its influence on policy is evident in the engaged research of other authors. Three engaged research efforts illustrated in Table 12.1 were conducted with youth, specifically on HIV/AIDS and youth empowerment, youth development, and health education. Youths who participated claimed the importance of using the assets of youth for empowerment, health benefits and participatory decision-making. Policies targeting health and youth development target the youth themselves as relevant resources and assets for action in the implementation of such policies. Engaged research can also address security matters by generating participatory knowledge about crime, substance abuse, gender-based violence, and so on.

Four engaged research projects, Chapter 8 by Andargachew Moges, Chapter 9 by Adugna Abebe, Chapter 10 by Kerebih Asres and Chapter 11 by Demelash Kassaye, emphasize youth participation in high schools, youth health education, student councils and community policing in a university environment. The concerns of youth participating in these projects were crimes that affect their life such as drug abuse, gender-based violence, petty thefts and problems of reproductive and sexual health. Formulation of policies that demand the protection of young people from being involved in crime or becoming victims of crime are critical issues. Chapter 3 by Yania Seid-Mekiye and Chapter 4 by Abiot

Simon are specifically about women's issues call up the importance of policy that should emphasis women's empowerment from both gender and economic perspectives. Chapter 5 by Getaneh Mehari and Getu Ambaye and Chapter 7 by Samson Chane focus on marginalized groups, specifically social discrimination experience by persons with leprosy and the situation of poor elders. Both chapters explore the economic and social challenges faced by marginalized groups face and the way in which local communities try to address these challenges. Both chapters inform the need for comprehensive social protection policy that provides guidance in addressing the economic and social needs of specific groups. Finally, Tadesse Gobesho in Chapter 6 emphasizes the role of local associations in improving the livelihood of members. His work challenges community and social development policy to consider the contributions of local associations for development.

Future Scholarship and Models of Social Change

Engaged/participatory research in which students and community participants were involved shaped the future scholarship of many doctoral students. Their participation led them to apply principles of engaged research and models of social change to their dissertations. Based on the knowledge and research skills they acquired, students identified important areas around social development, community development, community assets, social networks, and community partnership, all of which dealt with social development or models of social change in one way or another. Dissertations that emerged from their involvement in engaged research conducted with specific community groups are summarized in Table 12B. The common concepts used both in engaged research and dissertation projects are related to community development, assets, social networks, and poverty alleviation, which are elements of social development and models of social change. The list is not exhaustive. There are many other doctoral graduates of the School of Social Work at Addis Ababa University whose work is not featured in this book, but who conducted their dissertation and/or other research directly linked to their exposure to engaged research through coursework and required assignments in engaged research.

Table 12B: Common Concepts Used in Engaged Research and Dissertations

Author	Engaged Research in Coursework	Dissertation that Emerged from Engaged Research
Abiot Simon	Women and Economic Development	Social Development
Andargachew Moges	Exploring Assets of Youth for the Prevention and Control of HIV	Concept Mapping of Youth Development Assets
Tadesse Gobesho	Supporting People in Poverty Through a Local Association	Asset Based Community Development
Solomon Alemu	Engaged Research in University-Community Collaboration: Implications for the Ambo University Collaboration with Ubuntu in the Ethiopian City of Ambo	Ubuntu: Locality-Based Small-Scale Social Development through a University-Community Partnership: An Autoethnographic Approach
Wassie Kebede	Research as a catalyst for asset-based community development: Assessing the skills of poor women in Ethiopia	Social networks and sexual practices: Applying social network analysis techniques to understand adolescent sexual experiences.
Getu Ambaye	Leprosy: Stigma and Discrimination in an Ethiopian Sub-city	Social Networks

Source: Author.

Implementing Engaged Research in Social Work and Related Disciplines

As we discussed in Chapter 1, engaged research goes by various names, indicating different types or methods of engaged investigation. Nonetheless, all these approaches and methods consider community at the center of the research. Some of the engaged research methodologies and approaches commonly used in student research included Participatory Action Research, Community-University Partnership, Collaborative Inquiry, Participatory Research, Action-Oriented

Research and Action Learning Research. Although often used in research engagement under a common umbrella of action research or university-community partnership, these approaches although commonly mentioned in textbooks and other literature are not taught specifically in the classroom.

The experience we have gained from the engaged research projects conducted by faculty members and students from Addis Ababa University, School of Social Work leads us to recommend that engaged research should be included both in research courses, such as graduate courses on qualitative research and action research and models of social change for doctoral students. Doctoral and master's students need to be well acquainted with specific methods, techniques and skills to engage in community-based engaged research. Lessons can be drawn from the experiences of the Gedam Sefer community-university partnership in Addis Ababa, Ethiopia, from which a number of publications were produced both from student-supervised research and joint research involving faculty and students (e.g., Kebede & Butterfield, 2009; Kebede, 2010; Butterfield, Kebede & Gessesse, 2009).

Engaged research has now become a center of attention for Addis Ababa University, as exemplified by its establishment of the Community Engagement Office (CEO). This office encourages schools and departments to identify communities with which to establish partnership and engage in collaborative research. The intent is to adapt problem-solving engagement in which community groups become drivers of their own problem identification, analysis, project planning, and project implementation efforts. At the time of writing this book, the School of Social Work is identified as one of the leading schools and departments to initiate such engaged projects, and based on its previous experiences it was tasked with developing a meaningful plan for seeking support from the CEO. This research engagement will involve faculty members, master's and doctoral students in collaboration with communities. The success of these efforts will depend on whether faculty members and students develop the required knowledge and skills to employ engaged research methods and approaches. In this way, the School of Social Work and Addis Ababa University will become a center of excellence by participating in long-standing research engagement with communities. Student theses, dissertations, term papers and even field practicums can be designed in line with community-engaged research.

The studies discussed in the preceding chapters can be considered as prototypes for other similar post-graduate research undertakings in social work and related fields. Many of the authors of these studies, which they completed as partial fulfilment for the course "Action Research and Models of Social Change" later expanded their coursework assignments and exercises into dissertation projects. Some doctoral students built their action research directly into dissertation projects, and while others made some modifications related to issues and target groups. All confirmed that their engaged action research projects informed their future scholarship areas. They identified their dissertation topics and its related methodologies as having a direct impact on their engagement in action research. In relation to the course, students were required to develop an action research proposal, prepare an annotated bibliography, and conduct engaged research. Together, these exercises enabled students to link theory with practice. Specific course sessions included topics on action research, social development, diffusion of innovation, social networks, community development, Asset Based Community Development, community conversations, concept mapping and higher education partnership. For student learners, these topics widened possible areas of interest in which action research could be employed. A review of the engaged research conducted by doctoral students who contributed chapters for this book demonstrates that course-embedded mini-research projects can lead to areas of future scholarship. Although students acknowledged that the nature of such engaged research is labor intensive, burdensome and requires ample time and commitment to sustain an active partnership with community groups, the benefits are worthwhile.

For graduate students to use their engaged research project as a foundation for future scholarship, they need to be guided properly by their course instructors or research supervisors. Faculty should be aware that supervising students in engaged research requires intensive review and feedback. The authors who were able to use their engaged research for publication, as well as to identify the role of their research in defining or building their future areas of scholarship, were guided by the editors to reflect on the concepts of action research that they internalized through implementing their projects. The editors, as course instructors to these cohorts of doctoral students, were committed to providing not only theoretical knowledge, but also acting together with students during data collection, analysis, and writing research outcomes to prepare these book chapters.

Due to their reluctance to fully participate in collaborative learning, some students who were in the same cohort with those who produced chapters for this book, were unable to promote their research assignment into book chapters or other publications. Such lack of full commitment to engage in engaged research could be due to poor understanding of the nature of engaged research which is time intensive and burdensome for both students and faculty. As noted by Ministry of Education Canada (2013), if students need to succeed in their future scholarship, their active participation in research is essential. Involvement in collaborative inquiry can have paramount importance in developing their future careers in research and areas of development. Our experience demonstrates that for engaged research to happen with a given community, engagement between students and their instructors is vital. Close collaboration among students and instructors is a necessary requirement in proceeding with community-engaged research. In our experience, for those students who participated fully in community-engaged research, it paved the way for them to conduct their dissertations and future scholarship in a similar fashion by immersing themselves with communities and making community members their co-researchers.

Using this Book for Teaching Engaged Research

Engaged research is linked with teaching research-related courses including action research or and methods courses, particularly qualitative research. To involve students in engaged research, appropriate course syllabi with clear and specific procedures, tasks and responsibilities for students and instructors should be developed. Our teaching of action research through an engaged approach is summarized here as an example and sample syllabi are annexed at the end of the book.

Block teaching was the model we applied whereby one course was taught at a time, and specific times were blocked for certain activities. This model is different from a semester-based teaching approach in two ways. First, the time given to complete the contents of the course (lectures, book and article reviews, preparatory assignments, one-on-one consultation, and so on) was not more than a month. For their engaged research, students were given additional time after the first month to go out to the community and conduct their research, and this was followed up with a week of meeting back in the classroom for project presentations and consultation on writing a final report. Second, the block teaching method allowed students to fully dedicate themselves to their engaged research project. However, to complete the engage research component of the course, students should identify their own schedule to avoid time conflict with a course that follows the action research course we had taught. Such freedom given to students to follow their own schedule sometimes resulted with unnecessary relaxation in completing their assignments. To avoid this, we made deadlines to submit the final report for the engaged research (not more than 30 calendar days after completion of the course work). This helped students to be abided by course rules.

Using block model the course "Action Research and Models of Social Change" at Addis Ababa University, School of Social Work was first taught by international professors where the model was similarly used to teach all courses in the doctoral program and initially in the master's program as well. For Visiting Professors who find it difficult to teach in a 15-week traditional semester-based approach, the block teaching model was effective in allowing international faculty to use their vacation times or other mechanisms that released them from teaching for a shorter period than 15 weeks. The block teaching model that started in the School of Social Work was adopted by Addis Ababa University at large and become a policy for all departments and schools to teach at the postgraduate level.

Our action research course designed for PhD class consisted of the following: Course introduction, educational objectives, course assignments, list of reference and reading materials, guidelines for scholarly engaged research, and course topics. Offering the course followed specific steps that encouraged engagement in research. First, the course syllabus with reading materials were virtually shared with students three to four weeks prior the timetable assigned to teach the course. This allowed students to understand its content and accomplish preliminary readings. An assignment on introductory readings was due at the beginning of the in-class sessions. The next sequence was to conduct intensive lectures during which student-lecturer interaction is rigorous to cover major theoretical and applied contents. Then students had offered to break for a few days from in-class lectures and use the time to complete reading assignments, and work on preparing a concept paper for engaged action research (see Table 12B). During this break from classroom instruction, they were encouraged to go out to the community and explore possibilities and begin the process of engagement in action research.

In the final round of lecture days, students presented and discussed their assignments, which were also submitted in writing. This period of in-class instruction was a particularly important time for students to meet individually with the Instructors to discuss their engaged research topic, community connections, strengths and challenges. Time was allocated for students to go to field to start and/or continue their engagement in action research. This allowed students to interpret the theoretical knowledge learned in class directly through its application through collaborative research with the community groups that they had identified as research partners. During this fieldwork, each student or student group met individually with the Instructors on regular basis to discuss and share their engagement in the field, lessons learned and the preliminary outcomes of their engaged research. Table 12C below summarizes the segments of the course and expected durations to complete each segment.

Table 12C: Course Segments and Allocated Time/Period for Block Teaching

Course Segments	Allocated Time/Period	Remark
Lecturing (student-lecturer interaction in classroom)	Average 12 days	Direct student-professor interaction in classroom
Consultation and one-on-one support	Average 5 days	Continuous throughout the course period but a cumulative equivalent of five full days
Review of students' book and/or article-based assignments	Average 5 days	Professors' independent review of student assignments and providing written feedback
Engaged participatory research in the field	Average 30 days	Student-led engaged/action research with closer supervision by course professors. In some cases, field visits by professors were included
Review of engaged participatory research projects	Range 8-12 days (depending the number of PhD students in a cohort	Professors' independent review of engaged/action research reports and providing written feedback

N.B: The timeline varied slightly during different cohorts of teaching depending the effective self-coordination of students to conduct their engaged research, days spend by international professors for the block teaching and available spare days between end of one course and start of the next course.

Engaged research as a model of teaching action research or qualitative research can be used specifically in graduate programs (PhD and MSW). The use of engaged research to teaching PhD and MSW students are drawn from our experience of teaching in the USA (University of Illinois at Chicago) and Ethiopia (Addis Ababa University). This book as a recommended text to teach engaged research is a result of our participation of teaching of action research for PhD and MSW students. The experience of teaching action research helped us revisit and update the course syllabus on regular basis; information from fieldwork provided new insights for integrating and applying theoretical knowledge with local contexts. Since we started teaching action research at Addis Ababa University in 2007 and later at the University of Illinois at Chicago in 2019, the course syllabi were revised many times. To make use of expanded access to online materials instead of books, the course syllabus was further revised in teaching action research at the University of Gondar in Ethiopia.

The Challenge to Social Work Education & Human Service Professionals

Conceptually, engaged research and social work research share common features but also differ in important ways. A core characteristic of engaged research is the researcher-community partnership so as to address community problems and enhance community life. A common definition of social work research is a research that:

> Involves the study of preventive interventions, treatment of acute psychosocial problems, care and rehabilitation of individuals with severe, chronic difficulties, community development interventions, organizational administration, and the effects of social policy actions on the practice of social work (Teater, 2017, p.6).

Social work professionals, like those in other social and behavioral fields, are needed today to make a positive difference in people's lives given that economic, political, and socio-cultural challenges are more volatile than ever before. Social workers and other human service professionals can contribute to social change in many ways. These include through direct practice with individuals and families, organizational and community practice, teaching and research, and especially by engaging in community development initiatives to ensure economic well-being and social development to enhance human and behavioral well-being. To facilitate the overall development of society, there is a pressing need for problem-solving research that involves the direct and active participation of communities. Scholars have recommended the importance of participatory action research for social change and transformation (Altpeter, Schopler, Galinsky, & Pennell, 1999; Dhavaleshwar, 2016; Gray, O'Brian, & Mazibuku, 1996; Healy, 2001).

Social work engaged research can contribute to development, and social workers should be at the forefront of such community-engaged research endeavors across the world be it in socio-economically advanced nations or in countries where both economic and social development are in an emerging state. Social workers are agents of social change whose involvement in engaged research, particularly participatory action research, will enhance evidence-based practice at the individual, family, organizational, community, and society levels. By considering the benefit of engaged research to empower both researchers and community members, educators are encouraged to foster engaged research in order to promote development. Engaged research, by its very nature, encourages social workers and other human service professionals to pay as much attention to developmental social work rather than more traditional and remedial forms of practice. At present, countries in the global South face huge development issues, which are more complex than what is captured simply by economic growth. Social development encompasses issues of social, political, and human development, including human capital development, and engaged research can be a starting place to address these issues.

Engaged research can enhance the decision making and problem-solving power of the community and contribute to its empowerment, which is both a pre-requisite for and part and parcel of development processes. It is our hope that social work and human service educators, researchers, and practitioners will work together to promote engaged research. In this way, knowledge of contemporary issues and their potential remedies can be co-created with community groups who are experiencing those issues. It is incumbent for all social work schools and professionals in each country of the world to put into action the principles of engaged research, thereby contributing to the overall development agenda of their nation. Engaged research is premised on the necessity of researchers interacting with stakeholders, whether through virtual means or direct person-to-person involvement throughout the research process. Community-engaged research focuses on enabling a community, either geographic or a community of interest, to actively participate in the process of participatory action research. Community-engaged research benefits not only the community but also the academics who co-create the research idea, plan with and analyze findings with members of the community.

This book is beneficial for teaching postgraduate Master's and PhD students about engaged/participatory research and conducting community-partnered research. Chapters in this book can serve as specific guides for students to shape their scholarship areas including theses or PhD dissertation projects. The book also will serve social and other human service work practitioners in shaping their practice in community engagement through the co-creation of knowledge with community members.

References

Altpeter, M., Schopler, H.J., Galinsky, J.M., & Pennell, J. (1999). Participatory research as social work practice: When is it viable? *Journal of Progressive Human Services, 10(2),* 31-53.

Avila-Linn, Rice, K., & Akin, S. (2012). Designing community-based courses: A guide for instructors to develop community partnerships and create engaged public scholarship courses. Available at https://publicservice.berkeley.edu/sites/default/files/pdf/Faculty_Toolkit_brief_update_Nov_2015.pdf

Bahir Dar University, Research and Community Services (2014). Research thematic areas. Available at https://bdu.edu.et/sites/default/files/Themes.pdf

British Council (2018). Research and PhD capacities in Sub-Saharan Africa: Kenya report. Available at https://www.britishcouncil.org/sites/default/files/h233_02_south_africa_final_web.pdf

Butterfield, A.K, Kebede, W. & Gessesse, A. (2009). Research as a catalyst for asset-based community development: Assessing the skills of poor women in Ethiopia. *Social Development Issues, 31(2),* 1-14.

Debre Markos University (n.d). Research thematic areas. Available at http://www.dmu.edu.et/research-and-community-service/research/research-areas-thematic/

Dhavaleshwar, C.U. (2016). The role of social worker in community development. *International Research Journal of Social Sciences*, 5(10), 61-63.

Fenta, K., & Getachew, H. (2015). Community-based organizations and their role in empowering their members: experiences from Dire Dawa. *Developing Country Studies*, 5(1), 7-23.

Gray, M., O'Brian, F., & Mazibuku, F. (1996). Social work education for social development. *Journal of Social Development in Africa, 11(1),* 33.42.

Haromaya University. (2014, May). Haromaya University research thematic areas Office of the Vice President for Research Affairs. Available at http://www.haramaya.edu.et/wp-content/downloads/announcement/Research%20Thematic%20Areas%20Final%20Abrigded-2014.pdf

Healy, K. (2001). Participatory action research and social work. *International Social Work, 44*(1), 93-105.

Institute for Evaluations and Social Analyses (n.d). Evaluation of cross-cutting themes in the Czech International Development Cooperation. Retrieved from https://www.mzv.cz/file/2426640/Evaluation_of_crosscutting_themes_Operationalization.pdf

James, P. (n.d). Engaged research. Institute for Culture and Society. Sidney: Western Sidney University. Available at https://www.westernsydney.edu.au/__data/assets/pdf_file/0009/1149876/Engaged_Research.pdf

Jones, N., Tafere, Y., & Woldehanna, T. (2010, October). *Gender risk, poverty and vulnerability in Ethiopia: to what extent is the productive safety-net programme making a difference?* London: Overseas Development Institute. Retrieved from https://www.odi.org/sites/odi.org.uk/files/odi-assets/publications-opinion-files/6250.pdf.

Kebede, K. (2010). *Social networks and sexual practices: Applying social network analysis techniques to understand adolescent sexual experiences.* Germany: Lap Lambert Academic Publishing.

Kebede, W. & Butterfield, A.K, (2009). Social networks among poor women in Ethiopia. *International Social Work Journal, 52(3), 357-374.*

Kloos, H., Wuhib, T., Haile-Mariam, D. & Lindtjorn, B. (2003). Community-based organization in HIV/AIDS prevention, patient care and control in Ethiopia. *Ethiopian Journal of Health Development, 17(3), 3-31.* doi: 10.4314/ejhd.v17i4.9819,

McDonald, N.M. (n.d). Practicing community-engaged research. Available at https://www.mededportal.org/publication/1127/

Midgely, J. (2014). *Social development: Theory and practice.* Thousand Oaks: Sage.

Ministry of Education Canada. (2013). Students as researchers: Collaborative inquiry action-research toolkit. Available at http://www.edugains.ca/resourcesSV/StudentsAsInquirers/StudentsasResearchersToolkit/StAR_Toolkit.pdf

Miriti, G. (2009). *The Role of Community-Based Organizations in Transforming Peoples' Lives: A Case Study of Omega Child Shelter in Mwingi Central District.* (Master's thesis). University of Nairobi: East African Collection. Available at http://erepository.uonbi.ac.ke/bitstream/handle/11295/5112/Miriti_The%20role%20of%20Community%20Based%20Organisations.pdf?sequence=1

Monash University (2020). Monash University Research Agenda 2020. Available at: https://www.monash.edu/__data/assets/pdf_file/0008/1782044/monash-university-research-agenda.pdf

Nayak, K.B. (2014). Unemployment in Ethiopia: A call for an action. *International Journal of Management and Social Science Research, 3(4), 34-40.*

Patel, L. (2015). *Social welfare and social development.* (2nd Ed.). South Africa: Oxford University Press.

The Research Council of Norway (n.d). Roadmap for cooperation on research and education with China 2018-2020. Available at https://www.forskningsradet.no/contentassets/0aa5c0c035d3480d9c74afccf32939d8/chinaroadmapenglish.pdf

Scripps Translational Science Institute & Scripps Whittier Diabetes Institute (n.d). *Toolbox for conducting community engaged research.* Available from https://www.scripps.edu/ files/pdfs/science-medicine/translational-institute/community-engagement/training-and-tools/Community Engaged Research Toolbox.pdf

Stuer, F., Okello, O.F., Wube, M. & Steinitz, Y.L. (2012). From burial societies to mutual aid organizations: The role of Idirs-traditional burial societies in Ethiopia-in ensuring community-level care and protection of vulnerable children. *Journal of HIV/AIDs and Social Services, 11*(1), 57-76.

Teater, B. (2017). Social work research and its relevance to practice: The gap between research and practice continues to be wide. *Journal of Social Service Research, 43:5, 547-565.* Available at https://www.researchgate.net/publication/318638110 Social Work Research and Its Relevance to Practice The Gap Between Research and Practice Continues to be Wide

Young, J., & Shaxson, L. (2006). The research policy connection: Using research-based evidence to improve development policy, programs, and practice. Available at https://www.odi.org/sites/odi.org.uk/files/odi-assets/events-documents/2906.pdf

AN OVERVIEW OF THE METHODOLOGICAL APPROACH OF ACTION RESEARCH

O'Brien, R. (2001). Um exame da abordagem metodológica da pesquisa ação [An Overview of the Methodological Approach of Action Research]. In Roberto Richardson (Ed.), *Teoria e Prática da Pesquisa Ação [Theory and Practice of Action Research]*. João Pessoa, Brazil: Universidade Federal da Paraíba. (English version). Complete Report available at: http://www.web.ca/~robrien/papers/arfinal.html

Introduction

"If you want it done right, you may as well do it yourself." This aphorism may seem appropriate if you are a picky housekeeper, but more and more people are beginning to realize it can also apply to large corporations, community development projects, and even national governments. Such entities exist increasingly in an interdependent world and are relying on

Action Research as a means of coming to grips with their constantly changing and turbulent environments.

This paper will answer the question "What is Action Research?", giving an overview of its processes and principles, stating when it is appropriate to use, and situating it within a praxis research paradigm. The evolution of the approach will be described, including the various kinds of action research being used today. The role of the action researcher will be briefly mentioned, and some ethical considerations discussed. The tools of the action researcher, particularly that of the use of search conferences, will be explained.

What is Action Research?

Definition

Action research is known by many other names, including participatory research, collaborative inquiry, emancipatory research, action learning, and contextural action research, but all are variations on a theme. Put simply, action research is "learning by doing" - a group of people identify a problem, do something to resolve it, see how successful their efforts were, and if not satisfied, try again. While this is the essence of the approach, there are other key attributes of action research that differentiate it from common problem-solving activities that we all engage in every day. A more succinct definition is,

> "Action research...aims to contribute both to the practical concerns of people in an immediate problematic situation and to further the goals of social science simultaneously. Thus, there is a dual commitment in action research to study a system and concurrently to collaborate with members of the system in changing it in what is together regarded as a desirable direction. Accomplishing this twin goal requires the active collaboration of researcher

and client, and thus it stresses the importance of co-learning as a primary aspect of the research process."[1]

What separates this type of research from general professional practices, consulting, or daily problem-solving is the emphasis on scientific study, which is to say the researcher studies the problem systematically and ensures the intervention is informed by theoretical considerations. Much of the researcher's time is spent on refining the methodological tools to suit the exigencies of the situation, and on collecting, analyzing, and presenting data on an ongoing, cyclical basis.

Several attributes separate action research from other types of research. Primary is its focus on turning the people involved into researchers, too - people learn best, and more willingly apply what they have learned, when they do it themselves. It also has a social dimension - the research takes place in real-world situations and aims to solve real problems. Finally, the initiating researcher, unlike in other disciplines, makes no attempt to remain objective, but openly acknowledges their bias to the other participants.

The Action Research Process

Stephen Kemmis has developed a simple model of the cyclical nature of the typical action research process (Figure 1). Each cycle has four steps: plan, act, observe, reflect.

---

[1] Thomas Gilmore, Jim Krantz and Rafael Ramirez, "Action Based Modes of Inquiry and the Host-Researcher Relationship," Consultation 5.3 (Fall 1986): 161.

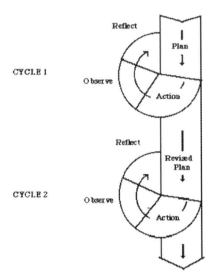

Figure 1 Simple Action Research Model (from MacIsaac, 1995) [2]

Gerald Susman (1983) gives a somewhat more elaborate listing. He distinguishes five phases to be conducted within each research cycle (Figure 2). Initially, a problem is identified, and data is collected for a more detailed diagnosis. This is followed by a collective postulation of several possible solutions, from which a single plan of action emerges and is implemented. Data on the results of the intervention are collected and analyzed, and the findings are interpreted in light of how successful the action has been. At this point, the problem is re-assessed, and the process begins another cycle. This process continues until the problem is resolved.

---

[2] Dan MacIsaac, "An Introduction to Action Research," 1995, http://www.phy.nau.edu/~danmac/actionrsch.html (22/03/1998).

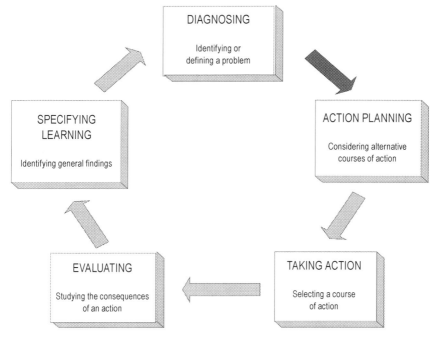

Figure 2 Detailed Action Research Model
(adapted from Susman 1983) [3]

Principles of Action Research

What gives action research its unique flavour is the set of principles that guide the research? Winter (1989) provides a comprehensive overview of six key principles.[4]

1. *Reflexive critique*
   An account of a situation, such as notes, transcripts or official documents, will make implicit claims to be authoritative, i.e., it implies that it is factual and

---

[3] Gerald I. Susman, "Action Research: A Sociotechnical Systems Perspective," ed. G. Morgan (London: Sage Publications, 1983) 102.

[4] Richard Winter, <u>Learning from Experience: Principles and Practice in Action-Research</u> (Philadelphia: The Falmer Press, 1989) 43-67.

true. Truth in a social setting, however, is relative to the teller. The principle of reflective critique ensures people reflect on issues and processes and make explicit the interpretations, biases, assumptions and concerns upon which judgments are made. In this way, practical accounts can give rise to theoretical considerations.

2. *Dialectical critique*
    Reality, particularly social reality, is consensually validated, which is to say it is shared through language. Phenomena are conceptualized in dialogue; therefore a dialectical critique is required to understand the set of relationships both between the phenomenon and its context, and between the elements constituting the phenomenon. The key elements to focus attention on are those constituent elements that are unstable, or in opposition to one another. These are the ones that are most likely to create changes.

3. *Collaborative Resource*
    Participants in an action research project are co-researchers. The principle of collaborative resource presupposes that each person's ideas are equally significant as potential resources for creating interpretive categories of analysis, negotiated among the participants. It strives to avoid the skewing of credibility stemming from the prior status of an idea-holder. It especially makes possible the insights gleaned from noting the contradictions both between many viewpoints and within a single viewpoint

4. *Risk*
    The change process potentially threatens all previously established ways of doing things, thus creating psychic

fears among the practitioners. One of the more prominent fears comes from the risk to ego stemming from open discussion of one's interpretations, ideas, and judgments. Initiators of action research will use this principle to allay others' fears and invite participation by pointing out that they, too, will be subject to the same process, and that whatever the outcome, learning will take place.

5. *Plural Structure*

The nature of the research embodies a multiplicity of views, commentaries and critiques, leading to multiple possible actions and interpretations. This plural structure of inquiry requires a plural text for reporting. This means that there will be many accounts made explicit, with commentaries on their contradictions, and a range of options for action presented. A report, therefore, acts as a support for ongoing discussion among collaborators, rather than a final conclusion of fact.

6. *Theory, Practice, Transformation*

For action researchers, theory informs practice, practice refines theory, in a continuous transformation. In any setting, people's actions are based on implicitly held assumptions, theories and hypotheses, and with every observed result, theoretical knowledge is enhanced. The two are intertwined aspects of a single change process. It is up to the researchers to make explicit the theoretical justifications for the actions, and to question the bases of those justifications. The ensuing practical applications that follow are subjected to further analysis, in a transformative cycle that continuously alternates emphasis between theory and practice.

When to Use Action Research

Action research is used in real situations, rather than in contrived, experimental studies, since its primary focus is on solving real problems. It can, however, be used by social scientists for preliminary or pilot research, especially when the situation is too ambiguous to frame a precise research question. Mostly, though, in accordance with its principles, it is chosen when circumstances require flexibility, the involvement of the people in the research, or change must take place quickly or holistically.

It is often the case that those who apply this approach are practitioners who wish to improve understanding of their practice, social change activists trying to mount an action campaign, or, more likely, academics who have been invited into an organization (or other domain) by decision-makers aware of a problem requiring action research, but lacking the requisite methodological knowledge to deal with it.

Situating Action Research in a Research Paradigm

Positivist Paradigm

The main research paradigm for the past several centuries has been that of Logical Positivism. This paradigm is based on a number of principles, including: a belief in an objective reality, knowledge of which is only gained from sense data that can be directly experienced and verified between independent observers. Phenomena are subject to natural laws that humans discover in a logical manner through empirical testing, using inductive and deductive hypotheses derived from a body of scientific theory. Its methods rely heavily on quantitative measures, with relationships among variables commonly shown by mathematical means. Positivism, used in scientific and applied research, has been considered by many to be the antithesis of the principles of action research (Susman and Evered 1978, Winter 1989).

Interpretive Paradigm

Over the last half century, a new research paradigm has emerged in the social sciences to break out of the constraints imposed by positivism. With its emphasis on the relationship between socially-engendered concept formation and language, it can be referred to as the Interpretive paradigm. Containing such qualitative methodological approaches as phenomenology, ethnography, and hermeneutics, it is characterized by a belief in a socially constructed, subjectively-based reality, one that is influenced by culture and history. Nonetheless it still retains the ideals of researcher objectivity, and researcher as passive collector and expert interpreter of data.

Paradigm of Praxis

Though sharing a number of perspectives with the interpretive paradigm, and making considerable use of its related qualitative methodologies, there are some researchers who feel that neither it nor the positivist paradigms are sufficient epistemological structures under which to place action research (Lather 1986, Morley 1991). Rather, a paradigm of Praxis is seen as where the main affinities lie. Praxis, a term used by Aristotle, is the art of acting upon the conditions one faces in order to change them. It deals with the disciplines and activities predominant in the ethical and political lives of people. Aristotle contrasted this with Theoria - those sciences and activities that are concerned with knowing for its own sake. Both are equally needed he thought. That knowledge is derived from practice, and practice informed by knowledge, in an ongoing process, is a cornerstone of action research. Action researchers also reject the notion of researcher neutrality, understanding that the most active researcher is often one who has most at stake in resolving a problematic situation.

Evolution of Action Research

Origins in late 1940s

Kurt Lewin is generally considered the 'father' of action research. A German social and experimental psychologist, and one of the founders of the Gestalt school, he was concerned with social problems, and focused on participative group processes for addressing conflict, crises, and change, generally within organizations. Initially, he was associated with the Center for Group Dynamics at MIT in Boston, but soon went on to establish his own National Training Laboratories.

Lewin first coined the term 'action research' in his 1946 paper "Action Research and Minority Problems",[5] characterizing Action Research as "a comparative research on the conditions and effects of various forms of social action and research leading to social action", using a process of "a spiral of steps, each of which is composed of a circle of planning, action, and fact-finding about the result of the action".

Eric Trist, another major contributor to the field from that immediate post-war era, was a social psychiatrist whose group at the Tavistock Institute of Human Relations in London engaged in applied social research, initially for the civil repatriation of German prisoners of war. He and his colleagues tended to focus more on large-scale, multi-organizational problems.

Both Lewin and Trist applied their research to systemic change in and between organizations. They emphasized direct professional - client collaboration and affirmed the role of group relations as basis for problem-solving. Both were avid proponents of the principle that decisions are best implemented by those who help make them.

---

[5] Kurt Lewin, "Action Research and Minority Problems," Journal of Social Issues 2 (1946): 34-46.

Current Types of Action Research

By the mid-1970s, the field had evolved, revealing 4 main 'streams' that had emerged: traditional, contextural (action learning), radical, and educational action research.

Traditional Action Research

Traditional Action Research stemmed from Lewin's work within organizations and encompasses the concepts and practices of Field Theory, Group Dynamics, T-Groups, and the Clinical Model. The growing importance of labour-management relations led to the application of action research in the areas of Organization Development, Quality of Working Life (QWL), Socio-technical systems (e.g., Information Systems), and Organizational Democracy. This traditional approach tends toward the conservative, generally maintaining the status quo with regards to organizational power structures.

Contextural Action Research (Action Learning)

Contextural Action Research, also sometimes referred to as Action Learning, is an approach derived from Trist's work on relations between organizations. It is contextural, insofar as it entails reconstituting the structural relations among actors in a social environment; domain-based, in that it tries to involve all affected parties and stakeholders; holographic, as each participant understands the working of the whole; and it stresses that participants act as project designers and co-researchers. The concept of organizational ecology, and the use of search conferences come out of contextural action research, which is more of a liberal philosophy, with social transformation occurring by consensus and normative incrementalism.

Radical Action Research

The Radical stream, which has its roots in Marxian 'dialectical materialism' and the praxis orientations of Antonio Gramsci, has a strong focus on emancipation and the overcoming of power imbalances. Participatory Action Research, often found in liberationist movements and international development circles, and Feminist Action Research both strive for social transformation via an advocacy process to strengthen peripheral groups in society.

Educational Action Research

A fourth stream, that of Educational Action Research, has its foundations in the writings of Thomas Dewey, the great American educational philosopher of the 1920s and 30s, who believed that professional educators should become involved in community problem-solving. Its practitioners, not surprisingly, operate mainly out of educational institutions, and focus on development of curriculum, professional development, and applying learning in a social context. It is often the case that university-based action researchers work with primary and secondary school teachers and students on community projects.

Action Research Tools

Action Research is more of a holistic approach to problem-solving, rather than a single method for collecting and analyzing data. Thus, it allows for several different research tools to be used as the project is conducted. These various methods, which are generally common to the qualitative research paradigm, include: keeping a research journal, document collection and analysis, participant observation recordings, questionnaire surveys, structured and unstructured interviews, and case studies.

The Search Conference

Of all of the tools utilized by action researchers, the one that has been developed exclusively to suit the needs of the action research approach is that of the search conference, initially developed by Eric Trist and Fred Emery at the Tavistock Institute in 1959, and first implemented for the merger of Bristol-Siddley Aircraft Engines in 1960.

The search conference format has seen widespread development since that time, with variations on Trist and Emery's theme becoming known under other names due to their promotion by individual academics and consultants. These include Dannemiller-Tyson's Interactive Strategic Planning, Marvin Weisbord's Future Search Conference, Dick Axelrod's Conference Model Redesign, Harrison Owen's Open Space, and ICA's Strategic Planning (Rouda 1995).

Search conferences also have been conducted for many different circumstances and participants, including: decision-makers from several countries visioning the "Future of Participative Democracy in the Americas"; [6] practitioners and policymakers in the field of health promotion in Ontario taking charge in an era of cutbacks;[7] and Xerox employees sorting out enterprise re-organization. [8]

Eric Trist sums up the process quite nicely -

> "Searching...is carried out in groups which are composed of the relevant stakeholders. The group meets under social island conditions for 2-3 days, sometimes as long as five. The opening sessions are concerned with elucidating the factors operating in the wider contextual environment - those producing the meta-problems and

---

[6] IIRM, "International Institute for Natural, Environmental & Cultural Resources Management," 26/08 1997, http://www.nmsu.edu/~iirm/ (24/03/1998).

[7] Ontario Prevention Clearinghouse, "Our Communities in a Global Economy: Under Siege and Taking Charge!" 03/06 1996, http://www.opc.on.ca/events/congressvii/index.html (22/3/1998).

[8] Ronald E. Purser and Steven Cabana, "Mobilizing Large-Scale Strategic Change: An Application of the Search Conference Method at Xerox," 19/10 1996, http://www2.wi.net/~rpurser/qualp.txt (12/04/1998).

likely to affect the future. The content is contributed entirely by the members. The staff are facilitators only. Items are listed in the first instance without criticism in the plenary session and displayed on flip charts which surround the room. The material is discussed in greater depth in small groups and the composite picture checked out in plenary. The group next examines its own organizational setting or settings against this wider background and then proceeds to construct a picture of a desirable future. It is surprising how much agreement there often is. Only when all this has been done is consideration given to action steps..."[9]

Figure 3 provides a schematic of a typical search conference.

Pre-conference process	• set up Advisory Group of local representatives • agree on process design and participants • use focus groups for preparation • invitations, distribution of introductory materials
Introductory plenary	introductions, review objectives, outline process, introduce first stage
Small group session 1	SCANNING THE ISSUE • past and present context • assess current situation • outline probable futures
Presentation plenary	reports from small groups, discuss directions, introduce second stage
Small group session 2	DESIRED FUTURES • long-range visions • alternative / preferred futures
Presentation plenary	reports, review progress, introduction to third stage
Small group session 3	OPTIONS FOR CHANGE • constraints and opportunities • possible futures

---

[9] Eric Trist, "Referent Organizations and the Development of Inter-Organizational Domains," 39th Annual Convention of the Academy of Management (Atlanta, 9/8, 1979) 23-24.

Presentation plenary	reports, define strategic tasks / actions, select key tasks, form task groups
Task Group sessions	TASK GROUP MEETINGS
Final plenary	Task Group reports, discuss future contacts, create new Advisory Group
Post-conference process	• report distributed • follow-up contacts • Advisory Group facilitates meetings of Task Groups • feedback on proposed actions • further search conferences • widen network • continuing evaluation of outcomes

Figure 3 - Search Conference
(adapted from The ABL Group, 1997)[10]

Role of the Action Researcher

Upon invitation into a domain, the outside researcher's role is to implement the Action Research method in such a manner as to produce a mutually agreeable outcome for all participants, with the process being maintained by them afterwards. To accomplish this, it may necessitate the adoption of many different roles at various stages of the process, including those of

planner	leader
catalyzer	facilitator
teacher	designer
listener	observer
synthesizer	reporter

The main role, however, is to nurture local leaders to the point where they can take responsibility for the process. This point is reached they understand the methods and are able to carry on when the initiating researcher leaves.

In many Action Research situations, the hired researcher's role is

---

[10] ABL Group, <u>Future Search Process Design</u> (Toronto: York University, 1997).

primarily to take the time to facilitate dialogue and foster reflective analysis among the participants, provide them with periodic reports, and write a final report when the researcher's involvement has ended.

Ethical Considerations

Because action research is carried out in real-world circumstances and involves close and open communication among the people involved, the researchers must pay close attention to ethical considerations in the conduct of their work. Richard Winter (1996) lists a number of principles:

- "Make sure that the relevant persons, committees and authorities have been consulted, and that the principles guiding the work are accepted in advance by all.
- All participants must be allowed to influence the work, and the wishes of those who do not wish to participate must be respected.
- The development of the work must remain visible and open to suggestions from others.
- Permission must be obtained before making observations or examining documents produced for other purposes.
- Descriptions of others' work and points of view must be negotiated with those concerned before being published.
- The researcher must accept responsibility for maintaining confidentiality."[11]

To this might be added several more points:

- Decisions made about the direction of the research and the probable outcomes are collective

---

[11] Richard Winter, "Some Principles and Procedures for the Conduct of Action Research," in New Directions in Action Research, ed. Ortrun Zuber-Skerritt (London: Falmer Press, 1996) 16-17.

- Researchers are explicit about the nature of the research process from the beginning, including all personal biases and interests
- There is equal access to information generated by the process for all participants
- The outside researcher and the initial design team must create a process that maximizes the opportunities for involvement of all participants.

Conclusion

This paper has presented an overview of action research as a methodological approach to solving social problems. The principles and procedures of this type of research, and epistemological underpinnings, were described, along with the evolution of the practice. Details of a search conference and other tools were given, as was an indication of the roles and ethics involved in the research.

SAMPLE ACTION RESEARCH SYLLABI

School of Social Work
Addis Ababa University

SWPH 701 Action Research & Models of Social Change

This course focuses on the distinctive nature of action research and practice models of social change in social work and social development. The course critically examines the purposes, context, procedures, and relationships within action-oriented research methodologies, including ethical issues, participatory data collection and analysis. Students will learn to examine action research from the standpoint of utility, feasibility, propriety, and rigor/accuracy. Emphasis is placed on advanced models of social change that build upon the assets and strengths of local communities through participatory, self-help, social network, and empowerment-based approaches. The course covers models of university-community engagement and interdisciplinary community development. Students will design and implement an individual action relevant to the social work and social development challenges faced by Ethiopia.

EDUCATIONAL OBJECTIVES

This course will provide students with the opportunity to:

1. Understand the role that action research can play in the development of knowledge for use in practice, policy, and research
2. Critically assess the various models, methods, and research designs of action research and community-based participatory research
3. Become familiar with advanced models and methods of social development
4. Understand the essential elements of building community capacity through asset-based, family-based, strengths-based, and capabilities approaches
5. Develop a perspective on university-community partnerships through teaching, service, and engaged research
6. Apply action research methods to a social work and social development challenge in Ethiopia

WRITING

Writing is a crucial component of policy work. In this course, you will be expected to produce professionally written products that demonstrate systematic and critical thinking, are well organized, respect rules of grammar, spelling, punctuation, and the use of nonsexist language. APA Version 6.0

COURSE ASSIGNMENTS

Assignment	Due	% of Grade
Class Participation		10
Action Research Proposal for review by		
Annotated Bibliography		20

Action Research Proposal Due		30
Final Paper		40
Total		100%

Class Participation (10%): Class participation emphasizes its importance in the learning process. Excellence in class participation includes the following:

- Regular attendance;
- Reading course materials;
- Compiling <u>summary notes of course readings for review by the instructor</u>;
- <u>Active participation</u> in asking questions, offering insights, and discussing issues.

Action Research Proposal (20%). Students will select one community group or an organization, which is undergoing a change process in Ethiopia. Students will select one model of social change (social development, asset-based community development, the capabilities approach, university-community partnerships, community-based participatory research, diffusion of innovations, family-based development, organizational networking, etc.) and prepare a rigorous action research project that is based on active engagement in the real activities of the community or organization under focus. The proposal should contain a review of the relevant literature related to action research and the substantive area of study. Guidelines for an action research proposal will be handed out in class.

Annotated Bibliography with Presentation (30%). Develop an annotated bibliography focusing on one or more of the following models of social change that are relevant for the "scholarship of engagement" in higher education: Higher education partnerships, Service Learning, and university-community partnerships. As part of your annotated bibliography, describe the process that you followed in carrying out the literature review. Prepare to make a brief presentation of your findings to the class.

Final Paper (40%). Students will prepare a final paper on their action research based on findings from the field. The paper should include: 1) an expanded literature review of at least 2 books, 10 refereed journal articles and government/organizational documents that support and/or contradict the findings from the field related to the selected model of social change and the substantive area of research; 2) a critical analysis of the methods and findings from the field, 3) a clearly stipulated process of the action research (level of participants' engagement and vice versa, etc). In general, the paper should be approximately 20-22 pages long, not including references, tables, and figures. Paper, references, and in-text citations should be formatted correctly according to the guidelines of the American Psychological Association (APA) version 5.0 or the referencing format required by the journal selected for publication. Submit a copy of the "Guide to Authors" from the selected journal with the final paper.

GUIDELINES FOR SCHOLARLY WORK

All students will be held accountable for adhering to academic and nonacademic standards of conduct. Plagiarism is academic dishonesty. A non-exclusive list of examples of plagiarism includes: 1) presenting work done for another class as original work; 2) failing to cite and reference previous papers that you have written, 3) failing to cite and reference other authors' works that have contributed to your paper in any way, and 4) failing to cite, reference and identify quotes and material directly taken from another work. In submitting a paper or a class project, the student warrants and affirms the following:

1. That the work presented is an original piece of research/scholarship/creativity done entirely by the listed author(s).
2. That the entire work, or a substantial portion thereof, is not copied or directly paraphrased from the published work of another author.
3. That all direct quotations, direct paraphrases, empirical research finding, and other suitable restatements of the research,

scholarship, or creative work of others is appropriately referenced with APA 5.0 citation methods.

4. That the work in question was prepared especially for the class assignment for which it is submitted, has not been submitted previously, and will not be submitted later in substantially its present form.

5. That in those instances when a similar or identical topic, theme, issue, population, problem or method is examined in the course assignments for two or more courses, the written consent or approval of both instructors has been obtained before the assignment is turned in. The instructor is under no obligation to provide their consent.

6. That appropriate credit is provided, in a footnote, for assistance provided by faculty, other students, etc. in preparing the paper.

7. That no part of the assignment was prepared by a commercial or nonprofit term paper preparation service or any web-based service, including papers from other students at any university or institution of higher education.

8. That the student has read or examined all sources cited and has personal knowledge that the quotations and findings attributed to those sources in the student's work are substantially correct.

COURSE TOPICS

Session 1: Overview of the Course

Bradbury Huang, H. (2010). What is good action research? Why the resurgent interest? *Action Research*, *8*(1), 91-109.

Bradbury, H., & Reason, H. (2003). Action research: An opportunity for revitalizing research purpose and practice. *Qualitative Social Work*, *2*(2), 155-175.

Session 2: ACTION RESEARCH -- Part I: Groundings

Boog, B.W.M. (2003). The emancipatory character of action research, its history and the present state of the art. *Journal of Community and Applied Social Psychology, 13*, 426-438.

Braun, K. L., Nguyen, T. T., Tanjasiri, S. P., Campbell, J., Heiney, S. P., Brandt, H. M., et al. (2012). Operationalization of community-based participatory research principles: Assessment of the National Cancer Institute's Community Network programs. *American Journal of Public Health, 102*(6), 1195–1203.

Macaulay, A.C., Jagosh, J., Seller, R., Henderson, J., Cargo, M., Greenhalgh, T., Wong, G., Salsberg, J., Green, L.W., Herbert, C.P., Pluye, P. (2011). Assessing the benefits of participatory research: A rationale for a realist review. *Global Health Promotion, 18*(2): 45–48.

Roberts, G., & Dick, B. (2003). Emancipatory design choices for action research practitioners. *Journal of Community and Applied Social Psychology, 13*, 486-495.

Session 3: ACTION RESEARCH -- Part II. Practices

Blitz, L. V., Kida, L., Gresham, M., & Bronstein, L. R. (2013). Prevention through collaboration: Family engagement with rural schools and families living in poverty. *Families in Society*, 94(3), 157-165.

Ferrera, M.J. (2017). Integrating principles of positive minority youth development with health promotion to empower the immigrant community: A case study in Chicago. *Journal of Community Practice*, 25(3-4), 504-523.

Freire, P. (1998). Cultural action and conscientization; The adult literacy process as cultural action for freedom. *Harvard Educational Review, 68*(4), 471-521. Reprinted.

Gehlert, S. & Coleman, R. (2010). Using community-based participatory research to ameliorate cancer disparities. *Health and Social Work, 35 (4),* 302-309

Grant, S. & Humphries, M. (2006). Critical evaluation of appreciative inquiry: Bridging an apparent paradox. *Action Research, 4*(4), 401-418.

Rhodes, S. D., Kelley, C., Simán, F., Cashman, R., Alonzo, J., McGuire, J. Reboussin, B. (2012). Using community-based participatory research (CBPR) to develop a community-level HIV prevention intervention for Latinas: A local response to a global challenge. *Women's Health Issues, 22*(3), e293-e301. doi: http://dx.doi.org/10.1016/j.whi.2012.02.002.

Session 4: ACTION RESEARCH -- Part IV: Skills

Maglajlie, R.A., & Tiffany, J. (2006). Participatory action research with youth in Bosnia and Herzegovina. *Journal of Community Practice, 14*(1/2), 163-181.

O'Brien, R. (2001). Um exame da abordagem metodológica da pesquisa ação [An Overview of the Methodological Approach of Action Research]. In Roberto Richardson (Ed.), *Teoria e Prática da Pesquisa Ação [Theory and Practice of Action Research].* João Pessoa, Brazil: Universidade Federal da Paraíba. (English version). Available at: http://www.web.ca/~robrien/papers/arfinal.html

Suleiman, A.B., Soleimanpour, S., & London, J. (2006). Youth action for health through youth-led research. *Journal of Community Practice, 14*(1/2), 125-145.

Wang, C. (2006). Youth participation in Photovoice as a strategy for community change. *Journal of Community Practice, 14*(1/2), 147-161.

Session 5: DIFFUSION OF INNOVATIONS

Assie-Lumumba, N.T. (2004). Sustaining home-grown innovations in higher education in Sub-Saharan Africa: A critical reflection. *Journal of International Cooperation in Education, 7*(1), 71-83.

Dearing, J.W. (2009). Applying diffusion of innovation theory to intervention development. *Research on Social Work Practice, 19*(5), 503-518.

Greenhalgh, T., Robert, G., MacFarlane, F., Bate, P., & Kyriakidou, O. (2004). Diffusion of innovations in service organizations: Systematic review and recommendations. *The Milbank Quarterly, 82*(4), 581-629.

Kebede, W., & Belay, S. (2017). The nexus between culture, indigenous knowledge and development in Ethiopia: Review of existing literature. *Global Journal of Human-Social Science: Sociology & Culture, 17*(4), 1-9.

Kerner, J.F., & Hall, K.L. (2009). Research dissemination and diffusion: Translation within science and society, *Research on Social Work Practice, 19*(5), 519-530.

Weir, S., & Knight, J. (2004). Externality effects of education: Dynamics of the adoption and diffusion of an innovation in rural Ethiopia. *Economic Development and Cultural Change, 53*(1), 93-113.

Session 6: SOCIAL NETWORKS

Ayuku, D.O., Kaplan, C., Baars, H., & de Vries, M. (2004). Characteristics and personal social networks of the on-the-street, shelter and school children in Eldoret, Kenya. *International Social Work, 47*(3), 293-311.

Kebede, W. (2009). *Adolescent Social Networks and Sexual Practices* (PhD Dissertation).

Kebede, W., & Butterfield, A.K. (2009). Social networks among poor women in Ethiopia. *International Social Work Journal, 52*(3), 357-374.

Murdoch, J. (2000). Networks—a new paradigm of rural development? *Journal of Rural Studies, 16,* 407-419.

Serneels, P. (2007). The nature of unemployment among young men in urban Ethiopia. *Review of Development Economics, 11*(1), 170-186.

Session 7: SOCIAL DEVELOPMENT

Gray, M. (2006). The progress of social development in South Africa. *International Journal of Social Welfare, 15* (Suppl. 1), S53-S64.

Green, S., & Nieman, A. (2003). Social development: Good practice guidelines. *Social Work/Maatskaplike Werk, 39*(2), 161-181.

Mequanent, G. (1998). Community development and the role of community organizations: A study in northern Ethiopia. *Canadian Journal of African Studies, 32*(3), 494-520.

Mequanent, G., & Fraser, T. (2007). The Big-Push approach to African development and local capacity building: Understanding the issues. *Canadian Journal of Development Studies, 28*(1), 9-26.

Pawar, M. (2014). Social work practice with local communities in developing countries: Imperatives for political engagement. *Sage Open*, 1-11.

Simeon, A., Butterfield, A.K., & Moxley, D.P. (2019). Locality-based social development: A theoretical perspective for social work. In M. Payne & E.R. Hall (Eds.), *Routledge Handbook of Social Work Theory* (pp. 294-307). Oxford: Routledge.

Session 8: SOCIAL DEVELOPMENT

Cronje, F., & Chenga, C.S. (2009). Sustainable social development in the South African mining sector. *Development Southern Africa, 26*(3), 413-427.

Kassahun, S. (2011). The urban poor and their willingness to participate in community development: The case study of Addis Ababa. *Easter Africa Social Science Review, 27*(1), 67-84.

Lyons, M., Smuts, C., & Stephans, A. (2000). Participation, empowerment and sustainability: (How) Do the links work? *Urban Studies, 38*(8), 1233-1251.

Patel, L., Kaseke, E., & Midgley, J. (2013). Indigenous welfare and community-based social development:

Lessons from African innovations. *Journal of Community Practice*, *20*(1-2), 12-31.

Teshome, E., Zenebe, M., Metaferia, H., & Biadgilign, S. (2014). Participation and significance of self-help groups for social development: Exploring the community capacity of Ethiopia. *SpringerPlus, 3*, 189.

Tonegawa, Y. (2014). Working for whose benefit? An analysis of local development NGOs in relation to the communities in Ethiopia. *Southern African Review of Education*, *20*(1), 7-29.

Session 9: CONSULTATION ON ACTION RESEARCH PROPOSALS

Session 10: CONSULTATION ON ACTION RESEARCH PROPOSALS

Session 11: COMMUNITY DEVELOPMENT

Bhattacharyya, J. (2011). Theorizing community development. *Community Development Society Journal, 34*(2), 5-34.

Butterfield, A.K., & Chisanga, B. (2008). Community development. In T. Mizrahi & L. Davis (Eds.). *Encyclopedia of Social Work, Volume I* (pp. 375-381). New York: Oxford University Press.

Ersing, R.L., Loeffler, D.N., Tracy, M.B., & Onu, L. (2007). Pentru Voi Fundatia: Interdisciplinary community development using social enterprise in Romania. *Journal of Community* Practice, *15*(1/2), 193-215.

Johnson Butterfield, A.K., & Korazim-Kőrösy, Y. (2007). Interdisciplinary community development: Setting the future course. *Journal of Community Practice, 15*(1/2), 239-245.

Karger, H., Iyiani, C., & Shannon, P. (2007). The challenge of community work in a global economy. *Journal of Sociology & Social Welfare, XXXIV*(2), 69-85.

Korazim-Kőrösy, Y., Mizrahi, T., Katz, C., Karmon, A., Garcia, M.L., & Smith, M.B. (2007). Towards interdisciplinary community collaboration and development: Knowledge and experience from Israel and the USA. *Journal of Community Practice, 15*(1/2), 13-44.

Session 12: ASSET-BASED COMMUNITY DEVELOPMENT

Butterfield, A.K., Kebede, W., & Gessesse, A. (2009). Research as a catalyst for asset-based community development: Assessing the skills of poor women in Ethiopia. *Social Development Issues, 31*(2), 1-14.

Butterfield, A.K., Yeneabat, M., & Moxley, D. (2016). 'Now I know my ABCDs': Asset Based Community Development with Ethiopian primary school children. *Children & Schools, 38*(4), 199-207. doi: 10.1093/cs/cdw031

Cunningham, G. (2008). Stimulating asset based development: Lessons from five communities in Ethiopia. In A. Mathie & G. Cunningham, G. (Eds.). *From clients to citizens: Communities changing the course of their own development* (pp. 263-289). Warwickshire, UK: Practical Action Publishers.

Mathie, A., & Cunningham, G. (2003). From clients to citizens: Asset-based development as a strategy for community-driven development. *Development in Practice, 13*(5), 474-486.

O'Leary, T. (2007). *Asset Based Approaches to Rural Community Development: Literature Review and Resources.* Scotland: International Association for Community Development for the Carnegie Trust UK. Available at: https://resources.depaul.edu/abcd-institute/publications/publications-by-topic/Documents/ABCD-IACDGlobal.pdf

Yeneabat, M., & Butterfield, A.K. (2012). 'We Can't Eat a Road': Asset Based Community Development and The Gedam Sefer Community Partnership in Ethiopia. *Journal of Community Practice, 20*(1/2), 134-153.

Session 13 COMMUNITY CONVERSATION

Ibrahima, A.B., & Mattaini, M.A. (2019). Social work in Africa: Decolonizing methodologies and approaches. *International Social Work, 62*(2), 799-813.

Tekletsadik, E., Fantahun, M., & Shaweno, D. (2014). Is community conversation associated with Human Immunodeficiency Virus voluntary counseling and testing service uptake in rural communities in Ethiopia? A comparative cross-sectional study. *North American Journal of Medical Sciences, 6*(2), 77-83. Available at: https://www.ncbi.nlm.nih.gov/pmc/articles/PMC3968569/

Gebre, A., & Admassie, Y. (2005, December). *HIV/ AIDS Community Conversations pilot projects in Alaba and Yabello: Assessment of the methodology.* Addis Ababa: UNDP Ethiopia.

Session 14 CONCEPT MAPPING

Butterfield, A.K., Tafesse, M., & Moxley, D. (2016). International Higher Education Partnerships: Concept mapping of the processes and outcomes of USAID funded projects in Ethiopia. *Social Development Issues, 38*(2), 47-67.

Petrucci, C.J., & Quinlan, K. (2007). Bridging the research-practice gap: Concept mapping as a mixed-methods strategy in practice-based research and evaluation. *Journal of Social Service Research, 34*(2), 25-42.

Ridings, J.W., Powell, D.M., & Johnson, J.E., et al. (2008). Using concept mapping to promote community building: The African American Initiative at Roseland. *Journal of Community Practice, 16*(1), 39-63.

Trochim, W.M.K. (1989). An introduction to concept mapping for planning and evaluation. *Evaluation and Program Planning, 12*, 1-16.

Session 15 SERVICE LEARNING

Golombek, S.B. (2006). Children as citizens. *Journal of Community Practice, 14*(1/2), 11-30.

Moxley, D. (2004). Engaged research in higher education and civic responsibility reconsidered: A reflective essay. *Journal of Community* Practice, *12*(3/4), 235-242.

These web resources provide a wealth of information and articles on service learning. Explore these websites and prepare an annotated bibliography of 10 articles and resources of good service-learning writings.

1. The National Service Learning Clearinghouse, which is part of the Corporation for National and Community Service, has some of the best definitions and overviews at: http://www.servicelearning.org
2. Campus Compact, the national organization for university community engagement, which again has great service learning resources and tools at: http://www.compact.org
3. The International Association for Research in Service Learning and Community Engagement, which is not so much a resource as an international organization to show them that this is an accepted international teaching and research focus: http://www.researchslce.org
4. The Carnegie Foundation for the Advancement of Teaching's new option community engagement classification, which has both an outreach and/or a curricular option. The curriculum is very much tied to service learning in higher education at: https://carnegieclassifications.iu.edu/

Session 16 HIGHER EDUCATION PARTNERSHIPS

Development of MSW and PhD Programs in Social Work & Social Development

Abye, T., & Butterfield, A.K. (2012). Can Africa learn from Africa? Can the world learn from Africa? Journal of Community Practice, 20(1-2), 3-11.

Butterfield, A.K., & Abye, T. (2012). Learning from Africa: Publication and research. Journal of Community Practice, 20(1/2), 211-217.

Johnson Butterfield, A.K. (2007). The internationalization of doctoral social work education: Learning from a partnership in Ethiopia. *Advances in Social Work*, 8(2), 1-15.

Johnson Butterfield, A.K., Tasse, A., & Linsk, N. (2009). The Social Work Education in Ethiopia Partnership. In C.E. Stout (Ed.), *The New Humanitarians: Inspiration, Innovations, and Blueprints for Visionaries*, Volume 2 (pp. 57-83). Westport, CT: Praeger.

Boyer, E. L. (1996). The scholarship of engagement. *Journal of Public Service & Outreach, 1*, 11-20.

Cox, D. N., (2000) Developing a framework for understanding university-community partnerships. *Cityscape: A Journal of Policy Development and Research,* 5(1), 9 – 25. http://www.community-wealth.org/_pdfs/ articles-publications/universities/article-cox.pdf

Pugh, M.B., & Spear, M.H. (2006). Can higher education partnerships teach a person to fish? *Journal of International Cooperation in Education*, 8(1), 45-69.

Sewpaul, V. (2003). Broadening horizons through international exchanges: Global and local discourses in the development of critical consciousness. In L. Dominelli and W.T. Bernard (Eds.), *Broadening horizons: International exchanges in social work* (pp. 297-232). Hampshire, England: Ashgate Publishing Company.

For Further Reading:

Cottrell, B., & Parpart, J.L. (2006). Academic-community collaboration: Gender, research, and development: Pitfalls and possibilities. *Development in Practice, 16*(1), 15-26.

Fisher, R., Fabricant, M., & Simmons, L. (2004). Understanding contemporary university-community connections: Context, practice, and challenges. *Journal of Community* Practice, *12*(3/4), 13-34.

Koehn, P.H., Demment, M.W., & Hervy, A. (2008). Enhancing higher education's engagement in international development. *Journal of the World Universities Forum, 1*(6), 127-139. [Includes higher education partnerships in Ethiopia].

Sifuna, D.N. (2000). Partnerships in educational assistance to African countries: Rhetoric or reality? *Journal of International Cooperation in Education, 3*(2), 3-21.

ADDITIONAL BOOKS ON THE COURSE TOPICS

Chaskin, R.J., Brown, P., Venkatesh, S., & Vidal, A. (2001). *Building community capacity.* NY: Aldine De Gruyter.

Checkoway, B.N., & Gutierrez, L.M. (Eds.). (2006). *Youth participation and community change.* Binghamton, NY: The Haworth Press.

Chibucos, T.R., & Lerner, R.M. (Eds.). (1999). *Serving children and families through community-university partnerships: Success stories.* Norwell, MA: Kluwer Academic Publishers.

Coghlan, D. (2005). *Doing action research in your own organization* (2nd Edition). Thousand Oaks, CA: Sage Publications.

Dubb, S. (2007, August). *Linking colleges to communities.* College Park, MD: The Democracy Collaborative at the University of Maryland. Retrieved October

27, 2009 from http://www.community-wealth.org/ pdfs/news/recent-articles/07-07/report-linking.pdf

Gladwell, M. (2000). *The tipping point: How little things can make a big difference.* Great Britain: Little, Brown, and Company.

Gladwell, M. (2008). *The outliers: The story of success.* New York: Penguin Group.

Green, G.P., & Haines, A. (2001). *Asset-building and community development.* Thousand Oaks, CA: Sage Publications.

Herr, K., & Anderson, G.L. (2005). *The action research dissertation: A guide for students and faculty.* Thousand Oaks, CA: Sage Publications.

Johnson Butterfield, A.K., & Korazim-Korosy, Y. (Eds.). (2007). *Interdisciplinary Community Development: International Perspectives.* Binghamton, NY: The Haworth Press, Inc.

Kane, M., & Trochim, W. M. K. (2007). *Concept mapping for planning and evaluation.* Thousand Oaks, CA: Sage.

Kretzmann, J.P., & McKnight, J.J. (1993). *Building communities from the inside out: A path toward finding and mobilizing a community's assets.* Chicago: ACTA Publications. (Book and DVD series).

Minkler, M., & Wallerstein, N. (Eds.). (2008). *Community-based participatory research for health: From process to outcomes.* (Second Edition). San Francisco: Jossey-Bass.

Nussbaum, M.C. (2000). *Women and development: The capabilities approach.* Cambridge, UK: Cambridge University Press.

Sachs, J.D. (2005). *The end of poverty: Economic possibilities for our time.* NY: The Penguin Press.

Soska, T.M., & Johnson Butterfield, A.K. (Eds.). (2005). *University-Community Partnerships: Colleges and Universities in Civic Engagement.* Binghamton, NY: The Haworth Press, Inc.

Strand, K., Marullo, S., Cutforth, N., Stoecker, R., & Donohue, P. (2003). *Community-based research and higher education.* San Francisco: Jossey-Bass.

Sullivan, M., & Kelly, J. (Eds.) (2001). *Collaborative research: University and community partnership.* Washington, DC: American Public Health Association.

Wiewel, W., & Guerrero, I. (1998). *Long-Term Collaboration: Building Relationships and Achieving Results in the UIC Neighborhoods Initiative.* Great Cities Institute Working Paper. Chicago, IL: University of Illinois at Chicago. http://www.uic.edu/cuppa/gci/publications

UNIVERSITY OF ILLINOIS AT CHICAGO
JANE ADDAMS COLLEGE OF SOCIAL WORK

SOCIAL WORK 565: RESEARCH II: ACTION RESEARCH

PREREQUISITES: SOCW 460   **Office Hours: By Appointment**

CREDITS: 3   **Remote Synchronous Learning**

DESCRIPTION

This course builds on the generalist curriculum and prepares students to demonstrate advanced competencies in designing participatory action research. Action research is a family of research methodologies that simultaneously pursues research objectives (knowledge, understanding), meaningful involvement of community members affected by the study focus, social action leading to change, and social policy formation. The action component and the direct involvement of the local community in the creation and implementation of research distinguish action research from other types of systematic inquiry. Involvement of those directly affected by the research issue makes this method of inquiry especially salient among economically disadvantaged; oppressed, racial and ethnic minorities; gay, lesbian, bisexual and transsexual populations; and other at-risk urban populations. Students will learn participatory action research perspectives and methods for assessing need, designing and evaluating programs and services, and generating knowledge for more effective practice, program development, and policy formulation in community and agency settings. Lectures and class discussions will emphasize critical thinking and the use of participatory action research methods in the context of a diverse urban environment. The course will emphasize utilization of current technology in the development of problems and empowering community capacity to conduct research and evaluation. This course is open to students of all concentrations except schools; students are encouraged to develop research projects that are specific to their concentration.

REQUIRED TEXT

Israel, B. A., Eng, E., Schulz, A. J., & Parker, E. A. (2012). *Methods for community-based participatory research for health* (2nd ed.). San Francisco, CA: John Wiley & Sons, Inc.

ADVANCED COMPETENCY OBJECTIVES

Building on the generalist social work foundation and consistent with the College's mission, this course will help students to acquire the following competencies related to participatory action research relevant to the student's concentration, with an emphasis on evaluation of programs for urban, at risk populations:

1. **Engage in Practice-informed Research and Research-informed Practice (Competency 4)** Social workers understand quantitative and qualitative research methods and their respective roles in advancing a science of social work and in evaluating their practice. Social workers know the principles of logic, scientific inquiry, and culturally informed and ethical approaches to building knowledge. Social workers achieve an advanced understanding of the importance and challenges of taking an evidence-informed perspective on practice with individuals, families, and groups within a community-building framework. They understand approaches to evidence-informed assessment, intervention, and evaluation processes in community-building and health promotion. They know and understand evidence-informed program models and policies related to health promotion within a community-building context. Social workers:

   - apply critical thinking to engage in analysis of quantitative and qualitative research methods and research findings;
   - engage and help empower community residents to identify and implement appropriate evidence-informed assessment,

intervention and evaluation processes and tools, and to encourage them to take action in solving individuals, families, and community problems within a health promotion context;

- apply research skills to the evaluation of health and human service programs aimed at individuals, families and communities building promotion strategies with individuals, families, and groups within a community-building and health promotion context.

2. **Evaluate Practice with Individuals, Families, Groups, Organizations, and Communities (Competency 9)** Social workers understand that evaluation is an ongoing component of the dynamic and interactive process of social work practice with, and on behalf of, diverse individuals, families, groups, organizations and communities. Social workers recognize the importance of evaluating processes and outcomes to advance practice, policy, and service delivery effectiveness. Social workers understand theories of human behavior and the social environment, and critically evaluate and apply this knowledge in evaluating outcomes. Social workers understand qualitative and quantitative methods for evaluating outcomes and practice effectiveness. Social workers:

- work collaboratively with participants and community to select and use appropriate methods for evaluation of intervention appropriateness and effectiveness.
- Work collaboratively with participants and community apply evaluation findings to improve practice effectiveness, engage in social action leading to change, and affect social policy formation.

3. **Engage Diversity and Difference in Practice (Competency 2)** Social workers understand how diversity and difference characterize and shape the human experience and are critical to the formation of identity. The dimensions of diversity are understood as the intersectionality of multiple factors including but not limited to age, class, color, culture, disability and ability,

331

ethnicity, gender, gender identity and expression, immigration status, marital status, political ideology, race, religion/ spirituality, sex, sexual orientation, and tribal sovereign status. Social workers understand that, as a consequence of difference, a person's life experiences may include oppression, poverty, marginalization, and alienation as well as privilege, power, and acclaim. Social workers also understand the forms and mechanisms of oppression and discrimination and recognize the extent to which a culture's structures and values, including social, economic, political, and cultural exclusions, may oppress, marginalize, alienate, or create privilege and power. Social workers:

- understand how issues of diversity, particularly among urban at-risk populations, affect client vulnerability and help-seeking behaviors;
- gain sufficient self-awareness to critically evaluate the influence of personal biases and values in working with diverse groups;
- implement assessment, intervention and evaluation tools that are appropriate to diverse clients
- gain an understanding of social justice and of the social determinants of health.

COURSE METHOD OF INSTRUCTION: This class will be delivered weekly via Zoom as a synchronous class on the designated day of Thursdays at the designated time of 1:00 pm – 3:50 pm. These sessions will be highly interactive, and your participation is essential. In addition to attending the required synchronous class sessions, you will be expected to devote additional time outside of class doing the following: 1) Completing weekly homework assignments which are due before each synchronous class; 2) Preparing for online class discussion which will include, for example, viewing videos, visiting webpages, assigned readings, participating in online discussion boards, and/or PowerPoint slides, and completing course assignments.

STUDENTS NEEDING ACCOMMODATION FOR RELIGIOUS REASONS: Students needing accommodation for religious reasons should notify the instructor by email at the beginning of the semester.

EVALUATION -- BASIS FOR GRADING: All students will be held accountable for adhering to academic and nonacademic standards of conduct. Plagiarism is academic dishonesty. A non-exclusive list of examples of plagiarism includes: 1) presenting work done for another class as original work; 2) failing to cite and reference previous papers that you have written, 3) failing to cite and reference other authors' works that have contributed to your paper in any way, and 4) failing to cite, reference and identify quotes and material directly taken from another work.

WRITING: In this course, you will be expected to produce professionally written products that demonstrate systematic and critical thinking, are well organized, respect rules of grammar, spelling, punctuation, and the use of nonsexist language. Use APA Version 6.0.

CLASS PARTICIPATION: ONLINE COURSE COMMUNICATION GUIDELINES (NETIQUETTE): Class participation emphasizes its importance in the learning process. Graduate students are expected to demonstrate "good citizenship" and professional behavior. This includes regularly attending scheduled class sessions, being prepared to discuss scheduled topics and participating actively. If you are unable to attend class, please notify the instructor immediately before or after the class you miss. Absences in more than three classes may result in the final grade being lowered by one or more letter grades. Excellence in classroom and group participation includes the following: 1) Regular attendance; 2) Prepare for class by completing the required readings; 3) Ask questions, offer insights, discuss issues, and participate actively in groupwork. The Instructor reserves the right to assign an individual grade reduction to students who do not actively and equally participate in remote learning or in as a group member in group assignments.

1. All classes will be recorded and students who miss a class must view the recorded class prior to the next scheduled session. Recorded classes will be posted on Blackboard. <u>Students who miss a class are required to watch the recorded class session.</u>
2. Students must be fully present (on video and audio) in a secure, confidential, and appropriate location and engaged for all class meetings.
   a. Turn off cell phones and remove yourself from other distractions.
   b. Whenever possible please locate to a private, not public space.
   c. You must appear on camera in a stationary and secure location and maintain confidentiality for the duration of the class meeting.
   d. Mute your microphone unless talking.
   e. Virtual backgrounds may be used.
   f. Do not operate a moving vehicle during class sessions.
3. To the greatest extent possible, children, coworkers, site supervisors, family, or friends other than the student should not be present during class meetings.
4. Students should refrain from using phones and other electronic devices that distract them from class meetings unless they are your method for participating in class.
5. To the greatest extent possible, you should be in a location that is appropriate for a class meeting, such as a desk, table, or another stable surface to avoid an unsteady video feed (i.e. not in bed).
6. Students must refrain from smoking, vaping, and the use of alcohol during class time.
7. Students are required to be appropriately dressed for your class.
8. Students must fully participate in the synchronous remote class meetings. Students are expected to be actively engaged in class discussion, breakout groups, and other class related activities.

9. Students may turn your video off as needed for breaks or to attend to something that would be distracting were the video on; however, students are expected to have their video on during the majority of class in order to actively participate.

10. Discuss any questions or concerns regarding these requirements with the Instructor.

ASSINGMENTS

Assignment	Type of Assignment	Due	% of Grade
Classroom & Group Participation		Weekly	- 2 points per class missed after more than 1 absence.
Reading Assignments (12)	Individual	Session 1 – Session 12	36% (3 points each)
Concept Idea for Action Research	Individual or Small Group	March 3	N/A
Human Subjects Training & Reading	Individual	April 15	9%
Poster Presentation of Proposal	Individual or Small Group	April 22; April 29	15%
Action Research Proposal	Individual or Small Group	May 7	40%
Total			100%

1. **Reading Assignments (36%).** Students will complete (12) Reading Assignments on action research. Reading Assignments are posted under the Assignments Tab on Blackboard™ and due at 11:59 pm on the day before class. Since these assignments relate directly to synchronous remote learning, <u>no late assignments will be accepted</u>.

   a. **Assignment Format means**: Name at top of page. Name file: Last Name, Reading #. Limit answers to two (2) pages (<u>350-500 words in MS Word format</u> not pdf format). <u>Single space answers with double space between paragraphs</u>. Assignment responses are not essays, but include short paragraphs, critical reflection, questions for discussion, as well as bulleted points and short phrases.

2. **Human Subjects Protection Training (9%).** Human Subjects Protections knowledge is required to successfully complete the Action Research Proposal assignment. Human Subjects Protection training is sponsored by the Office of the Vice Chancellor for Research, entitled "CITI Initial Course". The link for this training is https://research.uic.edu/human-subjects-irbs/education-training/citi-training/ Students who have completed the CITI Initial Course one year ago or less (***On or after January 14, 2020 to Present***) may take the CITI Refresher Training. Upon completion of the CITI Initial Course Training <u>or</u> Refresher Course, students will receive a report. <u>Full details of this assignment are located in Session 13</u>. Submit Assignment by **April 15, 2021.**

3. **Poster Presentation (15%).** Students will develop a Poster Presentation of their Action Research Proposal. There are templates and examples for developing the Poster Presentation available in the Course Resources tab on Blackboard™. Poster Presentations are submitted for grading under the Assignments Tab. Posters will be presented to the class on April 21 or April 29, 2021.

4. **Action Research Proposal (Final Assignment) (40%). Due: May 7, 2021.** The final assignment is an Action Research Proposal. To maximize participation and learning, students may work individually or in groups of two (2) or three (3). The purpose of this project is to formulate a community based participatory action research (CBPR) proposal focused on community-based organizations, groups, or communities. The Action Research Proposal requires approval by the instructor and use of research methodologies that are compatible with participatory action research. <u>Students will send a 1-page Concept Idea by email to the Instructor by March 3, 2021</u>. Final Proposals must include complete references, recruitment

tools and any instruments developed and /or used for the data collection, analysis, and dissemination processes. **An Outline and a Template for the Action Research Proposal is available on Blackboard™.**

TOPICAL OUTLINE

Session 1: Overview of the Course

Topic: Course Introduction and Review of Syllabus.

PPT: Overview of the Course

Handout on Blackboard™· Traditional versus community-based research.

Community-Based Participatory Research: AMOS Health and Hope https://www.youtube.com/watch?v=vPzz-E-61xc

Detroit Urban Research Center - Advancing Partnerships, Research, and Equity in Detroit https://www.youtube.com/watch?v=QLlL5xRzXKA&feature=youtu.be

Session 1 Reading Assignment (3 points): 1) Read Bradbury Huang (2010) and Bradbury (2017). List and summarize the core features and characteristics of action research. 2) Read Flanagan (2020). Identify Flanagan's argument for participatory service user research. Discuss the reason(s) that social work has not moved substantially in this direction. Briefly describe a problem in your field placement or in human services that potentially could be addressed through service user research. [Assignment Format].

Bradbury Huang, H. (2010). What is good action research? Why the resurgent interest? *Action Research*, *8*(1), 91-109.

Bradbury, H. (2017). Introduction: How to situate and define action research. In H. Bradbury (Ed.), *The Sage Handbook of Action Research* (3rd Edition) (pp. 1-9). Thousand Oaks, CA: Sage.

Flanagan, N. (2020). Considering a participatory approach to social work—Service user research. *Qualitative Social Work*, *19*(5-6), 1078-1094.

Session 2: ACTION RESEARCH – Groundings

Topic: Introduction to Participatory Action Research – An overview of participatory action research, including the definition, history, values, and philosophy. Differences between mainstream/traditional research methods and community-based participatory research.

PPT: CBPR History, Values, Philosophy

PPT: Foundation Research Review: Theory & Mixed Methods

Session 2 Reading Assignment (3 points): 1) Review O'Brien (2001). Summarize the Process of Action Research & the Principles of Action Research. Select One: 2) For Minkler & Wallerstein (2008): What are the contributions of various participatory research traditions, (for example, Freirian theory and practice, feminist participatory research, Lewinian action research, and so forth) to community-based participatory research for health? Which type or types of research resonates with your future as a social work practitioner? 3) For Bradbury & Reason (2003) describe First Person, Second Person, and Third Person research, including an example of each. Which type or types of research resonates with your future as a social work practitioner?

O'Brien, R. (2001). Um exame da abordagem metodológica da pesquisa ação [An Overview of the Methodological Approach of Action Research]. In Roberto Richardson (Ed.), *Teoria e Prática da Pesquisa*

Ação [Theory and Practice of Action Research]. João Pessoa, Brazil: Universidade Federal da Paraíba. (English version). On Blackboard. Complete Report Available at: http://www.web.ca/~robrien/papers/arfinal.html

Select One:

Minkler & Wallerstein (2008). Chapter 2: The theoretical, historical and practice roots of CBPR, (pp. 26-46).

Bradbury, H., & Reason, H. (2003). Action research: An opportunity for revitalizing research purpose and practice. *Qualitative Social Work, 2*(2), 155-175.

Videos for Class Remote Learning

- Highlander Research & Education Center - Folk Alliance International Lifetime Achievement Award 2012 https://www.youtube.com/watch?v=dAUCZH-r3KQ
- Paulo Freire and Myles Horton: Conversations on Education and Social Change https://www.youtube.com/watch?v=vSTiG3x-Pl4
- Paulo Freire Documentary Seeing Through Paulo's Glasses: Political Clarity, Courage and Humility https://www.youtube.com/watch?v=U4jPZe-cZgc
- Paulo Freire: An Incredible Conversation https://www.youtube.com/watch?v=aFWjnkFypFA

Session 3: ACTION RESEARCH – Groundings

Topic: Introduction to Participatory Action Research -- Altering mainstream/traditional research methods and making them more participatory in nature. Engaging in community planning and participatory research and its usefulness for social work and service delivery.

PPT: Models, Challenges & Examples of CBPR

PPT: Foundation Research Review: Quantitative: Sampling— Experimental & Quasi-experimental Designs

Handout: CBPR Conceptual Model (On Blackboard)

Session 3 Reading Assignment: 1) Read Braun et al. (2012). Identify four (4) challenges in operationalizing community-based participatory research. 2) Select One: Blitz et al. (2013) or Gehlert & Coleman (2010) or Rhodes et al. (2013) or Lee et al. (2016). Drawing on the Braun article, critique the use of engaged or participatory research in the article you have selected. Identify the article's strengths and challenges for planning and service delivery. [Assignment Format]

Braun, K. L., Nguyen, T. T., Tanjasiri, S. P., Campbell, J., Heiney, S. P., Brandt, H. M., et al. (2012). Operationalization of community-based participatory research principles: Assessment of the National Cancer Institute's Community Network programs. *American Journal of Public Health, 102*(6), 1195–1203.

Select One:

Blitz, L. V., Kida, L., Gresham, M., & Bronstein, L. R. (2013). Prevention through collaboration: Family engagement with rural schools and families living in poverty. *Families in Society*, 94(3), 157-165.

Gehlert, S. & Coleman, R. (2010). Using community-based participatory research to ameliorate cancer disparities. *Health and Social Work, 35 (4),* 302-309

Lee, S. J., Hoffman, G., & Harris, D. (2016). Community-based participatory research (CBPR) needs assessment of parenting support programs for fathers. *Children and Youth Services Review, 66,* 76-84.

Rhodes, S. D., Kelley, C., Simán, F., Cashman, R., Alonzo, J., McGuire, J. Reboussin, B. (2012). Using community-based participatory research (CBPR) to develop a community-level HIV prevention intervention for Latinas: A local response to a global challenge. *Women's Health Issues, 22*(3), e293-e301.

Session 4: ACTION RESEARCH – Practices

PPT: Principles of Action Research

Video – *The People's Report: Street Participatory Action Research.*

Session 4 Reading Assignment: TBA

Session 5: ACTION RESEARCH – Practices

PPT: Theory & Practice in Small Groups

Session 5 Reading Assignment: 1) Read Israel et al (2012). List the twelve (12) elements of group dynamics that are relevant to CBPR partnerships. Describe the characteristics of CBPR partnerships that make group process so useful. 2) Read Ludema et al. (2006). Identify and discuss the phases of Appreciative Inquiry. Why is the power of the positive question important for action research? 3) Select One: For Fieldhouse & Onyett (2012) discuss the small group process strategies and outcomes of applying appreciative inquiry with the Community Involvement Subgroup (CIS). For Eckstein & Pinto (2013) discuss the strategy and outcomes of applying small group processes with young men. [Assignment Format]

Israel, Eng, Schulz, & Parker (2012). Chapter 3. Strategies and techniques for effective group process in CBPR partnerships. (pp. 69-96).

Ludema, J.D., Cooperrider, D.L., & Barrett, F.J. (2006). Appreciative inquiry: The power of the unconditional positive question. In P. Reason and H. Bradbury (Eds.), *The Handbook of Action Research* (pp. 155-165).

Select One:

Fieldhouse, J., & Onyett, S. (2012). Community mental health and social exclusion: Working appreciatively towards inclusion. *Action Research, 10*(4), 356-372.

Eckstein, J.J., & Pinto, K. (2013). Collaborative participatory action strategies for re-envisioning young men's masculinities. *Action Research, 11*(3), 236-252.

Session 6: ACTION RESEARCH – Skills

PPT: Photovoice. Guest Speaker: Photovoice - TBA

Session 6 Reading Assignment: 1) Read Israel et al. (2012). Look at how the Photovoice project was implemented using a CBPR process. How was the data collected and analyzed? What is the relationship between the data and the Quality of Life (QOL) Framework? 2) Select One: Hamilton et al. (2017) or Redwood et al. (2010) or Trott (2019) or Valdez et al (2019). Discuss the process for collecting and analyzing the Photovoice data. Describe and summarize the way in which the Photovoice data was used for social change.

Israel, Eng, Schulz, & Parker (2012). Chapter 15: Photovoice as a CBPR method, (pp. 489-514).

Select One:

Hamilton, K.C., Richardson, M.T., Owens, T., Yerby, L.G., Lucky, F.L., & Higginbotham, J.C. (2017). Using Photovoice to identify the physical activity practices of children residing in Alabama's Black Belt Region. *Journal of Community Practice, 25*(3-4), 488-503.

Redwood, Y., Schulz, A. J., Israel, B. A., Yoshihama, M., Wang, C., & Kreuter, M. (2010). Social, economic, and political processes that create built environment inequalities: Perspectives from urban African Americans in Atlanta. *Family & Community Health, 33*(1), 53-67.

Trott, C.D. (2019). Reshaping our world: Collaborating with children for community-based climate change action. *Action Research, 17*(1), 42-62.

Valdez, E.S., Korchmaros, J, Sabo, S., Garcia, D.O., Carvajal, S., & Stevens, S. (2019). How the U.S.-Mexico border influences adolescent substance abuse: Youth participatory action research using photovoice. *International Journal of Drug Policy, 73*, 146-155.

Session 7 Partnerships and Oppressed Communities

Topic: Partnerships and Oppressed Communities – Defining research objectives, including working community gatekeepers, initial formation of community partnerships, defining roles and responsibilities, organizational structure, and decision-making frameworks.

Session 7 Reading Assignment: 1) Read Minkler & Wallerstein (2008). How do issues of racism and other intersecting oppressions, such as class, gender, and sexual orientation connect with issues of power in community engaged research? Describe ways that you think these issues affect the CBPR research process. 2) Read Israel et al. (2012). Identify and describe the challenges for partnering. List and describe three (3) strategies or skills that may be useful for organizing and building authentic partnerships. 3) Select One: Cottrell & Parpart (2006) or Gerassi et al. (2018) or Letiecq & Schmalzbauer (2012). Identify and discuss the issues in applying community partnerships. What skills, methods, or processes did the researchers use or recommend to address these issues?

Minkler & Wallerstein (2008). Chapter 5: The dance of race and privilege in CBPR, (pp. 91-105).

Israel, Eng, Schulz, & Parker (2012). Chapter 2: Developing and maintaining partnerships with communities, (pp. 43-68).

Select One:

Cottrell, B., & Parpart, J.L. (2006). Academic-community collaboration: Gender, research, and development: Pitfalls and possibilities. *Development in Practice, 16*(1), 15-26.

Gerassi, L.B., Colegrove, A., & McPherson, D.K. (2018). Addressing race, racism, and commercial sexual exploitation in practice through an action-based research partnership. *Action Research, 17*(2), 220-236.

Letiecq, B., & Schmalzbauer, L. (2012). Community-based participatory research with Mexican migrants in a new rural destination: A good fit? *Action Research, 10*(3), 244-259.

Session 8 Partnerships and Oppressed Communities

Topic: Partnerships and Oppressed Communities (Cont.) – Continuation with an increased focus on issues and challenges that arise from community partnerships and differences between institutional, organizational, and community culture with an emphasis on skill-building and coalition-building.

Session 8 Reading Assignment: 1) Read Israel et al. (2012). List the methods used in Action Oriented Community Diagnosis (AOCD). What are the pros and cons of using AOCD in the initial phase of designing a study or planning a program? List the roles and responsibilities of community partners, both while conducting AOCD and after its completion. Why is it important to note differences between the views of Insiders from those of Outsiders? 2) <u>Select One</u>: For Ferrera (2017) describe and reflect on the effectiveness of critical consciousness raising in working with a marginalized community. Why was the Youth Health Service Corps (YHSC) campaign effective? For Katz-Wise et al. (2018) describe and reflect on the lessons learned from community-based research with transgender and nonconforming youth and their families. Why was the Trans Teen and Family Narratives Project effective? For Wright et al. (2017) describe and reflect on the lessons learned from community-based research in establishing a partnership to support lesbian, gay, bisexual and transgender ageing in place. Why was the Seniors

Using Supports To Age In Neighborhoods (SUSTAIN) effective?

Israel, Eng, Schulz, & Parker (2012). Chapter 5: Insiders and outsiders assess who is "The Community": Participant observation, key informant interviews, focus group, interviews, and community forum (pp. 133-160).

<u>Selection #1</u>:

Ferrera, M.J. (2017). Integrating principles of positive minority youth development with health promotion to empower the immigrant community: A case study in Chicago. *Journal of Community Practice*, 25:3-4, 504-523.

Katz-Wise, S.L., Sansfacon, A.P., Bogart, L.M., Rosal, M.C., Ehrensaft, D., Goldman, R.E., & Austin, S.B.

(2018). Lessons learned from a community-based participatory research study with transgender and gender nonconforming youth and their families. *Action Research*, *17*(2), 186-207.

Wright, L.A. et al. (2017). Lessons learned from community-based participatory research: Establishing a partnership to support lesbian, gay, bisexual and transgender ageing in place. *Family Practice*, *34*(3), 330–335.

Session 9 Action Research Design and Methods

Topic: Methodology– Design, data collection, qualitative and quantitative methods, and training of community partners in research methods.

PPT: Foundation Research Review: Qualitative Research

Due: Update on the Development of the Action Research Proposal

Session 9 Reading Assignment: 1) Read Minkler & Wallerstein (2008). Identify and describe three (3) methods of community-driven asset identification and issue selection. In view of the action research proposal that you are developing, identify and describe two (2) ways that you could use to identify natural leaders and research partners. 2) Select One: For Alvarez et al. (2006) list and describe the process of minority recruitment used by the authors. Identify the strengths and challenges of this approach. How might this process be used in your proposal? 3) For Giachello et al. (2003) describe the training components and the process used with natural leaders and research partners. Identify the strengths and challenges of this approach. How might this process or some parts of it be used in your proposal?

Minkler & Wallerstein (2008). Chapter 9: Community-driven asset identification and issue selection (pp. 153-169).

Select One:

Alvarez, R.A., Vasquez, E., Mayorga, C.C., Feaster, D.J., Mitrani, V.B. (2006). Increasing minority participation through community organization outreach. *Western Journal of Nursing Research*, *28*, 541-560.

Giachello, A.L. et al. (2003). Reducing diabetes health disparities through community-based participatory action research: The Chicago Southeast Diabetes Community Action Coalition. *Public Health Reports*, *118*, 309-323.

For Further Detail of CBPR Methods see Appendices in Israel, Eng, Schulz, & Parker (2012):

Appendix A. Instructions for Conducting a Force Field Analysis, pp. 581-583.

Appendix B. Full Value Contract, pp. 585-587.

Appendix C. Collaborative Revised Bylaws, pp. 589-599.

Appendix D. Community Member Key Informant Interview Guide, pp. 601-604.

Appendix E. Measures by Survey Categories...Source of Identification for Inclusion and Scale Items, pp. 605-611.

Appendix F. Focus Group Summary Analysis Form, pp. 613-617.

Appendix G. Field Notes Guide, pp. 619-621.

Appendix H. In-Depth, Semi-structured Interview Protocol, pp. 623-626.

Appendix I. Closed-Ended Survey Questionnaire, pp. 627-637.

Appendix J. Philosophy and Guiding Principles for Dissemination of Findings, pp. 639-643.

Appendix K. Fact Sheet and Informed Consent Form for Study Participants, pp. 645-650.

Appendix L. Informed Consent Form for Adults who May Appear in Photographs, pp. 651-653.

Appendix M. Partnership Agreed-Upon Mechanism for Deciding on Research Activities, pp. 656-657.

Session 10 Action Research Design and Methods

PPT: Focus Groups & Key Informant Interviews

Topic: Methodology (cont.) – The use of traditional/mainstream research methods within a PAR context; ethics, values, and the protection of human subjects in PAR (relationships, communication, participation, and inclusion); principles of privacy, justice, and safety of subjects.

Session 10 Reading Assignment: 1) Watch *Moderating Focus Groups* on YouTube and review Kreuger (2002). Describe three (3) important skills or methods for conducing focus groups. Discuss the potential use of focus groups in your action research proposal. 2) Read Israel et al. (2012). This chapter's case study research design intentionally built community capacity. Provide an example and discuss how capacity building was integrated into each phase of the focus group process. 3) Select One: For Langford (2000) identify the list of safety issues and discuss how you might address these issues in your action research proposal. For McKenna & Main (2013), identify and discuss criteria and challenges in selecting key informants. For Owen et al. (2015) describe the Nominal Group Technique. Identify is similarities and differences to focus groups. For Rabiee (2004) review focus group analysis and outline a potential method of analysis that you could use in your action research proposal.

Richard Krueger. Moderating Focus Groups. https:// www.youtube.com/watch?v=xjHZsEcSqwo

Kreuger, R.A. (2002). *Designing and conducting focus group interviews.* University of Minnesota. Available at: https://www.eiu.edu/ihec/Krueger-FocusGroupInterviews.pdf

Israel, Eng, Schulz, & Parker (2012). Chapter 9: The application of focus group methodologies to CBPR, pp. 249-276.

Select One:

Langford, D.R. (2000). Developing a safety protocol in qualitative research involving battered women. *Qualitative Health Research, 10(1),* 133-142.

McKenna, S.A., & Main, D.S. (2013). The role and influence of key informants in community-engaged research: A critical perspective. *Action Research, 11*(2), 113-124.

Owen, A., Arnold, K., Friedman, C, & Sandman, L. (2015). Nominal group technique: An accessible and interactive method for conceptualizing the sexual self-advocacy of adults with intellectual and developmental disabilities. *Qualitative Social Work, 15*(2), 175-189.

Rabiee, F. (2004). Focus-group interview and data analysis. *Proceedings of the Nutrition Society, 63,* 655-660.

Spring Break –No Class

Session 11 Data Analysis, Dissemination, and Change

PPT: Foundation Research Review: Program Evaluation

Topic: Analysis, Data Dissemination, and Change – Clarification of meaning and group processes for interpreting issues, disseminating results, and planning for change. Moving from data to social action and enacting the project vision.

Session 11 Reading Assignment: 1) Watch "A Bridge Between Communities…" and read Israel, Eng, Schulz, & Parker (2012). Based on the experience and lessons learned from the Detroit URC, identify methods you plan to use to evaluate your action research proposal (for example, the use of multiple methods, formative, participatory, internal or external evaluation). Discuss the strategy you would use to implement your evaluation methods. 2) <u>Select One</u>: For Ferrara et al. (2015), <u>or</u> Minkler et al. (2008), <u>or</u> Wilson et al. (2008): Describe the outcomes of CBPR. Describe the process used in disseminating results. Discuss the way or ways that the CBPR process led to social action or change.

> A Bridge Between Communities: The Detroit Community Academic Urban Research Center SD https://www.youtube.com/watch?v=P64TPPZyhhQ
>
> Israel, Eng, Schulz, & Parker (2012). Chapter 13. Documentation and evaluation of CBPR partnerships: The use of in-depth interviews and closed-ended questionnaires. (pp. 369-398).
>
> <u>Select One:</u>
>
> Ferrera, M. J., Sacks, T. K., Perez, M., Nixon, J. P., Asis, D., & Coleman, W. L. (2015). Empowering immigrant youth in Chicago: Utilizing CBPR to document the

impact of a youth health service corps program. *Family & Community Health, 38*(1), 12-21. (Note: Whole Issue is on CBPR and youth).

Minkler, M., Hammel, J., Gill, C. J., Magasi, S., Vasquez, V. B., Bristo, M., Coleman, D. (2008). Community-based participatory research in disability and long-term care policy. *Journal of Disability Policy Studies, 19*(2), 114-126.

Wilson, N., Minkler, M., Dasho, S., Wallerstein, N., & Martin, A.C. (2008). Getting to social action: The youth empowerment strategies (YES!) project. *Health Promotion Practice, 9*(4), 395-403.

Session 12 Participatory Models and Innovative Practices

Session 12 Reading Assignment: 1) Read Chapter 11 or Chapter 15 of Israel, Eng, Schulz, & Parker (2012). Describe the study's multiple methods and how these methods contributed to triangulating the data. Identify and discuss the lessons learned and implications for practice. 2) Select One: For Minkler & Wallerstein (2008) discuss the experiential processes used to involve the community in data analysis and interpretation of results. Identify the strengths and challenges of this level of involvement. For Tremblay & de Oliveira Jayme (2015) list the process of training community participants for video development. Discuss the role of participants in data analysis and interpretation of results.

Select One:

Israel, Eng, Schulz, & Parker (2012). Chapter 11. CBPR and ethnography: The perfect union (pp. 305-334).

Israel, Eng, Schulz, & Parker (2012). Chapter 15: Collaborative data collection, interpretation, and action planning in a rural African American community: Men on the Move (pp. 436-462).

Select One:

Minkler & N. Wallerstein (2008). Chapter 16: Analyzing and interpreting data with communities. (pp. 285-302).

Tremblay, C., & de Oliveira Jayme. (2015). Community knowledge co-creation through participatory video. *Action Research*, *13*(3), 298-314.

Session 13: Action Research – Ethics and Critical Analysis and Reflection

Consultation on Posters and Action Research Proposals. Students are not required to participate in remote learning. Any individuals or groups that want feedback should email the Instructor that they plan to meet on Zoom and schedule a time slot for feedback.

Session 13: Human Subjects Training & Reading. 1) Read Brydon-Miller & Greenwood (2006). Describe and reflect on three (3) challenges inherent in action research and the human subjects review process. [Assignment Format]. 2) Complete the CITI Training. The link for this training is https://research.uic.edu/human-subjects-irbs/education-training/citi-training/ Submit your Certificate for Human Subjects Training and Reading Assignment through Blackboard™.

Topic: Overview of Ethics in Action Research. ***Topic:*** Critical Analysis of PAR: Reflection of PAR, its effectiveness and utility as a research approach, and its place with traditional/mainstream research methods. Focus on how PAR use could be increased.

Brydon-Miller, M., & Greenwood, D. (2006). A re-examination of the relationship between action research and human subjects review processes. *Action Research,* *4*(1), 117-118.

Meyer, I. H., & Bayer, R. (2013). School-based gay affirmative interventions: First amendment and ethical concerns. *American Journal of Public Health, 103*(10), 1764-1771.

Session 14 & Session 15: Action Research – Exemplars

Project Presentations. Present your Poster Presentation during class.

AUTHOR BIOGRAPHIES

Abiot Simeon is an Assistant Professor in College of Social Science and Humanities, Debreberhan University. He received his PhD in Social Work and Social Development from Addis Ababa University. His dissertation examined Mission for Community Development Program, a local NGO as a locality-based social development organization in Ethiopia. His scholarship focuses on social development, organizational development, social policy, and community development. Dr. Abiot is the Career Service Director at Debreberhan University since 2017. He is also a General Assembly Member of Mission for Community Development Program. He can be reached at abiotsimeon@gmail.com

Adugna Abebe Bihonegn is an assistant professor at the Department of Social Work, University of Gondar, Ethiopia. He also serves as the coordinator of the PhD Program. His scholarship focuses on positive youth development, community development, social movements, and indigenous knowledge. His research includes youth development, youth movement, disability, street people, indigenous social welfare practice, grief and bereavement. Dr. Adugna also serves as the coordinator of Faculty Development at Mastercard Foundation Scholars Program, a 10-year project for collaborative partnership between University of Gondar (Ethiopia) and Queen's University (Canada). Dr. Adugna has played a leading role in developing doctoral curriculum and launching the PhD degree in social work education at the University of Gondar. He received the Civil Society Scholars Award from Open Society Foundations in 2016/17 and 2019/2020. He can be reached at adugna78@gmail.com

Alice K. Butterfield is a professor at the Jane Addams College of Social Work, University of Illinois at Chicago. Her scholarship focuses on homelessness, social policy, international social work education, and community development. She is an author of *Practicing as a Social Work Educator in International Collaboration* (2017); *Dynamics of Family Policy* (2010), *Social Development and Social Work: Learning from* Africa (2013); *Interdisciplinary Community Development* (2007); *University-Community Partnerships: Colleges and Universities in Civic Engagement* (2005). She leads the Social Work Education in Ethiopia Partnership (Project SWEEP), resulting in a the first-ever MSW and PhD degrees in Social Work and Social Development in Ethiopia. Her practice includes Asset Based Community Development) and the Integrated Community Development and Child Welfare Model of Practice [http://www.aboutsweep.org]. Dr. Butterfield has served as a Fulbright Specialist with Assam Don Bosco University in Northeast India, and on the Council on Social Work Education's Commission on Global Social Work Education. She received the Distinguished Alumni Award from Washington University in St. Louis in 2007, and Career Achievement Award from the Association for Community Organization & Social Administration in 2014. She can be reached at akj@uic.edu

Andargachew Moges Agonafir is an assistant professor of Social Work and Social Development, Bahir Dar University, Ethiopia. His scholarship focuses on positive youth development, counseling, social policy and voluntarism. He is the author of an article: Perceived barriers to undergoing voluntary HIV counseling and testing among university students, and two book reviews, *The Short Guide to Social Work* and *Journeying Together: Growing Youth Work and Youth Workers in Local Communities*. He coordinated a project on Situation Analysis of School Related Gender-Based Violence and Its Impact on Learning and served as a Principal Investigator for a research project on sexuality education. He served as a coordinator of two international projects Bridging the Education Quality Gap in Africa; Leadership and Management of Ethiopian Universities, and Environmental Education. He received basic consultant certificate on Positive Psychotherapy. He received

Certificate of Recognition for contributing to the academic success of female students at Bahir Dar University. He can be reached at amoges02@yahoo.com

Dr. Cmdr. Demelash Kassaye is an associate professor at the School of Social Work, Addis Ababa University. His scholarship focuses on criminology, policing, criminal justice and restorative justice. He is an author of the *Scaffolding of Police Corruption* (2014); *I Fought the Law and the Law Won* (2018); *Challenges Facing the Implementation of Children's Rights in Primary Schools in Ethiopia* (2019); *Causal Attribution of Athletes on Their Success and Failure in Distance Running* (2014). Formerly, Dr. Demelash was a Commander of the Ethiopian Police. He led different departments and delivered trainings designed to advance community policing in the country. He is a Visiting Professor at Wolega, Gonder, Mekele, and Jima Universities of Ethiopia and Kutztown University of Pennsylvania, USA. He teaches courses of Criminal Justice and Correctional Administration, Human Behavior and the Social Environment for both the graduate and undergraduate programs. Currently, he is chairman of Ethiopian Police Reform Task Force and Ethiopian Police Doctrine Team. Dr. Demelash has presented research papers in various international and national conferences. His area of research interest is Criminology, Policing, Human Rights and Organized Crime. He can be reached at zmekdelawit@gmail.com

Getaneh Mehari is an assistant professor at College of Social Sciences, Addis Ababa University, Ethiopia. His research interest focuses on gender, women's reproductive health and rights, legal pluralism, and food security. Some of his publications are: *Anthropology and Graduate Research in Ethiopia: Changes and Continuities at Addis Ababa University* (2018); *Cursed or Blessed: Female Genital Cutting in the Gamo Cultural Landscape, South Western Ethiopia* (2016); *and The Role of Women in the Household Economy, the Dorze Case* (2006). Dr. Getaneh is a co-author of *Civic and Ethical Education* textbooks for grades 9, 10, 11, and 12, published in 2010. He was a visiting research fellow at the Asian and African Area Studies (ASAFAS), Kyoto University, Japan in 2017. Dr.

Getaneh won the Adaptive Problem-Solving Research Award from Addis Ababa University, for a research project entitled *'Smallholders' Responses to Food Insecurity in Ethiopia'* in 2016. He can be reached at getanehmeh@gmail.com.

Getu Ambaye Teshale is an assistant professor in the Department of Social Work, College of Social Sciences and the Humanities, University of Gondar. He received his PhD in Social Work and Social Development in 2015. Getu teaches several different courses and serves as an advisor of graduate students working their thesis on a range of topics and issues. His publications include: *Social Development: Theory and Practice.*; *Analyzing Social Networks*; and *The Role of Indigenous Association for Promoting Local Development Initiatives: A Case Study of Indigenous Association among Agaws in Awi Zone of Amhara Regional State* (2019). His research interests include community development, indigenous knowledge, conflict resolution, social development, social capital, social network analysis, and displaced populations. In 2009, Getu received Certificate of the Completion of Six Months of Intensive Training and the Application of Skills in an integrated approach to social work, child welfare and community development. In 2016, he received a Certificate on Elections Management and Monitoring Course held at Peace and Conflict Studies School, Nairobi, Kenya. He can be reached at getuambay@yahoo.com

Kerebih Asrese is an associate professor in the Social Work department, Bahir Dar University, Ethiopia. His scholarship focuses on social network and health behavior, social policy, and urbanization and livelihoods. Selected publications include Quality of Intrapartum Care at health centers in Jabi Tehinan District, North West Ethiopia: Clients' perspective (2020); Online activities as risk factors for problematic internet use among students in Bahir Dar University, North West Ethiopia: A hierarchical regression model (2020); Rethinking collapse of micro and small enterprises in Bahir Dar City, North West Ethiopia: A grounded theory approach (2019); Social network correlates of risky sexual behavior among adolescents in Bahir Dar and Mecha Districts,

North West Ethiopia: An institution-based study (2018); and Women's social networks and use of facility delivery services for uncomplicated births in North West Ethiopia: A community-based case-control study (2017). Currently, he is working research on Gender socialization in Amhrara Regional State, North West Ethiopia, social norms and adolescents' reproductive health, and quality of intrapartum care services at health facilities. He can be reached at kerebiha@bdu.edu.et

Samson Chane, PhD, is an assistant professor in the Department of Social Work at Bahir Dar University, Ethiopia. Dr. Samson received his PhD in 2014 from Addis Ababa University. He served as Academic Vice Dean for the Faculty of Social Sciences, at Bahir Dar University for three years from 2015 to 2018. Dr. Samson teaches Social Work Theories & Methods, Qualitative Research Methods, Contemporary Social Problems & Issues, and Social Work with Group, Community and Organizations to MSW students. He contributed a co-authored book and articles titled *Elder Abuse in Ethiopia: A Sign of the Times*; Factors contributing to elder abuse in Ethiopia. (2015); 'Death is better than misery"; Elders' accounts of abuse and neglect in Ethiopia. (2016); Giving voice to at risk elders in a developing nation: Collecting phenomenological narratives. (2017); and *Family and Kin Care of Elders in Sub-Saharan Africa* (2020). His areas of research interest are ageing, social justice, death and bereavement. He can be reached at chanesamson@gmail.com

Tadesse Gobosho Gerba is an assistant professor at the School of Social Work, College of Social Sciences and Humanities, Jimma University, Ethiopia. His scholarship focuses on mobilizing and utilizing the assets of local associations for community development, and traditional conflict resolution. Currently, he is the Social Work Post Graduate Program Coordinator in the School of Social Work. He is also a Research Review Board member in the College of Social Science and Humanities. His practice focuses on improving the life of local communities by forming local associations, especially those farmers who lose their farmland and are unable to continue their livelihood due to the expansion of towns and investments. Dr. Tadesse's interest is intervention research to improve the life of people with disabilities through creating support network among local individuals, associations and institutions. He can be reached at tgobosho@gmail.com

Wassie Kebede, MSW, PhD, is associate professor of social work and social development at Addis Ababa University, School of Social Work. He teaches Community and Social Development, Integrated Social Work Methods, Knowledge Building and Models of Social Change, Mixed Methods Research and Community Mobilization and Organization. He is a visiting professor of social work at the University of Gondar in Ethiopia since 2010 and University of Eswatini, former Swaziland, from 2016-2019. He contributed to the social development sector in Africa by his involvement in academic capacity building in Eswatini and Ghana. Dr. Wassie renovated social work programs in these two countries to maintain the international standards in curricula, staff capacity and teaching. He has served on the Board of Directors of the International Association of Schools of Social Work (IASSW) and as Secretary for the African Association of Schools of Social Work (ASSWA). Dr. Wassie is on the editorial board member of the *International Social Work Journal* and *Journal of Community Practice*. He is associate editor of the *Ethiopian Journal of Social Sciences and Humanities* (EJSSH) at Addis Ababa University. He is passionate in using mixed methods and social network analysis in engaged research. He can be reached at wassiek7@gmail.com

Yania Seid-Mekiye Seid-Ali is an assistant professor at the School of Social Work, Addis Ababa University. She has served as Field Education Coordinator and Head of the School of Social Work. Her scholarship focuses on gender and diversity in social work; community development, gender and Islam/Muslims; culture, religion and human rights. Her research includes *The Socio-Economic Causes and Impacts of Halaba Women Seeking for and Engagement in Causal Work at "Sew Tera" area at Halaba Kulito City Administration*; and *The Traditional Community Support System at Halaba Community, Ethiopia*. In

2018/2019, she engaged in the regional research focusing on the challenges and solutions for the Southern Region of Ethiopia. Dr. Yania is the Director of the Office of Community Engagement at Addis Ababa University. Her practice focuses on community development with special focus on integrated community development. She is also a member of Peace Ambassadors Committee working for bringing lasting solution for the Southern region of Ethiopia. She can be reached at yaniaseidmekiye@gmail.com

INDEX

consensus, 96, 217, 244–45, 303

consequences, negative, 49–50, 239, 257

constructivist theory, 210

consultation, 18, 64, 272, 284, 286, 295, 321, 352

context, 53, 57, 63, 67–68, 77, 79, 110, 115, 117, 119, 127, 131, 135, 140, 142, 180, 183, 208, 217, 219, 221, 223, 238–39, 306, 327, 329

control, 22, 35, 61, 64, 88, 159, 165, 183–85, 188–89, 197, 218, 233, 246, 249, 274, 280, 291

cooperation, 19, 64, 151–52, 190, 210, 235, 271–72, 292

co-researchers, 116, 119, 152, 159, 214, 226, 258–61, 283

corruption, 22, 33, 36, 43–45, 51, 54–56, 58

coursework, xviii, 280

credit, 99, 105, 329

crime, 50, 251–55, 257, 260–68, 275, 278

cross-cutting themes, 269, 271–76, 290

cultural values, 173, 186, 197, 222

culture, 27, 41, 69, 78, 196, 200, 217, 222, 238, 270, 291, 301, 318, 331, 360

cyclical process, 116, 119–20, 258

D

data collection, 5, 71, 92, 118, 120, 170, 185, 191–92, 258, 283, 337, 346

Delphi processes, 105

developing countries, 10, 19, 32, 51, 54, 57, 63, 87, 89, 102, 139, 149, 249, 276, 320

development, 17–19, 25, 31–37, 39, 41, 43, 53, 55, 58, 79–80, 84, 86, 88, 90, 104–5, 107, 147, 149, 165, 187–90, 206–10, 212, 219–22, 226–27, 271–72, 287–88, 304–5, 322–23, 325–29, 344

international, 43, 55, 327

organizational, 171, 355

professional, 262, 304

social work and social, xv–xvi, 103, 139, 141–42, 184, 246, 311–12, 355–56, 358, 360

women and economic, 22, 33, 280

development activities, 199, 216

development issues, xviii, 21, 31, 288

development processes, 18, 22, 209, 227, 288

dialogue, 11, 71, 111, 119–20, 153–54, 206, 209, 213, 215–18, 220, 222, 225, 227, 229, 239, 245, 259–60, 270, 298, 308

disabilities, 38, 41, 50, 122, 129, 275–76, 331, 351, 355, 360

discrimination, 22, 33, 63, 108–14, 117–22, 124–27, 131, 133–34, 136, 140, 274–75, 280, 332

discussion, 7, 61, 69–71, 78, 80–81, 93–96, 100–101, 118, 134, 154, 171–72, 191–93, 195, 216, 223–24, 229, 240, 244, 259–60, 299, 336

disease, 49, 108–9, 111, 113–14, 121–29, 131–34, 136–37, 142, 236, 247

dissemination, 2, 5, 15, 35, 159, 217, 348, 350

dissertations, xvii, 82, 103, 160, 162, 201–2, 247, 276, 279–80, 282–83, 319, 355

diversity, 38, 46, 54, 67, 81, 263, 272, 331–32, 360

drug use, 186, 195, 197, 204, 275

E

economic development, 17, 19, 22, 31, 33–34, 37, 41, 54, 57, 88–90, 106, 150, 276–77, 280

economic growth, 32–33, 35–36, 42, 46, 53, 58, 88, 288

education, 6, 9–12, 22, 24–25, 29, 32–38, 41, 44–45, 47, 49, 53, 56–57, 61–64, 229, 233, 235–36, 238, 244, 318, 321, 326–27

    peer, 217, 223, 236–37

effectiveness, 18, 39, 91, 208, 257, 331, 345, 352

elders, 47, 174, 178, 194, 275–76, 359

Emancipatory design choices, 85, 316

emancipatory research, 2–3, 5, 12, 294

employment, 34–35, 45, 48–50, 59, 86–88, 90, 96–97, 136, 168, 257, 272

empowerment, 5, 34, 60–61, 63–64, 78, 80–81, 115, 134–35, 187–89, 206–7, 212, 214, 220, 223, 228, 271, 278, 288, 320

    economic, 32, 86–88, 97, 102, 106, 274

    women's, 61, 63–64, 68, 81, 279

engaged research, xvii–xviii, 1–4, 6, 21–23, 26–27, 31–33, 53, 61, 63, 81–83, 89, 92, 100, 102–4, 115–16, 134, 136–40, 151–52, 158–63, 187, 190, 199–201, 246–47, 258, 269–71, 273–88, 291–92

engagement, xvii, 2, 21, 39, 46, 69, 103, 110, 118, 137–38, 140, 170–72, 179, 181, 213, 219, 224–27, 230, 259, 264, 269, 277, 282–83, 285

    scholarship of, 3, 6, 313, 326

entrepreneurship, 21, 52, 102

environment, 8, 17, 35, 79, 98, 140, 162, 210, 238, 253–54, 258, 263, 272, 277

    social, 49, 236, 238, 303, 331, 357

evaluation, 5, 7, 9, 56, 104, 175, 178, 192, 204, 212, 230–31, 236, 271, 290, 307, 324, 328–31, 333, 350

exclusion, 41, 62, 91, 110, 126–27, 131, 133

experts, 171, 190, 226, 255

F

facilitator, 70–71, 80, 92–94, 146, 152–53, 172, 192, 216, 218, 226, 306

families, leper, 122, 129–30

family engagement, 316, 340

family members, 48, 77–78, 80, 89, 121, 129, 167

farmers, 32, 43, 53, 359

fathers, 72, 77, 130–31, 302, 341

Feminist Action Research, 3, 5, 304

FGDs (Focus Group Discussion), 60, 70, 80, 83, 144, 153, 156, 185, 191, 193, 197, 240, 251, 261

Focus Group Discussion. *See* FGDs

focus groups, 12, 60, 84, 153, 191, 193, 240, 261, 345, 348

Freire, 8–9, 25, 119, 138, 141, 266, 268, 317

G

gender, 60–61, 64, 73, 81–85, 117, 278–79, 327, 332, 343–44, 346, 357, 360

gender equality, 32, 34, 67–68, 81, 272, 274

gender inequality, 61–62, 71, 75–76, 78, 87, 114

GOs. *See* governmental organizations

producing, 117–18

strengths, 3, 80, 101, 115, 134, 136, 153, 158, 166–67, 169–73, 178–79, 186–89, 195, 199–202, 211, 215, 218, 220, 224, 227, 244–45

student engagement, 22, 33, 201, 206, 212, 226–27, 251, 253, 274

support, 18, 20, 32, 38, 40–41, 77, 81–82, 100–103, 167–68, 171, 173–75, 177–78, 180, 183, 199–200, 228, 232–33, 237, 241, 243, 262, 264, 275–76, 281

sustainability, 162, 170, 201–2, 320

sustainable development, 57, 63, 273

T

teaching, xvi, 10, 22–23, 68, 100, 177, 264, 283–84, 286–87, 312, 325, 360

team, 199, 215, 225, 227

themes, 71, 120, 193, 215, 218, 268, 270, 272, 275, 294, 315

training, 9, 18, 33, 35, 47, 56, 71, 78, 80, 92, 99–101, 103–4, 156, 158, 190, 242, 336, 346, 352

trust, 19, 80, 134, 179, 181, 251, 255, 262, 267, 277

U

unemployment, 22, 32–34, 36, 43, 47, 49–52, 54–55, 58, 89, 91, 185, 197, 291, 319

university-community partnerships, xvii–xviii, 3, 280–81, 312–13, 328, 356

university researcher, 199–202

V

validity, 11, 95, 192, 225

values, 5, 43–44, 73, 78, 107, 120, 135–36, 151, 187–88, 196, 199,

212, 214, 217–18, 222, 235, 260, 332, 338, 348

vulnerability, 41–42, 56, 88, 137, 164–65, 275, 291

W

women, 5, 32–33, 35, 52, 60–92, 96, 98–99, 101–2, 106–7, 114, 149, 167, 186–87, 239, 247–48, 274–78, 328, 357, 359

women empowerment, 63, 85

women in Islam, 63, 69, 71, 74, 76, 80, 82

women's rights, 72, 74, 76, 85

women's status, 63, 67, 71–72, 84

women students, 70, 73, 75–77, 81–82

Y

youth, 22, 35, 52, 55, 157, 185–91, 193–211, 220–21, 227, 229–35, 239, 242, 246–48, 253, 262, 274–75, 278, 280, 317, 351

engaging, 188, 206–7, 212, 227, 230

youth assets, 190, 194, 197–98, 201, 275–76, 278

youth associations, 185, 194, 196

youth development, 200, 204, 210, 229–30, 274, 278, 355

youth participation, 211, 229, 278, 327

Printed in the United States
by Baker & Taylor Publisher Services